SOMERSET VILLAGES

OTHER BOOKS IN THE VILLAGE SERIES

Somerset Villages

PAUL NEWMAN

ROBERT HALE · LONDON

© *Paul Newman 1986*
First published in Great Britain 1986

ISBN 0 7090 2579 3

Robert Hale Limited
Clerkenwell House
Clerkenwell Green
London EC1R 0HT

British Library Cataloguing in Publication Data

Newman, Paul
  Somerset villages — (Village series)
  1. Villages — England — Somerset —
  History   2. Somerset — History
  I. Title   II. Series
  942.3′8′009734   DA670.S5

  ISBN 0-7090-2579-3

Photoset in North Wales by
Derek Doyle & Associates, Mold, Clwyd.
Printed in Great Britain by
St Edmundsbury Press, Bury St Edmunds, Suffolk

Contents

The author would like to acknowledge the authors of numerous local guides and histories of parish churches; contributors to the *Visitor* magazine of Castle Cary (edited by Patrick Dunion); Mrs J.M. Hoyle of the Economic Development and Tourist Unit of Taunton Deane for promptly answering queries; and David Bromwich of the Taunton Local History Library for providing useful source material. Also, for helping with transport and accommodation, many thanks to Graham Thomas of Shepton Mallet, Ann Jenkins of Clevedon and David Salaman of Bradford-on-Avon.

List of Illustrations

Introduction

Generalizations about any English county are of dubious value. In the case of Somerset this is especially true, for the old county has been truncated, and the northern coastal towns of Weston-super-Mare, Clevedon and Portishead, together with an ample slice of the Mendip Hills, have been incorporated in the new county of Avon formed in 1974. Having been born and brought up in Clevedon, then styled 'the gem of sunny Somerset' and likened to Rome on account of its seven hills, I was placed in the curious situation of having to drive some twelve miles south and over the River Axe at Lympsham (marked by the Viking sign of the Hobb's Boat Inn) in order to attain the county of my birth. The change-over enraged many traditionalists – 'I invite you to join the growing number of people who refuse to call Somerset anything but Somerset,' urged a letter addressed to me at the time. One automatically sympathizes with such a view but unfortunately the packaging and re-allocation of boundaries is as old as history. What is the Domesday Book if not a gargantuan labour of petty bureaucracy?

Even allowing for the dramatic depletion in the extent of the county, it remains an excitingly varied place, difficult to pin down with any specific image. What does Somerset imply? Simply different things to different people. To the Powys brothers it meant the dusky-gold Hamstone villages of Montacute and Tintinhull where gloving girls and dairymaids with cowslips in their hair dallied with local youths on flower-starred greens. But to the novelist Henry Fielding, born at Sharpham Park in the shadow of the Poldens, it probably signified grey stone and red-tiled villages where peat was dug and where Glastonbury Abbey was once the supreme landowner. R.D. Blackmore's Somerset is dramatically different again, conjuring up the sheep-cropped, buff-green uplands of Exmoor where clusters of thatched cottages overlook gushing trout-streams. But many would call Exmoor, with its luxuriant combes and aura of cream teas, more typical of Devon and draw attention instead to the alluvial Vale of Taunton Deane, where cider orchards abound and corn grows tall. This was the region that nurtured the poet Samuel Daniel, a contemporary of Shakespeare, and Thomas Young, who developed the science of optics and helped decipher the hieroglyphs on the Rosetta Stone.

So what exactly is typical Somerset? Perhaps the most apposite clue is the name itself, derived from 'Seo-mere-seatan – 'dwellers by the sealakes'. This alludes to the early settlers at the lake villages of Glastonbury and Meare who raised wooden huts on grassy mounds above the marshes which provided such rich ground for fishing and hunting. The area is now called Sedgemoor and is characterized by its millions of intersecting drains, locally called rhynes, which form a glistening network separating fields and farms. The villages of these plains are slightly solemn, pervaded by a plodding, hoof-heavy atmosphere of unvarying agricultural routine, and the most persistent music is the sullen dong of milk churns banging their metallic torsos as they are jostled along by farm wagons. The buildings are of grey limestone or severely whitewashed, while the churches, made splendid by the power of the 'Golden Fleece', may be pinnacled, exuberant, with a rich show of statuary and gargoyles.

Geographers tend to classify villagers according to the pattern of their layout: 'nucleated', 'dispersed' and 'polyfocal' are specimens of the incantatory jargon used to intimidate the layman. An example of a nucleated village might be Nunney, tightly wedged in its combe, the houses clinging like iron filings around the magnet of the castle, while Spaxton on the Quantocks could be classed as dispersed, consisting as it does of hamlets and farms scattered over a large area. Martock can be seen as polyfocal, for it has several distinct, interlocking units of development straggled along its main street. And then there are spring-line groupings, such as Brent Knoll and East Brent, and open-field-type settlements like Hinton St George where strips of land follow up behind the backs of houses. But in general such scientific classifications have been avoided here, for they are almost impossible to demonstrate without detailed mapping and extensive analysis. This book aims at impressionism rather than microscopic scrutiny.

Many chapter divisions in the present volume are self-explanatory. Exmoor, the Quantocks and the Brendon Hills are homogeneous regions with their own flora, fauna and microclimate. The same could be argued of the Blackdown Hills and the Poldens, which form a low, thin ridge across the Sedgemoor plain. Taunton Deane is a large administrative area embracing the flatlands to the east as well as the red-soiled Tone valley and parts of the enclosing hills. Sedgemoor is truly extensive, necessitating a separate chapter dealing with the Northern Levels and further chapters describing the *zoy* parishes and the Curry villages. In certain instances an area has been designated after a major settlement, notably in the chapter detailing the villages around Frome. On other occasions a physical feature has been used, such as the Brue meadows, the Sheppey valley or that region, dominated by the twinkling spectre of Arthur, traversed by the tiny River Cary and guarded by the wooded ramparts of Cadbury Castle. These strategies have been resorted to in order to draw together disparate elements which inevitably occur in so geologically complex a county as Somerset where hills are continually giving way to plains, and rocks vary from chalk, flint and greensand to red sandstone, lias and oolite.

1

The Northern Levels

Formerly it was the graceful, silver-curving Avon that marked the northern boundary of Somerset, but since the creation of Avon county (1974) it has been the murkier, less distinguished Axe. My village tour begins at this north-west corner, only two miles from the estuary, at Bleadon Bridge, with the benign brow of Brent Knoll nodding in the distance. This is the coastal belt where the Mendips have given way to alluvial plains ending in dunes and sandy beaches by the Bristol Channel. The nearest coastal community, Brean, lies some three miles to the east across the flats, and its function as a holiday centre is dictated by its closeness to Weston-super-Mare.

Happy Days Caravan Park – one of the numerous such sites – establishes the tone of well-being traders are anxious to promote. Judging by the numbers of these mobile units, their sales drives have proven effective; like vivid-hued robotic cattle, they stand in silent ranks congregating about the water-holes of grocery shops and inns.

Ribbon development predominates. Warren Road (rabbits once formed the staple diet) is lined by modern bungalows, many gleaming-gabled, ultra new, others having a clapboard, quickly nailed-together air – indeed, whole sections of them were delivered by the incoming tide. The name of the pebbledash pub, the Beachcomber, refers to the practice of hoarding useful objects the sea deposits each day. Names of the houses, such as Silver Haze (sea mist?), Toiler's Rest (on the Down's steep slopes) and Hidaway (surely not any longer?), invoke the familiar seaside muse.

15

There is a cheerful incongruity about some of the buildings, most notably in a florid chocolate-painted bungalow featuring crenellations, Ionic motifs rendered in gold, and a resplendent wrought-iron gate: an enterprise bringing to mind confectionery rather than brickwork.

The coast road terminates in a low grey building which is the bird garden. 'DON'T MISS THE BIGGEST COLLECTION OF BIRDS FOR MILES' proclaims a sign, while 'THESE PREMISES ARE PATROLLED BY GUARD DOGS' deters any felon from stealing in at night and coming out with a flamingo or cockatoo concealed beneath his shirt.

Evidence of the mildness of the climate can be seen in the stunted palms occupying the gardens; they sprout like shocks of green daggers, and marram grass – an effective soil-fixing agent – is rife on the dunes. At low tide the pale brown sand, staked with wooden posts, is left bare and desolate. Beyond it one glimpses the plains of dark-pocked mud and the slaty sea. But the real presence here is the Down itself, fissured and gullied with limestone battlements. Beside it the chalets and bungalows of the shoreline exude a faintly insubstantial, shanty town atmosphere; they are simply not made to endure like this enormous battleship of a headland.

Seeming almost as old as the Down, and certainly more substantial than most of the surrounding architecture, Brean church is a grave and simple building with a cradle-beam roof and an ancient piscina in the form of a shamrock – an allusion perhaps to its patron, St Bridget, who was abbess of a monastery and nunnery at Kildare in the sixth century. The fabric dates from the thirteenth century and has a richly carved pulpit and an eagle lectern contributed by W. Sperring, who was churchwarden for forty-seven years. Lightning struck the tower in 1729, and it was shortened and fitted with a saddleback.

The big seaside resort of this coastal region is Burnham-on-Sea, a curious place, not discreetly developed but energetically uglified with big emporiums sellings glass ashtrays, digital watches, enormous rubber tarantulas and cheap varnished shells. Then there are the ice-cream vans, the fish-and-chip shops, the hamburger stalls, the fairgrounds and amusement arcades – all evoking the worst parts of Weston. But the town has its compensations – miles of sandhills stretching north to Brean and the pathetic lighthouse-on-legs which stands sentinel on the beach. Furthermore, there are intrusions of Victorian elegance, such as Catherine and Julia Terraces, named after the daughters of a nineteenth-century developer, and Stert House where the old baths were established.

Berrow village has almost merged with Burnham. No intervening space breaks up the line of guest houses and bed-and-breakfast notices. A Caravan Club site indicates the general tone of *bonhomie*, but solitude can also be found among the dunes where marram grass grows thick, locals walk their dogs, and driftwood accumulates in abundance. Old buildings are few and far between in Berrow, which is predominantly Victorian, Edwardian and contemporary, but there is (for those who feel truly desperate) a hundred-year-old pig-sty at Barton Farm which has been honoured with a preservation order.

Berrow church hides shyly among the sandhills, as if forgotten by all but the vicar – a rugged little building with a stout, battlemented tower. Parts date from 1300 but the interior is mainly Jacobean, and the churchyard has two crude stone figures, abraded by sand, wind and rain to featurelessness, and yet:

O, indeed
The skill-less hand that carved it had belonged
To a most yearning and bewildered brain:
There was such desolation in the work
And through its utter failure the thing spoke
With more of human message, heart to heart,
Than all these faultless, smirking, skin-deep saints,
In artificial troubles picturesque,
And martyred sweetly, not one curl awry.

(Lord de Tabley)

The Burnham and Berrow golf course is famous throughout Britain and has an unusual anecdote attached to it. No golfer was allowed to drive the long five-hole past Berrow church on the Sabbath, so an extra four-hole was designed for use on Sundays, making this a nineteen-hole course. But today the five-hole is no longer used and the golf course has forfeited its eccentricity.

Brent Knoll, like Burrow Mump and Glastonbury Tor, is one of those shale and limestone outliers; it rises 450 feet above the north Somerset plain and is crowned by an Iron Age fort. The settlements clustering on the slopes of the hill, East Brent and Brent Knoll village, are typical spring-line groupings. Excavations in the low ground of the Somerset Levels confirm extensive flooding in the third and fourth centuries (local names like Lake Farm bear this out), and the drier upland areas must have attracted cultivation as the strip lynchets on the south and south-west of the fort testify.

Nowadays the solitary hill-fort adjoins the M5 rest area. The contrast is abrupt: the slumbrous rural community set aside the hurtling, frenetic cars and lorries. One seems almost absurdly composed; the other rushing, hysterical, neurotic.

Brent Knoll's parish church, dedicated to St Michael, is renowned for its savagely satirical bench ends; they are usually construed as a veiled reference to the rapacious nature of the monks at Glastonbury Abbey, depicting Reynard the Fox dressed as an abbot, attended by three monks in cowls who have the heads of swine. Grouped around him are various geese, presumably parishioners, who in the end string him up: thus the greedy prelate is executed by those he intended to despoil.

Equally striking is the monument to John Somerset and his two wives, having a kind of naïve literal quality reminiscent of the Cookham resurrection sequences painted by Stanley Spencer. There are trumpeting angels, mild-eyed spouses, one with a broad-brimmed hat, and John Somerset himself, both as a recumbent husband and as a risen soul, shrouded, shaking off his gravesoil and arising from the tomb. In fact, Somerset was a brave, tenacious fellow, who, as a captain in the Royalist army, led the villagers of Brent against the plundering Roundhead troops. He was imprisoned for this show of resistance and died in 1663.

The village of Brent Knoll consists of a string of stone farmhouses – Tableland, Shrub, Burton Row and Chestnut

Farm – belted round the lower slopes of the hill and backed by meadows and orchard. Between them lie traditional cottage rows and the manifold infillings of the last hundred years: substantial bungalows with artistic pretensions, a village hall, a junior school and some lofty Victorian structures by the church.

Situated prominently on the hillside, overlooking a rather prosaic red-brick estate, the manor house stands out like a sober-suited Victorian gentleman amid a group of off-the-peg commoners. John Norton designed it in Elizabethan style, and its cautious, restrained harmonies reflect this architect in one of his less abandoned moods: to savour Norton's more tempestuous Gothic phases, examine Tyntesfield, near Wraxall, (1862–4) which is contemporary with the Brent Manor but spikily exuberant and vaguely unnerving.

East Brent, although similarly straggled, occupies more of the low, fenny ground, suggesting a slightly later settlement pattern after drainage operations had been effected. Early farming confined itself to the Knoll; only during medieval times, when the rhynes had been cut, was it possible to regard the flats as regular meadowland.

Offering fewer vistas of stone farmhouses framed by wooded slope, East Brent has more the feel of a typical Sedgemoor village. The Knoll is less prominent, and it is less dispersed along a single road. A nucleation occurs around the village green and Knoll Inn. At one corner, facing the road, there is a memorial to soldiers of the First World War, depicting officers and men, carved in full relief, standing against the panels of an octagonal cross; a flagstaff, railing surround and poppy wreath complete the composition. The surrounding houses are cream-plastered, limewashed or just plain red brick, fairly uninspiring, yet varied by Victorian intrusions such as Rossholme Girls' School, the Wesleyan chapel (1871) and the Baptist chapel (1850) at Rooksbridge.

Visual relief is provided by the slenderly beautiful spire of St Mary the Virgin. The interior is astonishingly light and elegant, almost Georgian Gothic, with the plaster ceiling of the nave (1637) adorned with pendants interconnected with quatrefoil ribwork. In the north wall of the chancel is a

stained glass window, where, among Christian symbols, can
be clearly picked out a set of stumps, a ball and pair of
wicket-keeping gloves, commemorating the Reverend
Archdale Palmer Wickham, who kept wicket for Somerset
CCC from 1891 to 1907. A former vicar of Martock and
known to his team as 'the Bishop', he retired to the living of
East Brent when his cricketing days had ended. Collecting
moths and butterflies was a secondary passion, and he would
visit Shapwick and Loxley Woods hunting for specimens.
Villagers often glimpsed his lantern glowing at night on the
slopes of the Knoll as *Lepidoptera* innocently fluttered to
eternal life.

A certain swaggering ostentation characterized Wickham's appearance on the field. His stance at the wicket was
low, his legs wide apart, and he wore black-topped pads,
grey flannels sashed by a black cummerbund, a Harlequin
hat that just peeped above the stumps – attire that, when
combined with Victorian side-whiskers and a heavy
soup-strainer moustache, guaranteed a degree of conspicu-
ousness.

Another celebrated vicar of East Brent was Archdeacon
Denison (d. 1896) who started the vogue for Harvest Homes.
In Maxwell Fraser's book *Companion into Somerset* (1947)
there is a full description of this festivity which smacks
faintly of heathenish gluttony but without the orgiastic
sequel.

Bounded on the north by the River Axe, Lympsham
connects to East Brent by West Lane and a track passing
Lower Farm and Beck's Farm. A bland, slightly flat
peacefulness pervades this village, with its working
blacksmiths and tidy orchards, which encourages one to
adopt a retired shuffle while exploring its corners and
byways. There are ancient houses such as The Grange, which
may have been used by the monks of Glastonbury as a
summer retreat, and modern estate development near
Coppice End Corner. By far the most flamboyant edifice is
the neo-Tudor manor house set in grounds with an
ornamental lake. Traceried windows and pinnacles dance
amok in this delightful bit of fakery. Inscribed obelisks
make yet another enhancing feature. The building was the

upshot of Joseph Stephenson's (rector 1809–37) penchant for romantic Gothic, and it went up around 1828 along with several estate cottages inscribed with the letter S. His son, Joseph II, carried on the good work by erecting the manor hall (1875) at a cost of £1,800, and the school, another fine example of philanthropic Gothic. Joseph II died in 1901 and was succeeded by Edmond Stephenson (rector 1901-12).

To the south of Brent Knoll, amid the mazelike interconnections of rhynes and rivers, Huntspill (its name derived from 'Hun's creek') hides with a modesty befitting its demure appearance. Groups of red-tiled houses create an almost Dutch landscape which evening light can instil with that vague pastoral melancholy one associates with a symphony by Butterworth. One is never far from the grumbling susurrations of the old grey Channel and the plaints of curlew and snipe which haunt the mud-steeped estuaries.

Huntspill is divided into two parts, Huntspill and East Huntspill, the latter lying on the edge of Mark Moor, and the former west of the motorway cut near the Parrett. Until 1800 the villages did not exist at all, except as a sprinkling of isolated hamlets going by names such as Batts Bow, near Batts Farm, the Causeway, Cote, Withy Bow and Dotts.

St Peter's Church is an early fifteenth-century building, with an embattled western tower buttressed against the sea. It was restored in 1876, during the incumbency of the Reverend James Gylby Lonsdale, then burnt down two years later, on 9 December 1878. The red-stained pillars inside testify to the ferocity of the conflagration; so does the cracked shield of a knight, who has lain beside his lady since the fourteenth century.

Only a little way south of Huntspill, Pawlett (locally called Pollet) presents a similar Dutch or East Anglian aspect: farmsteads, embanked cottage rows and a forlorn feeling of space and solitude. The village is nucleated around a triangle of roads where brick houses and renovated cottages mingle. It hugs the high ground below which rhynes form a silver web and the M5 motorway cleaves across level farmland. Pawlett Hams were once renowned as 2,000 acres of fertile pasture land, 'the richest in England', dating back to the twelfth century, when Robert Gaunt 'embanked from the sea a thousand acres'. In the fourteenth century Pawlett was owned by John of Gaunt. The great prince's will alludes to his Somerset estate: 'I, John o' Gaunt, do give and bequeath from me and mine to thee and thine all that portion of land known as Pawlett's Ham.' It should be added that in 1922 the Hams were broken up and sold in small parcels of land. Gaunt Road runs over the bare, houseless summit of Pawlett Hill to Gaunt's Farm; an old tombstone was dug up here recently, indicating that a small church or burial ground may have occupied the site. The end of the road trails off into a track running beside White House Rhyne down to the River Parrett. Nearby are the ruins of the White House Inn, formerly an important junction for stage-coaches in the West Country. From here travellers were ferried across the river to Combwich, and horses were fed, rested and changed. One feels keenly the depletion of the place's significance: no sign of life or bustle now; saltgrass, mud, water, crumbling stumps of stone and gulls making arcs in the long grey sky.

A ghost story is attached to the White House. During a night of dense, driving rain, a stage-coach full of passengers was hurrying towards the inn. Visibility was minimal; the sky was a black, pillowy mass of cloud. A sudden thunderclap made the horses bolt forward in a panic; they swept past the coaching yard and into the river, where they all perished. The incident is said to repeat itself on such wild nights: horses, driver and passengers endlessly thundering over those muddy banks followed by the long, bleak, soapless bath.

Readers of *Tom Jones* may recall the chapter dealing with the man from Mark, a village Fielding knew at first hand – for he lived at the not-too-distant Sharpham – which has been variously called March (a marsh), Merk (a boundary) and Mercon. A regular approach is by branching off the M5 at Brent Knoll and heading due east across the wetlands. The countryside is pleasant if unremarkable, with modern bungalows, cottage farmhouses and sporadic council rows, jumbled and juxtaposed in random fashion. Artificial causeways are evident, fringed by willows and waterways. Eventually the road curves round by a group of houses and the White Horse Inn, followed by the modern estates of Merryfield and Churchlands Close. Few of the buildings are notably attractive, but rich umbellifer-bordered meadows sweeten and aerate a scene which falls slightly short of total dullness. Carry on about a hundred yards, past the post office and local shop, until Myrtle House, a jaunty pink Georgian dwelling, is reached. Hereabouts is the Packhorse Inn, faintly severe in black and white, and a small stream crossing the road – a listless, immobile strip of water from which a stagnant smell arises.

The church of the Blessed Virgin Mary commands the view. Its handsome tower dominates the humble garage-and-joinery business across the way. Green spear-tipped railings enclose the graveyard, and the entrance is guarded by two lean, vigilant lions, symbols of St Mark. This raises a small query over the original dedication. Traditionally it is assumed St Mark was the patron saint, his figure occupying a niche in the east wall of the tower, but a chaplain of Mark, in his will dated 1425, requested that he might be interned in 'the Chapel of the Blessed Virgin Mary of Merk'. This was probably the Lady Chapel which has a cross-shaped incision on the north wall, evidence supporting the idea that here was a *Capella Sanctae Crucis* referred to in an ancient document.

The interior of the church is no disappointment. The north-aisle roof has magnificent Tudor carvings: twenty-four cherubim with outspread wings carry alternately the crown of glory, instruments of the Passion and the Book of Life. The nave roof has carvings of King Alfred and his wife, Queen Alswith, and the Danish King Guthrum – all distinctively executed from wood taken from the long-devastated forest of the Mendip. The extension and beautification of the fabric took place during the fourteenth century, following the Black Death, 1340–9. The pestilence swept through Bristol and Bath, overspilling into Somerset, interrupting the progress of church-building, but after the disease had abated, labour acquired increased validity, and a new class of farmer and free worker arose who drained the moors, bred cattle and paid generous tithes. The influx of new wealth, allied to the prospering wool trade, enabled churches to be endowed with rich and gracious features. An example is seen, in the elegant sculptured pillars capped by flat Tudor rose-bands in the north arcade and the bold tower of alternate bands of blue lias and brown stone from the upper beds.

The Isle of Wedmore is an uplift of land occupying the area between the Mendip and Polden Hills. It is bounded on the east by the River Axe, and to the west is the network of rhynes that join up with the River Brue as it heads somnolently towards the sea at Highbridge. A dry, fertile rise seldom exceeding 200 feet, it provided a sanctuary for prehistoric settlers (stone tools have been found) who fished and hunted in the encircling marshes. The Romans, too, during a drier historical period, used Wedmore as a base, establishing a look-out post near Heath House and another foundation at West End.

But it was the Saxons who gave Wedmore its name, variously translated as 'wet moor', 'moor for hunting' and 'moor of agreement or reconciliation'. The last refers to the 'Peace of Wedmore', treaty that followed the baptism of the Danish chieftain Guthrum at Aller in AD 878. Wedmore was part of Alfred's estate, and there was probably a kind of rudimentary royal hunting lodge in the area to accommodate the feasting and formulation of the pact. The Danish king accepted the Christian faith and agreed to settle within defined boundaries and co-exist peacefully with his Saxon hosts.

The village centre displays a dignity and amplitude more befitting a small spa town. The buildings, too, have an ostentation that takes one by surprise. The National Westminster Bank in Church Street is Venetian Gothic, and the nearby chemist's is an Italianate daydream with round-headed windows, pilasters, a wrought-iron balcony and entablature.

Westhovers lies at West End, which branches off Pilcorn Lane. A converted stone building with Tudor-style mullioned windows and a cock weathervane, it is socially significant because it was once an early lunatic asylum, founded by John Westhover (b. 1616), a farmer, surgeon and dentist who lived next door in Porch House.

A medieval cross stands in the part of the village called the Borough. Dating from the fourteenth century, it has a slender octagonal shaft crowned by a canopy and bears sculptures of the Holy Rood, Madonna and Child, a knight and an ecclesiastic. Pilgrims to Glastonbury are believed to have gathered here, and there is a small rectangular stoup for holy water.

The church is banked high above the road and dominates the street with its implacable force of outline. It is lofty-towered, austere and grim, with three chapels incorporated in its cruciform plan. Above the pulpit is an old mural painting of St Christopher carrying the infant Christ. There are actually two such portraits, the later effort superimposed on the older, one *c.* 1460 and the other *c.* 1520. Details of fishes, mermaids and ships recall a similar well-painting at Ditcheat. There are tablets and brasses to the Boultings, Hodges and other families, including a brass with the figure of a heart and the following inscription:

Wounded not Vanquisht

Sacred to the memorie of Captain Thomas Hodges of the county of Somerset, esq.; who at the siege of Antwerp, about 1583, with unconquered courage wonne two ensignes from the enemy, where, receiving his last wound, he gave three legayces: his soule to his Lord Jesus, his body to be lodged in Flemish earth, his heart to be sent to his deare wife in England.

Here lies his wounded heart, for whome
One kingdome was two small a roome:
Two kingdoms therefore have thought good to part
So stout a body and so brave a heart.

Wedmore has a reputation for liveliness and revels. Being a former royal borough, governed by portreeves chosen at the annual court, when bread-weighers, ale-tasters, a swineherd and bailiffs are appointed, it has a tradition of feasting and fun-making that is continued in the present day. The old Wedmore Revels, drunken and gluttonous celebrations, were stopped by the Reverend W. White in

1830 — owing perhaps to increased violence and the dangerous custom of single-stick fighting, but the Wedmore fairs continued to be held twice a year outside the George. There were a number of stalls and a shooting-gallery, lit at night by naphtha flares, and gypsies attended, showing off the paces of their horses to find a buyer. These deals often resulted in flashing fists, bared teeth and bloody faces. Hannah More and her sisters, who opened up a school in Pilcorn Street in 1799, described the farmers as 'savage and depraved' — epithets that came rather too readily to her lips whenever she witnessed rustics at play.

During her time, and right down through the Victorian era, Wedmore was a very different community from the stable, land-locked village, full of small service industries, that the visitor sees today. At least once a year the peat moor flooded, and people took to boats to get to work or go to church. Eels were then caught and carried on long withy poles, and during other seasons the moors provided a rich diet of wild duck and snipe. Peat kept the homefires burning, and nearly all the farms made their own butter and cheese.

All this has gone, yet Wedmore is proud of its heritage and boasts that the average life of a newcomer is only one month — then he is absorbed by all the neighbourliness and activity. There is a cricket club, floral art club, pre-school playgroup, badminton club and bridge club as well as a multitude of church societies. And for those who wish to indulge in a little of the traditional excess, where religion combines with genteel revelry, there is the annual harvest home celebration.

To the south of the Wedmore rise are the flatlands of northern Sedgemoor, drained by the Brue and subsidiary rhynes and extending unbroken to the narrow ridge of the Poldens. This damp, low-lying area includes some 6,000 acres of peat moor. Peat, or 'turf' as it is called locally, has been dug in Somerset since prehistoric times. Even today there are hand-diggers left who arrange the turf into mumps to dry. But nowadays machines do most of the work, and the peat is employed for horticultural purposes rather than for domestic fuel. Near Meare, Catcott and Westhay vast quantities of peat have been excavated, a process attended by continuous pumping to reduce the water-table. Once the operation is complete, the water trickles back, leaving a long, deep trench of ebony liquid.

The digging of peat has not enhanced the appearance of the flats but it has resulted in some useful discoveries. Westhay – a hamlet of scattered farms – is archaeologically important for the Sweet Track, a prehistoric footpath dating from 4,000 BC first discovered in 1970 by a sharp-eyed peat-cutter, Mr Ray Sweet. He was clearing ditches when he came across some ancient waterlogged timber and a flint arrowhead. Guessing the importance of this find, he reported it, and the oldest known trackway in the world was brought to light. These routes must be envisaged as rudimentary gangways, made of poles or rails held in place by large, sharpened side-pegs and strengthened by turf padding, enabling early fishers and hunters to cross the huge areas of reed and sedge swamps.

Westhay is part of the extensive parish of Meare, which was formerly an island called 'Feramere' just as Westhay was known as 'Westeie' (the 'eye' meaning 'island') and Godney 'Godenere'. Meare is set on a gentle elevation above the Brue some three miles north-west of Glastonbury. The name derives from the ancient saltmarsh drained during the Middle Ages.

The plan of the village is elementary. Confined on all sides by marshland, the cottages were nucleated on the higher ground in rectangular rows. The pattern is not spectacularly evident today, when vernacular dwellings mingle with Regency residences, split-level bungalows, routine red-brick estates and Victorian essays in civic decorum. The Countryman and the Ring of Bells are the two locals, and the latter, as its name implies, stands next to the church, which is entered by a double row of limes.

The church's south door has medieval wrought ironwork, black, spidery and muscularly writhing, and the interior contains a stone carving of the Holy Grail. Across the way is Meare School, built by public subscription in 1840, a grey stone edifice with a dull, teacherly air and a slightly crumbled belfry tower. Near at hand, and far more characterful, is the old manor house: stout grey walls, a two-storeyed porch and the figure of a stone bishop – could it be Abbot Bere? – perched on a gable. This was a manorial residence of the abbots of Glastonbury, erected about 1300 and improved by Abbot Bere, until it became a farmhouse at the Dissolution.

The most curious relic of medieval Meare is the fourteenth-century Fish House, an austere, gabled dwelling with Gothic windows, where the chief fisherman of Glastonbury Abbey stored his catch and lived with his family. He would have fished the big lake called Meare Pool, which was five miles round in the seventeenth-century, and donated most of his catch to the monks. The lower floor was where he salted and dried the fish; in the upper he slept and dined. There was no staircase connecting the floors – access was via an outside ladder.

2

The North-West Mendips

The Mendip Hills, aptly described by Thomas Hardy as 'a range of limestone rocks stretching from the shore of the Bristol Channel into the middle of Somersetshire', are designated an Area of Outstanding Natural beauty and display the typical scenery of karst: dry gorges – the spectacular remnants of collapsed cave systems at Cheddar, Burrington and Ebbor; smooth, domelike summits with thin calcareous soil; disappearing streams and swallet holes – features that attract the rider, hiker, camper and caver. Although the high plateau is sparsely habited, the perimeter is belted round by main roads along which are strung compact and populous settlements: Axbridge, Cheddar, Draycott, Shipham, Westbury and Wells on the westerly scarp face; Shepton Mallet, Frome, Mells and Chewton Mendip on the gentler eastern side.

The northern fringe of the Mendips reaches its extremity at Churchill, Avon, lying on the A38 Bristol road beneath the Iron Age encampment of Dolebury Warren. A former turnpike road forks off from here (established 1827 by the Wedmore Trust), taking one past a round-windowed Gothic toll-house and into Shipham, Somerset, a name recalling the early sheep fairs.

The hilltop village is centred around the square, which has a clean, spacious, utilitarian look. It is presided over by the late-Victorian court house, the Miners' Arms free house, a group of terraced council homes and the dazzling white Penscot Hotel and Restaurant. But the apparent orderliness of Shipham is belied by exploration: the plan of the village is random, haphazard, comprising a maze of crisscrossing lanes. Go up Hollow Road and branching off to the right, not far from the Community Hall, are Allens Lane, Court Lane, Hindpits Lane and Folly Lane, all looping in and out and converging.

The names Hollow Road and Hindpits Lane hold the clue to the expansion of the village in the eighteenth century. Calamine was the basis for its sudden trebling of population and rash of cramped cottage dwellings. The ore yielded zinc which, alloyed to copper, produced brass – thus supplying the busy foundries of Bristol, already dependent on South Wales for copper and north-east Somerset for furnace-coal. It was mined in pits and lateral grooves, and in 1792 Collinson observed 'upwards of 100 mines, in the streets, in the yards and in the very houses of Shipham'. The last observation bears a veiled reference to the citizens of the village – traditionally regarded as lawless – sinking shafts beneath their own kitchens in the hope of avoiding paying the Lord of the Minery his dues. Common land during this period became rapidly in-filled with squat and boxy miners' cottages (today spruce, colour-washed buildings) approached by narrow and intersecting lanes, a feature which gives Shipham its distinctive cellular plan.

Hollow Road leads out of Shipham, climbing a hill on which derelict mining cottages stand and finally emerging in the hamlet of Rowberrow. Here the parish church and manor house stand adjacent, a mellow pair of buildings, lichen-stained and reddish-grey in colour. Clinging to the brow of a sheer-sided hill, they are most effectively seen from the flanks of Dolebury Warren.

Dedicated to St Michael, Rowberrow church was rebuilt in 1865, but the tower, an effective piece of Perpendicular work, dates from the original thirteenth-century foundation, although capped with Victorian pinnacles inferior to the originals which decorate the churchyard. On a corbel, fixed in the interior north wall, is a stone carved with interlaced and serpentine designs, obviously Saxon in origin. Quite possibly it is part of a cross, and the Ringerlike coils may have constituted the tail of the primeval serpent who was cast out of Heaven by the church's patron.

The manor house, although coeval with the church, is one of those hardy buildings designed to endure Mendip weather. Its one decorative feature is an oak mantelpiece carved with dolphins, probably Jacobean, which was moved from an upper floor to ground level. The rectory, screened by limes and elms, stands in spacious grounds, a large pink-washed Georgian building dating from 1790. Near it is the Swan Inn, an unpretentious free house around which several renovated cottages are grouped.

Dotted about the valley in Rowberrow are ruined homesteads, where daffodils once grew profusely, adding a touch of Hebridean melancholy to the landscape. They bring home vividly the situation in 1822 when nearly every man in the village was engaged in mining, except for about six who worked the land. But calamine-roasting was a dreadful trade, producing poisonous fumes that shrivelled trees, tainted pasturage and shortened lifespans. Only the spoilheaps and choked shafts survive today; fortunately many of them are effectively concealed by Rowberrow Woods, 545 acres of Corsican pine, Norwegian spruce and Sitka spruce, planted by the Forestry Commission in 1939.

The road from Shipham to Cheddar descends into the gorge of Callow Hill Quarry. Spoilheaps and scars loom; machinery clanks and shudders; lorries churn up lime dust; year by year the skyline is lowered by blasting. The demand for aggregates is still rising, and the quarries have been granted large concessions: no doubt in time Callow Hill and Sandford Hill will be reduced to hollowed-out stumps.

The main road from Bristol to Cheddar bypasses Shipham and Rowberrow. It hooks round Shute Shelve Hill, a former place of execution where felons were hung in chains, and clings to the lower slopes above the floodplain of Axbridge Moor. From here the Cheddar Reservoir, like an immense blue coin, glimmers crisply.

The name 'Cheddar' derives from the Old English 'che', 'high ground', and 'dwr', 'water' – features that have recommended the site from earliest times. Prehistoric man occupied the gorge over 10,000 years ago, and one imagines the Celts viewed this awesome green-robed chasm, rife with subterranean rumours, as a place of sanctity and terror. The

Romans, more commercially inclined, exploited the water-supply by establishing a wharf at Hythe on the Wedmore Road, whereby lead mined at Charterhouse was shipped down the Rivers Yeo and Axe to the port of Uphill on the Bristol Channel. Water-power also made an important contribution to trade in the eighteenth century, turning thirteen grist and paper-mills, while the rich pasturage of the valley encouraged cheese-making.

When the railway was opened in 1869, the cult of the picturesque had already established Cheddar as a place of prodigious spectacle. So the new branch line served two important purposes: effecting the efficient transport of local produce (strawberries, cheese and butter) and bringing in more tourists from such wealthy towns as Bath and Bristol. The gorge attracted sightseers who liked to eat and drink and take home keepsakes: hence Cliff Street evolved into a kind of market-place of diverse wares, many of which are so incongruous as to be almost irritating: Gough's Motor Museum, Joke Jewellery, Wurzel Zider and Country Wines, Home Made Corn Dollies – a veritable banquet of gimcrackery and knicknackery. There is much at Cheddar that is strangely inappropriate. Why is there a restaurant and 'nitespot' named after a famous French criminal? Why is there another eating house called 'The Norseman'? Why is there yet a third called 'The Edelweiss'? To sum it up, Cheddar is a blend of natural sublimity and human tawdriness.

The magnet of all the business is the caves. At the entrance to the Fantasy Grotto (discovered by Mr Cox in 1837) there is a plaster model of a snarling wolf tucking in to the carcase of an unfortunate deer, no doubt serving to remind the tourist, possibly sedated by an overdose of natural wonders, that the subterranean lifestyle of early man was beset by bloody hazards. Cox's Cave is considered to have the more exquisite formations: Marble Curtain, Peal of Bells, Bunch of Carrots, Lady Chapel, Mermaid and Mummy, Home of the Rainbow. Gough's Cave, on the other hand, goes all out for sublimity: St Paul's, the Fonts, the Frozen Waterfall – names transcending the human scale of things.

This then is a sketch of Cliff Street, Cheddar, but the larger part of the village is separated from the gorge. Exploring roads like the Lippiat, Church Street, Silver Street (after the Roman god Sylvanus?), one encounters casemented cottages, elegant Georgian townhouses with scalloped entrances, stone-built Victorian mansions with bargeboard gables – an architectural variety of surprising richness.

The omphalos of the old town is the market cross – a fifteenth-century monument encircled by a colonnade of six arches and covered by a roof. Medieval merchants sold their wares from here, and itinerant preachers vented their sermons. Not far away is the parish church of St Andrew's, noted for its 110-foot tower; also its chantry chapel dedicated to the Fitzwalter family and the canopy tomb with brasses to Sir Thomas de Cheddre (d. 1442) and his wife Isabella (d. 1474).

A lane from the churchyard leads to the Kings of Wessex Upper School – a centre for cultural and further educational activities – adjoining the excavated site of an old Saxon palace. Cheddar was one of the royal forests used by the kings for hunting, and there is an account (941 AD) of King Edmund chasing a flying stag to where 'a certain wood covers a mountain of great height, which being separated at its summit, exhibits to the spectator an immense precipice and horrid abyss, called by the local people Cedderclyff'.

Not far from the school, in Lower North Street, is Hannah More's Cottage, now the property of the Evergreen Club. In 1789 she founded the first day school at Cheddar assisted by the statesman William Wilberforce. She thought Cheddar even worse than Shipham: 'There is as much knowledge of Christ,' she commented, 'in the interior of Africa as there is to be met in this wretched place.' In a letter she noted that she saw one Bible in the whole of the parish 'and that was used to prop up a flower pot'. Nowadays there is a County First School at Hillfield for the village, Fairlands Middle School at Fairlands Way and the Kings of Wessex (Church of England) for the surrounding area, together with a county library, a modern Catholic church, a Baptist and Methodist church, an informal group of Christian Scientists who meet in Cathay Lane and a dozen more civilized facilities. Confronted with all this, even Hannah More might have felt a prick of nostalgia for the hard primitivism of her day.

Draycott conjures up the appealing image of strawberry fields; unfortunately the physical evidence – equidistant rows of polythene cloches – is not visually delectable. A native of Cheddar, Sam Spencer, was among the first to recognize that the rich red strip of loam skirting the foot of the north-west Mendips was ideal for market gardening; it combined long hours of sunshine and a humid climate, together with a sheltered position. The strawberry trade was particularly intense during the 1880s, when the Cheddar railway was known as the Strawberry Special. The original luxuriant brand known as the Black Prince did not carry well; in transit it tended to bruise and leak – hence tougher strains such as the Gauntlet were developed.

Market gardening still flourishes here; numerous homesteads have allotments advertising the sale of onions, leeks, potatoes, cabbages and carrots. Otherwise one receives the impression of a tidy village lacking an integral centre. The A371 cuts between the succession of farmhouses, often spankingly refurbished, and the odd stone-built Victorian villa. The main part of the village lies west of the main road and consists of four parallel routes: Back Lane, the Street, West Lane and Bay Lane. These meet up in Station Road; from here a minor road crosses the old railway bridge and strikes out across the moors, looping round Nyland Hill, one of those evocative tree-studded outliers of the Mendips.

As a hamlet and ecclesiastical parish, Draycott was formed in March 1862 out of the parishes of Cheddar and Rodney Stoke. One of its major industries was quarrying 'Draycott marble', a conglomerate found in layers one to four feet thick and used for posts and steps but capable of taking a high polish and impervious to weather. The church, chapel and school, plus miscellaneous gateposts and quoins, together with the plinth of the memorial to John Card (d. 1729, the donor of a local charity) in the churchyard, are composed of this attractive golden stone.

Draycott almost imperceptibly merges with Rodney Stoke, its sister village, yet possessing a quite different atmosphere, an entrenched tranquillity. The village is built largely of Dolomitic conglomerate and comprises a church, manor, post office, Baptist chapel and junior school. Lining the main road there is a string of red-brick council homes; they exude a slightly raw sunset glare, modified only by their neat, well-tended gardens.

But the arresting feature is the church, a restrained and sober building displaying the familiar roofing appeals. Its highlight is the Rodney Chapel, comprising the tomb chest of Sir Thomas Rodney (1478), armoured and slumbering under an open canopy of cusped arches; of Sir John Rodney (1527), looking less comfortable under a Tudor cusped arch; and of Anna (1630), wife of George Rodney, under an arch supported by four columns. Finally there is the wall tomb and monument to George Rodney (1651), youngest son of Sir Edward, complete with angel statuettes and figure rising up from the coffin. There is something almost eerily affecting about these monuments. Not the fact that they bring the past to life. Rather it is their frozen inertia, their total deadness, that is unsettling. All that ornate sorrowing; gilded grief; a hopeless bid to achieve immortality by means of alabaster and elaboration.

From Draycott the New Road branches off, ascending the steep scarp face of the plateau, passing scattered tumuli, isolated farmstead, eroded hillfort. Colours here are muted greys, browns and greens. The terrain has a weathered, planed-down aspect; dazzling knuckles of limestone protrude through the turf, and sheep are strewn over the rough pasture like bits of cloud. After passing a quarry and reservoir, the road levels out and crosses the West Mendip Way, emerging on the B3135 about one mile from Priddy.

This village is the capital of the Mendips. Lying 800 feet up in a sheltered basin, it appears at first glance a harsh, grey-walled community grouped around a spacious green on which a stack of hurdles is placed, awaiting the annual sheep fair. In such a context, the word 'village' is almost a misnomer, hardly applicable to these straggled settlements that have sprung up in this wild country owing to the presence of water, adequate pasturage or mineral wealth. There is such quietness here. No tight Devonshire grouping of rose-embowered cottages, church and manor house; here buildings stand separate, self-contained, reminding one there is work to be attended to and little time for neighbourly gossip.

Arranged around the green are the New Inn, a sprinkling of slated, colour-washed cottages, St Cuthbert's Farm, Manor Farm, the post office and – discreetly isolated on a low eminence – the church of St Lawrence. Built in the Early English style, it stands boldly against the skyline, the western tower with pierced trefoiled parapets and pinnacles, making a powerful impression in its bare and barren setting. The font is early Norman, squat yet decorative, and there is a notable pulpit about which there is a legend that, when a goose nested annually inside, the kind vicar did not disturb the bird's sojourn and confined his preaching to the lectern. Interesting too is a tablet recording the mending of the tower and 'to pinikls' in 1705, when Shavian spelling flourished.

Priddy gives its name to one of the four mineries of Mendip. They were enclosures to which the miners brought their ore to be processed. First it was washed in buddles (tanks) and then reduced to metal in furnaces. The flues and the chimneys for the latter were curious. Each flue ran for several hundred yards along the ground before ending in the usual high chimney to create the draught. The reason for this arrangement lay in the fact that lead was a volatile metal, and, if the vapours went straight into the atmosphere, much would be lost. The workers, however, could cool the flues and enter the tunnels to scrape out the condensed lead. Until fairly recently, Chewton or Waldegrave minery had a complete chimney, but now only the flues along the ground remain. The water-supply, on the other hand, is still intact, the large artificial pond being widely known as Priddy Pool. Today people fish in it and during cold winters go ice-skating; it is also a favourite place for naturalists, the nearby Stockhill Wood providing in autumn a fungi-collector's paradise.

As important as Priddy, and particularly rich in associations, prehistoric, Roman and medieval, is the scattered settlement of Charterhouse, set in a wide, empty landscape of rolling heather-covered hills, looking south over Velvet Bottom towards Cheddar. Around Charter-house, on the very top of Mendip, there is this feeling of ordered desolation. Compared with the lush dairylands of the Somerset plain, the terrain seems harsh, almost savage, especially where the turf has been ravaged by mining. There are few trees, only green-grey recessions of space, sweeping horizons, across which razoring winds hiss and sigh. Drystone walls crawl across the hillslopes in flinty files, oozing moss between their layers like emerald cement, and many of the roads and tracks they follow are ruler-straight, affording spectacular views towards the edge of the plateau.

The name 'Charterhouse' derives from the French 'Chartreuse', the spot, fourteen miles from Grenoble, where in 1084 St Bruno of Rheims founded the first Carthusian monastery. The conclave at Witham near Frome was the first in England, St Hugh of Lincoln being its most famous prior, and it owned land at Velvet Bottom, a valley near Charterhouse, which was probably worked by lay brothers as a sheep farm. The building is a long, two-gabled affair with stone-mullioned windows, a tiled roof and look of weathered severity: no pepperpot chimneys or spiky ornaments for this hard land. It was erected over the monastic foundation by one Robert May whose descendants included John May, Sheriff of Somerset. The present house dates from around 1600, and the May family held it until 1799; the new owner was granted the glorious title Baron Mendip. His descendant, Viscount Clifden, owns it today.

Once Charterhouse had a village school but this now serves as an outdoor activity centre. The Blackmore Educational Reserve owns several acres of the old minery and is an important focus for wildlife studies. Those interested in local architecture find themselves drawn to W.D. Caroe's most unusual church, erected 1908, with its roughcast exterior, vestigial spire and finely carved screen. Fittingly enough, it bears a dedication to St Hugh of Witham.

To the south of Priddy is Green Ore, a small hamlet situated on the crossroads where the Roman road from Charterhouse to Old Sarum and the Bristol-Wells turnpike road intersect. The land is irregular, with scooped-out troughs and bumpy depressions, the legacy of ancient leadworkings, and the hamlet consists only of a pub Druidically named 'The White Bull', a few bleached cottages and outlying farms, and the ruined mansion of Hill Grove (1850), once a sanatorium. This is a grimly atmospheric ruin, split-walled with high, echoing rooms in which old wallpaper hangs like gigantic flaps of skin and ghosts of elderly men and ladies intermittently appear.

One explanation of the name is that 'Green Ore' derives from the rare emerald-coloured deposits occasionally found in the local mines – Woodward mentions 'Mendip Green Ore, a lead ore of Poppinjay green colour'. But the hamlet was formerly called 'Greenworth', 'the green enclosure', referring to the Carthusians' grange and sheepwalks, but later corrupted to 'Green Ore' by reason of the mining.

The grange belonged to Witham Priory, the owners of the Charterhouse farm, and Green Ore was referred to in the census of 1841 as an 'extra-parochial district'. The farmhouse occupying the sight of the Carthusian grange is obviously a building of some antiquity; the windows are narrow and arched, arranged in groups of twos and threes, indicating a seventeenth-century origin which is confirmed by an inscribed stone near the entrance porch: 'PAX HUIC DOMINI 1655' ('Peace to this place O Lord').

Wookey Hole, derived from the Celtic *ogof*, 'cave', is recessed in a narrow Mendip valley two miles north-west of Wells. A wedged-in hamlet, always industrially active in a minor way, it had a paper-mill in 1610 close to where the Axe discharges itself from that immense stone vent that draws the jostling multitudes.

The cave is owned by Madame Tussaud's, who acquired it from Olive Hodgkinson in 1973. The Hodgkinsons developed the village during Victoria's reign and are responsible for its principal features. After a fire in 1855, William Samuel Hodgkinson rebuilt the paper-mill, founded a school and erected some trim workers' dwellings, a village club (1883) and a church dedicated to St Mary Magdalene. Installing themselves in the neo-Tudor mansion Glencot, the Hodgkinsons ran the estate and paper-mill (which in 1863 made paper for American Confederate bank-notes), and

Wookey prospered as a durable, self-sufficient community. It was George William Hodgkinson, the husband of Olive, who nurtured a dominant ambition to open up the great cave. Tourists in the Edwardian era were shown around the cave by a tenant farmer who would ignite the silhouette of the witch by throwing petrol over her. But in 1928 George William began the process of organizing visitors and opening up the caves commercially. The upshot of his entrepreneurial flare was the railings and rock-cut steps, the fern-fringed artificial lighting, and the rockeries and gardens that formalize the course of the Axe. But despite the feel of a touristic complex, complete with ice-cream kiosk, café, picnic area and toilets, it is generally acknowledged that a more restrained hand has been at work here than at Cheddar. There are fine nineteenth-century survivals, too: the paper-mill, in particular, overlooking the bowling green (now housing Lady Bangor's fairground collection and Madame Tussaud's attics), is made of local conglomerate and has a functional formality of line.

William of Worcester (1470) wrote of the image of a porter at the entrance to the cave. Each visitor asked permission of this figure to enter the hall, then went in carrying 'shevys of reed sedge' as torches. Michael Drayton (1612) poeticized about 'Ochy's dreadful hole' in language full of foolish, fantastic conceits, personifying the cave as suffering from a gross inferiority complex because she was not classed among the foremost wonders of the isle:

Yet Ochy's dreadful hole still held herself disgrac'd
With the wonders of this isle that she should not be plac't;
But that which vex't her most, was, that the Peakish cave
Before her darksome self such dignity should have ...

From 1908 to 1912 the pioneer Mendip speleologist H.E. Balch conducted an excavation of the floor of Wookey. This and subsequent investigations brought to light objects of craftsmanship in silver and bronze along with spindle whorls, loom weights, bracelets, querns, Samian ware and Romano-British pottery. What has intrigued people, especially those with a Hammer Films mentality, is whether the immense fissure was ever used for sacrificial killing. The eeriness of the cave recalls Lucan's description of the Druidical grove near Marseilles where 'water fell ... in abundance from dark springs. The images of the gods, grim and rude, were uncouth blocks formed of felled tree trunks ... often the subterranean hollows quaked and bellowed ...' Wookey would certainly have qualified as a place of foreboding and sanctity: H.E. Balch found a recess beneath the shoulder of the witch and a corresponding mark in the floor below, as if a stake had been implanted, but whether a human being or goat was once attached to it is an open question.

Wookey paper-mill is still operative. It is fun seeing the rags churning in troughs and the vatman and coucher at work, then the completed sheets being hung up for drying. One can sample the fairground collection as well, which has a Marenghi organ, a Ben Hur front, ice-cream barrow, walking donkeys – all nicely kitsch and mildly (to the present writer's way of reacting) headache-inducing. Finally Madame Tussaud's attics, also in the mill, where one can inspect the heads and assorted members of those now deprived of contemporary significance – all those names flighty fashion deified then deserted: George Brown, Ringo Starr, Twiggy, Lee Harvey Oswald, complete with labels fitted to their various parts so that, if the spotlight irradiates them once more, they can be reassembled correctly.

Wookey village, as opposed to the tourist-swallowing hole, is an expanding, little-visited place, two miles south-west of all the commercial activity. Situated at the eastern tip of that rambling, wriggling rise of land along which such hamlets as Theale, Bleadney and Henton are strung, it is a slightly reclusive community encased by modern housing estates, none of them large but substantial enough to have shifted the economic basis of the community from agriculture to commuting. The Preywater and Knowle roads converge forming the High Street where the Ring of Bells (a weekend drinking venue decorated with wagon wheels and suspended flower-baskets) joins company with Chantry Cottage and the post office stores. The great showpiece is Mellifont Abbey – a big, embattled, early nineteenth century manor with Gothic windows, red-brick dressing and imposing wrought-iron gates. Older fragments from the early medieval Court Farm are worked into the abbey; an early Tudor oriel window caught the eye of Pevsner, as did 'four spandrels of some trefoil arcading with, it seems, early 13th C sculpture'. Formerly this was the rectory, and it is overshadowed by the lean, sharp profile of St Matthew's Church, a thirteenth-century structure with an extended pinnacle that juts out dramatically from the embattled tower. The chancel was repaired in 1423, when Bishop Bubwith controlled the diocese, and a flat-headed south window, now removed to a wall of the south-east chapel, was installed. The interior is dark, claustrophobic and unnerving – an effect heightened by the glass case containing the body of a swift struck dead by lightning during a service. A cross was fashioned from the damaged roof timbers and is mounted on the north wall.

The road from Bath to Wells climbs by a series of long, undulant curves to Green Ore, then descends Nedge Hill, eventually to reach Chewton Mendip. A historically interesting place, cradled among hills yet hardly overshadowed by them, Chewton featured in the Will of King Alfred (d. 901), and the parish church incorporates Saxon stonework. Although it was essentially a sheep-farming community, lead was also intensively mined here, and local marl provided an excellent building-material. The infant River Chew washes by a ford and under a double-arched bridge; for part of its course it is walled in, and its twists and irregularities soften the starker aspects of the scene. Limestone here is dark, gritty, tinged with brown, lending a rather grim visage to Chewton during foul winter weather. But the approach from Wells makes a pleasant descent among sprawling deciduous boughs to the convergence of routes marked by the prominent Tor View Garage. There is also a post office and store at hand, several businesses, a cheese-making factory and the Waldegrave Arms, named after the East Anglian family who once owned the manor. On the Litton road stands a row of Victorian cottages with a stone and paint finish called Foxcroft; another notable building is Manor Farm, a substantial creeper-covered house (*c*.1700) with crossed mullions – possibly a former residence of a steward of the Waldegraves.

The Perpendicular tower is by far the church's most elaborate exterior feature. Leland in 1535 commented on the 'goodly new high tourred steple of Chewton Mendip'. It sweeps upwards a full 126 feet, with fifteen-foot corner pinnacles, making a very impressive sight, and on its west face is a group of figures representing Christ in Glory, with his foot resting on the globe, attended by angels with censers and feather-legged Seraphim clutching scrolls.

Less congenially situated – but memorably barren and bleak – the parish of Emborough is scattered south of Chewton and consists of various weather-beaten farms, an old tollhouse and a church and manor. The manor looks grey, damp, slightly woebegone, and the medieval church – a lonely stump of Christianity – makes a suitably doleful companion. Inside are memorials to the Hippisleys, a Georgian gallery and – on the sanctuary floor – a pathetic carving of two children's faces with the legend:

These pretty babes for long did play
Before the Lord called them away.

Emborough Pool is a tree-fringed lake, popular among fishermen, invigorating in sunny weather, but fiercely desolate on grey winter evenings when waves slap moodily in the clouting wind and ghouls gather at the water's edge and attempt to push one in.

3

The Polden Hills

The Polden Hills are an inspiring scenic incident never rising above 300 feet but affording spectacular views all the same, for they overlook the dyked flatlands of Glastonbury and Highbridge to the north and the similarly low-lying areas of King's Sedgemoor to the south. The axis of the range is approximately north-west to south-east, extending from Puriton to Somerton, a distance of over twenty miles. They are attractive hills, freckled by orchard and woodland and merging with the peat moors on the northern slopes but rising more steeply on the southern side. Bowered by chestnut, elm and oak, the ridge has (to quote Desmond Hawkins, 1973) 'a modestly sylvan atmosphere of occasional woods and copses and open parkland, with rooks flinging off into the wind or riding out over the marshland'.

Local lias is the predominant building material, although the red brick of Bridgwater creeps in here and there, and shades vary from icy grey to shadowed blues and lighter honey tones. Alien substances have been introduced, such as pebbledash and artificial stone, particularly along the main ridge road, where there is some rather obtrusive ribbon development, mainly centred upon Ashcott, Walton and Bawdrip. But still the Poldens remain a distinct miniature geographical region with their flora, folklore and follies.

Puriton is the most westerly of the villages strung along the northern slopes. The situation is lush, sheltered, backed by spinneys and coppices and salubrious ridge walks – yet the best has not been made of it. Here estates strike out and sprawl on the levelled hillside, and the huge Royal Ordnance factory provides employment for many. Industrially always an active parish, for it lies on a tidal bend of the Parrett, Puriton has featured as a centre for quarrying, cement-making, salt-mining and the manufacture of Bath bricks – derived from the exclusive slime of the murky river.

There is a profusion of new houses and roads but, partly because of the hilliness, the openness and casual loose-planned aspect, the effect is far from industrial or commercial – more a large, friendly, unfussy village. New architecture predominates but fragments of old Puriton are found in Rye Lane, where the parish church stands, a squat, sturdy building with a pyramid-capped tower.

East of Puriton is its twin village, Woolavington, overlooking the flat moors stretching away to the lighthouse tower at Burnham-on-Sea and the immense wave-like block of the Mendips. The village began in Saxon times on the site of the square and Lower Road, with strips of field running up the hill. The community was self-contained, focused entirely on the land, varied only by quarrying and lime-working. The most dramatic change came in the 1930s when the outbreak of war caused an estate to be built to house war-workers. Today the houses have been rebuilt, and many new ones added, so that the formerly quiet village, with its court house, windmill, duckpond and shady twisting lanes, is blocked out with extensive red-brick estates extending almost a mile from the foot to the summit of the hill.

The manor house is the nucleus of the old village and is at least 500 years old. A priest's hiding-place is inset in the dining-room chimney, and the heart-shaped stops on the oak beams are another special feature. William Pym lived here: his 1608 Will contains a remarkable tirade against his wife, Agnes, citing her various lovers but bequeathing her £10 and the justice of God. The Pyms were major landowners in Woolavington along with the Throckmortons. Their most famous representative was John Pym, who angered King Charles I by presenting a petition defending the privileges of the House of Commons.

An even older building than the manor is the Grange. An early Elizabethan manor house, originally granted by deed to the Woolavington family by Maud de Candos in the twelfth century, it is now divided into two parts with an extension at both ends and contains a cock-fighting pit – a round, stone structure with thick walls and plastered beams. By the Grange stands the fourteenth century church, which has a Norman chancel and a pulpit quaintly assembled from oak panels believed to come from Sharpham Park, the nearby Tudor manor where Abbot Whiting of Glastonbury was arrested and killed and where the poet Sir Edward Dyer and the novelist Henry Fielding lived at different periods. In the west wall of the church is a stone to Sir John Hody, Lord Chief Justice during Henry VI's reign, who died in 1441.

On a hill above Woolavington, in the grounds of a Georgian mansion, Knowle Hall, there used to be a folly tower which was built by Mr Benjamin Cuff Greenhill for his wife Pélagie, daughter of the Count of Breville. This exotic lady was so terribly homesick that Mr Greenhill, desperate to placate her with some pretty fancy, built this sham castle. It was blown up in 1949 because of its ruinous state, but there is a memorial to Pélagie in Puriton church; she lived to be seventy-three (dying in 1899), despite her chronic attachment to her native land.

Twinned with Woolavington is the neighbouring village of Cossington, for they share parish magazines, clubs and functions. Here is a satisfying grouping of cottages around the post office, church and manor. There is a walled-in stream, chestnut trees and a Victorian primary school with stone tracery in the main gable. Far more ostentatious is Cossington Grange, an imposing neo-Tudor concoction with a heavy central tower built in 1863; nowadays it houses a firm of building contractors. Writers on the Poldens draw attention to the rugged centrally placed elm under which John Wesley is alleged to have preached a sermon. No longer in its green-leafed glory, only a truncated stump set in concrete, this relic has also been cited as a hiding-place for the Duke of Monmouth after the Battle of Sedgemoor, 1685. One wonders how this fastidious, high-born nobleman enjoyed his sojourn among the squirrels and bird-droppings.

The manor house of Cossington adjoins the church. Although essentially Victorian in date and designs, this building has a Regency grace and lightness: tall chimneys, honey brickwork, lacy bargeboards – features markedly contrasting with the crustacean solidity of the church. The latter has a heavy, squareish tower – probably thirteenth century – shaded by tall firs and copper beeches. Inside is the brass-cut figure of John Brent (d. 1524), lord of the manor, and Maud Pauncefoot, his wife. They lived in the old manor, not the present building, and John's father, Robert, left the sum of 40s. 'to the glazing of a window of the parish church of Cosyngton'. One notes in the south-west window of the nave the heraldic wyvern argent of the Brents impaling the fleurs-de-lis of the Pauncefoots.

On leaving Puriton and ascending the ridge, the next most westerly village is Bawdrip, warming itself on the southern slopes and reflecting a slower pace altogether. To many people it counts only as a dispiriting row of houses encountered on the A39 Bridgwater-Street road, an interval of nondescript monotony before the road swoops uphill to join the old Roman way. From this point things improve – soft-curving hills, immense vistas of quilted fields with toytown farms, coppices, follies and wayside inns. Back to Bawdrip, however, which people remember as a halt on the Somerset and Dorset railway – a kind of shunting hesitation heightening the tedium of the journey. But this is not Bawdrip proper, whatever the signposts say, for the village nestles south of the road. A friendly slapdash scene meets the eye. Old cottages, some with moulting whitewash, a ladder against one where two men are engaged fitting slates, the chug of a tractor on a road which receives the imprint of cattle hooves as insistently as speeding tyres, a jolly primary school at play across the way from the thirteenth-century church – all these are facets of a scene so commonplace that it remains unforgettable. Below the school, at the junction of Bradney Lane and Church Road, there is an estate tucked away to the right, comprising large modern houses with half brick and half smooth yellow cement finish, amazingly inappropriate. Take this road round the back of the cottages and approach the church via a narrow alley of red-brick terraced dwellings.

St Michael's Church is cruciform with a central embattled tower, a combination of Norman strength and the stirrings of

English exuberance. In 1681 died Eleanor Lovell, a young woman of this parish, 'taken away by a sudden and untimely fate, at the very time of her marriage celebrations' – so that Latin inscription on the tablet behind the altar tells us. Also a chest was formerly kept in the church – a combination of factors that identifies the parish with the old song 'The Mistletoe Bough' which dealt with a family named Lovell and a young bride-to-be hiding in an oak chest. Unfortunately, when his beloved was found missing, it simply did not occur to the naïve young bridegroom that she had mistaken herself for a legal document and locked herself away. So when they did open it up, they found a severe deterioration in her condition:

> At length an oak chest that had long laid hid,
> Was found in the castle; they raised the lid,
> And a skeleton form lay mouldering there
> In the bridal wreath of that lady fair ...

Lying almost exactly between Cossington and Catcott is Chilton Polden, one of those unfocalized places where no definite centre is traceable. A long road called the Broadway careers past rows of elderly cottages, colour-washed terracotta, pink and Regency green; a linear straggle of bungalows; a former school building with a clock tower alarmingly jutting from it commemorating Edward VII and Queen Alexandra; and finally reaching the western end where most of the interest lies. Here is St Edward's Church, a building which consistently seems to evoke no comment whatsoever; it is in the Perpendicular style and was rebuilt in 1889 at the cost of £2,000. Opposite the church is the part-Tudor Sealey's Farm with a working cider-press in the barn. Also, facing the road, is Chilton House – an exquisitely unkept example of frozen Regency blancmange. It shimmers so pinkly one is almost tempted, like Hansel and Gretel, to bite a chunk from the wall.

But the real architectural outsider lies some way from the village on the main A39 ridge road. Known as Chilton Priory, it is an audacious battlemented folly, yet suffering from a certain cumbersome literalness, lacking the gay theatricality of the very best follies. It is, if anything, closer to low-budget Hollywood lunacy than real antiquarian passion. Backed by lawns and gardens that render it effective when seen from below, it was built by William Stradling in the early nineteenth century to house documents and oddments (including armour from the field of Sedgemoor) amassed during many years of travel and souvenir-hunting. The house was known as 'The Priory' because it is said to incorporate materials from an old Benedictine priory established here as a cell to the abbey of Glastonbury. This is probably true, for it incorporates just about everything that Stradling could beg, borrow or buy, including pinnacles from Langport, an iron-fitted door from Stogursey, a lump of Glastonbury Abbey, a finial from Chedzoy, grotesque heads from Enmore Castle – an enterprise smacking of Frankenstein rather than harmonious creation.

Catcott is many people's favourite Polden village. It has a maze of intersecting lanes reflecting an older, more haphazard pattern of growth. They provide perfect thoroughfares for exploring this haven of well-tended homes and gardens. Cottage façades gleam with freshly applied whitewash; gardens are scrupulously weeded; streets are spick and litterless. There is new primary school whose crisp, razorlike contours are not entirely sympathetic, and several stone farmhouses. Probably the most artistic feature is the war memorial, a slender, crocketed column supporting a carving of a First World War soldier. King William Road leads past the Royal Inn (a pub with white quoins at the angles and windows) to the church of St Peter, a building in the Norman style preserving its ancient stocks in the porch. Inside, it is white and unpretentious, with a Jacobean pulpit and chancel roof with carved oak bosses. On one wall, in old-fashioned lettering, is the sermon from Titus for the women of the village: 'The aged women likewise that they be in behaviour as becometh holiness, not false accusers; teachers of good things, that they may teach the young women to be sober, to be chaste, keepers at home, to love their husbands.'

Two miles south-east of Catcott, and connected by the same rambling, rolling roads, stands Shapwick, a village with a bluff, durable air long associated with peat-cutting and animal husbandry. There are recent buildings here, infilling along the road, and older cottages sprouting windows and extensions, but the impression created is of a restrained mingling of styles. Grey lias weathers well and softly contrasts with earth-red tiles and roses, yellow, pink and white, nimbly scaling the walls and porches. The main street is East Street, running from north to south, and many lanes branch from it at right angles to join the other main thoroughfare, West Street (farming communities do not strain their imagination when naming roads). An old map of 1764, available in the church, confirms how little this basic pattern has altered: strip-shaped smallholdings making blocks of interconnected rectangles. Locals of the period are enshrined in the nomenclature: Bartlets Lane, Poles Lane, Godfreys Lane, Durstons Lane, Richard Collins Lane, Pollards Lane, Tilliers Lane – tiny personalized routes running in to each other.

St Mary's Church stands south of Shapwick Manor alongside East Street. Grainy-grey weathered stone, the colour of stormclouds, surges up to form a massive, embattled tower – no prongs or pinnacles, just a blunt strength of form, essentially Norman, creating an impression of contained power. Inside are memorials to the Strangways family, who owned the estate from 1657 to 1944 when Miss Viall Strangways sold it to Lord Vestey, and also to the Bull family, former lords of the manor. A red bull's head marks their memorial stones, one of the finest of which commemorates Jane, wife of William Bull, who died 1657. The Bulls descended from Dr John Bull, chaplain to Henry VIII and Edward VI, who is said to have penned England's national anthem and to have embodied that horse sense and solidity which arouses patriotic pride in Englishmen and sends bilious shudders down the spines of artistic Frenchmen. The Bulls married into the Templer family, who married into the Strangways. Henry Bull Templer Strangways became premier of Australia, 1868–70. The altar rail is made of Australian oak especially shipped over in 1861 by this member of the antipodean elect.

The single thatched house in the village, 'Forsters', is

thought to have been the old vicarage. When it was re-thatched, in the nineteenth century, four silver christening-spoons (dated to the reign of Charles I) were found hidden in the roof, possibly the original church silver hidden by the vicar, fearful that they would fall into the hands of the King's soldiers or the Monmouth rebels after their defeat on Sedgemoor in 1685.

More imposing is the Jacobean Shapwick House, lying isolated and tree-shielded at the north-west corner of the village. It was built by Charles I in 1630 for his Chief Justice, Sir Henry Rolle, on the site of the old court house owned by Abbot John de Taunton. In the grounds is an impressive hexagonal dovecote, dating from around 1235 and now splendidly restored after a falling chestnut tree truncheoned the roof to splinters. The house itself is now adapted as a large luxury hotel.

Walton is the easternmost of the settlements occupying the Polden ridge before the main road descends to Street and Glastonbury. By no means a beautiful village, with too many examples of insensitive development and patchy infilling, it dates back to Saxon times. The name means either 'settlement of British serfs' or 'settlement in a wood'. The Domesday Book listed it, and later it came under the control of Glastonbury Abbey. When Henry VIII sequestered the massive ecclesiastical holdings throughout the land, Walton was sold to Sir John Thynne, an ancestor of the Marquesses of Bath.

Physically the village is concentrated around the main road. There are two pubs, the Pike and Musket (formerly the Globe) and the nautically furnished Royal Oak, a Methodist church, a garage, a converted windmill and the old vicarage. Near the middle is Teign Court, a wholly unsuitable row of neat red-tiled artificial stone houses with triangular timbered porches. At Broughton Close there is an estate of big, bold, gabled houses with ample garages and gardens – again unsuitable but very substantial to look at.

The church is rather big and dominant with a dwarf pyramidal broach spire. It was rebuilt in 1866 but still retains its Norman door with floriated ironwork and a fourteenth-century stone figure grasping a heart, with a long-eared dog as his partner in oblivion. The church was one of the few items that did not come under the hammer on 14 July 1939, when practically the whole village was auctioned. The Marquess of Bath had decided to sell his Walton estate through his agent, Thomas B. Gill, and it was split into 137 lots: arable land, orchards, quarry sites and a turbary (where peat is dug), together with farms, cottages, paddocks and the Globe Inn. The total profit, after the agents had docked their expenses, amounted to £61,665. 'The next time you speed through Walton,' wrote Christopher Nicholson (1983), 'give a thought to the villagers who left their cottages that line the road you are on, to walk to Street, not knowing who would own their cottages when they returned.'

Sunny and south-facing, with cottages clinging limpet-like to the steep road, a garage and testing-station, shop and post office, the plan of Moorlinch has been determined by its wedged-in position. The Saxon inhabitants cultivated the hillsides around the backs of the cottages or used the lower slopes for grazing and cultivating. The main street ascends sharply from the Ring of Bells, passing the church on its jutting shelf, then over the ridge to join the A39 – an exciting twisty ascent by foliage-shadowed cottages and tunnel-like banks. In the Braikenridge Collection at Taunton, there is a colour drawing showing Knoll Hill around 1840 crowned by a windmill. Large ridges are identifiable on the slopes – hence the 'linch' comes from lynchets or cultivation terraces. 'Moor' is said to come from 'mirie': thus the name has been translated as 'Happy Hillside', which sounds speciously folksy. Before the Sedgemoor marshes were drained, the sea flooded the valley. Local fishermen hauled their catch up to the village crossroads. The old cross, which was removed to the churchyard in 1860, was actually called Fish Cross.

After the Norman Conquest, Moorlinch was shared out between the Pyks and Glastonbury Abbey, the traditional landowner. A feud broke out in 1339, resulting in a bow-and-arrow fight between the Pyks and the abbot's men, an incident noted in the Glastonbury chartulary. (The stone effigy in the church, enshrouded in stiff drapery, is of Lady Eleanor de Beauchamp, wife of Richard Pyk.)

The partly Norman church is elevated on a hillock above

Sedgemoor, looking out towards Weston Zoyland. In July 1685 the parishioners watched the last battle on English soil, and Swayne's Leap, four stones sunk in the undergrowth on the outskirts of the parish, is said to mark the desperate jumps of Swayne, a Monmouth supporter who was captured and tortured.

Greinton hugs the southern slopes of the Poldens above King's Sedgemoor. Sited high and dry above the floodline, it formerly consisted of a straggle of farms arranged along the old drove linking Stawell, Moorlinch and Pedwell. But part of this was widened and tarmacked to accommodate the A361, which forcefully butts through the hamlet and on to Othery and Taunton.

The parish church, another St Michael's, is banked high above the main road. It is predominantly fifteenth century with superb oak doors dating from the Tudor period. Four ball-eyed gargoyles malevolently glare from the embattled tower with its pyramidal capping. An old Victorian street-lamp lights the entrance on dark evenings, and along the road is a pink-washed Georgian house, a Victorian-Elizabethan manor and the rose-embowered Church Farm. Backing the road are red-tiled barns around which bovine choirs rehearse their obbligato. At Greinton Gate Farm, a local man named Thomas Bryant provided rest and refreshment for the defeated Duke of Monmouth. He was rewarded with a Spanish snuffbox exquisitely inlaid with tortoiseshell, which his descendant, Miss Eileen Bishop, gave to the County Museum. No one seems to know the site of the farmhouse today, and a 1772 sketch of it exists showing it already in a ruinous state.

Stawell has been described as 'the jewel of the southern Poldens'. This is a slightly over-eulogistic description of the tiny hamlet that sits composedly at the west end of the narrow road linking up with Moorlinch and Greinton. Two pigmy eminences, Pendon Hill and Ball Hill (did they once light bale-fire here?), embosom the houses and farms. 'Stawell' derives from the Saxon meaning a 'stony stream', an allusion to the pond at Ford Farm which encrusts with lime any object immersed in it.

The hamlet amounts to little more than a long road dawdling past the red-brick Manor Farm – a Georgian building with a triangular pedimented entrance – and extensive orchards to which people drive to pick apples at the going price. The climax of the route is the small, stumpy church with the gabled tower overlooking the well-kept Walnut Farm and a row of agreeably rural cottage buildings with bushy, rose-petal whiskers and small, neat, black crosses on the walls, indicating supporting braces. Probably the church was begun in the twelfth century, and it is thought that the churchyard was built up from soil carted from the woods to avoid flooding. On the right-hand side of the door is a cross carved within a circle cut by a villager who wished to record that he had fulfilled his vow or received a special blessing.

Lying between Street to the north and Somerton to the south, Compton Dundon hails the motorist with the Castlebrook Inn, a popular stopping-place with a traditional wooden interior. Nearby stands Castlebrook Farm and the old tithe barn exuding the sober solidity of local lias. This stone, derived from the quarries of Keinton and Charlton, absorbs the light, markedly contrasting with the cream-plastered, colour-washed cob cottages of West Somerset and Devon. The effect might be austere were it not for the golden thatching, a noted feature of Dundon, and the twining roses clasping the exterior walls of almost every dwelling. At the corner of Ham Lane stands a gabled farmhouse with a long thatched roof: fringes of Norfolk reed, not the usual combed wheat reed, form aprons to accommodate the irregularly spaced windows.

The main road section is only part of Dundon. To get to the church, follow Ham Lane to Church Farm, a 400-year-old thatched cottage (now a completely renovated guest house advertising a spotlit 25-foot-deep well in the kitchen) standing opposite St Andrew's, a rugged fourteenth-century church with a rich, blue-grey, granular texture to its walls and battlements. A large yew shades the churchyard which nestles beneath Lollover Hill, a wooded eminence overshadowed by the neighbouring Dundon Beacon, a towering fort of the Iron Age bristling with oaks and ash. But the church does not mark the end of this scattered village – properly speaking an amalgamation of two hamlets – for there are half a dozen more crusty-gold thatched cottages with red-brick chimneys strung along the lane that skirts the hill fort.

The great landmark around Compton is the Hood Memorial Column which honours Samuel, Admiral Viscount Hood, whom Nelson described in 1795 as 'the best officer, take him altogether, that England has to boast of; great in all situations which an Admiral can be placed in'. Southey echoed this opinion in a fulsome epitaph (honouring all three nautical Hoods – Samuel, Arthur and Alexander) in Butleigh church:

> Yes, wheresoever hostile fleets have ploughed
> The ensanguined deep, his thunders have been heard,
> His flag in brave defiance hath been seen;
> And bravest enemies at Sir Samuel's name,
> Felt fatal presage in their inmost heart ...

The Column is 115 feet high and stands on Windmill Hill amid dramatic beeches. It is dark and daunting and the base consists of inscribed panels; the crown is a glass belvedere with men-of-war sail motifs. This is no jaunty folly but an expression of stark authoritarianism.

4

The Sheppey Valley and Batcombe

East of Wells are the cloth villages culminating in the towns
of Shepton Mallet and Frome tucked away in the hills.
Scenery varies according to the surface geology, and the
Wells-Frome road crosses a belt of Keuper marl and
Dolomitic conglomerate around Dinder and Croscombe,
lending a distinctive pinkish tinge to the buildings, then over
the lower lias beds of Shepton, where the stone varies from
Cotswold cream to gritty mottled textures, followed by bare
and beechclad domes of mountain limestone at Cranmore,
then rolling sheep hills extending in an ever-broadening
enclave from below the Frome basin up to Gloucestershire.
The country is rich with fuller's earth, once used for
purifying fleeces, and scored by streams that wash down
tiny valleys streamered with oak, ash and pine. Shepton
('sheep farm of the Malets', *c.* 1100) stands high in the centre
of this region and can be traced back to the eighth-century,
when Ina, King of the West Saxons, granted the manor to
the abbots of Glastonbury. The town prospered after 1500,
when the wool trade was expanding, and the course of the
River Sheppey became thick with leats and mills. Around its
banks arose blocks of weavers' cottages arranged side-upon-
back forming tiny self-sufficient units, and the town grew
from the amalgamation of these individual clusters. After
the cloth trade declined in the nineteenth century, Shepton
turned to such industries as brewing, bacon-curing and
manufacturing machine parts, and today its most famous
factory is Showering's, which displays as its mascot a little
twinkly hooved chamois with a blue bow around its neck

and the magical gift of transforming refined pear juice into hard cash.

Oakhill lies north of Shepton, on the fringes of the Somerset coalfield, abutting on the Fosse Way. It was formed into an ecclesiastical parish from the parishes of Ashwick, Shepton Mallet and Stoke Lane on 11 May 1866. Very much an industrial phenomenon of the late eighteenth and nineteenth centuries, it is dominated by an extensive brewery first established in 1767. Tanning was also important, as Tan Lane at the foot of the hill suggests. It is hardly a beautiful village; other, less hackneyed adjectives come to mind: dour, sturdy and characterful. In particular the outskirts are not prepossessing: concrete-shelled council homes and uniform bungalows spreading along the road and over the brow of the hill. But towards the centre the pattern diversifies with the first view of the brewery, slightly grim and prison-like; its pungent exhalations waft forth and overwhelm like a natural benzedrine. Used by Courage's as a gigantic malting-plant, the other brewery building, further down the hill, has been adapted by Massey Wilcox Transport Limited. Descending deeper into the valley, there is a turreted Victorian Gothic church, complete with bellcote and exuding an authentic atmosphere of the Transylvanian creepiness. Local lias here is a dark brownish grey which creates a stern Presbyterian feel. Yet Oakhill has verve, vitality and self-sufficiency, being well served by a local primary school and by such enterprises as the brewery and Mendip Mouldings. But it was the old Oakhill Brewery Company which essentially created the village, financing the building of several homes and the supply of gas, water and sewerage facilities. There was attached to the brewery 'a fire brigade, consisting of a captain and nine firemen, who have a powerful steam fire engine and appliances' (Kelly's Directory, 1931). It is a reasonable surmise that the fire brigade was installed to avoid the possibility of what took place in 1825 – a great fire which gutted the building.

Exactly half way between Wells and Shepton, Croscombe fits in its small and verdant valley like a bean in a pod. Like many grey-lias villages, in winter beneath a dripping sky, when the stream slurps along noisily and all the houses look dungeon-dark, it can appear far from compelling. But summer transforms it into the apotheosis of a happy valley. The road curves past stone and tile cottages, many retaining their fifteenth-century lintel doorways, and past the stream, formerly called the Croscombe water but renamed the Sheppey, which crosses and re-crosses the road and is marked by leats indicating where cloth-mills once stood.

The spiritual glory of Croscombe, St Mary's, is one of those leaping-spired examples of Gothic rigidity and tension. It has a dynamic sculptural quality, slightly hard and spiky, with its keen angles and crocketed finials. Inside are high oaken pews, some with poppy-headed bench-ends, contributed by the Fortescue family, lords of the manor from the early sixteenth century to the middle of the eighteenth.

The neighbouring Dinder is set back from the Wells-Shepton road beneath the hanging woods of Lyatt. To the south rises Dulcote Hill, around which the dismantled track of an old quarry line can be traced. Eastward lies the hamlet of Dulcote, where a natural spring spurts from a big rock at the crossroads.

Two Regency-period mansions, Dinder House (1803) and Sharcombe (1830), preside over the village, which strikes a note of tasteful orderliness. No cottage clusters or jumbled states of elevation but a long, straight, single-sided street of trim gabled houses built of local rose-tinged conglomerate. Here the tiny River Sheppey pours over a series of weirs and under a balustrated bridge. The houses overlook this formalized watercourse and beyond to the broad, parklike space of the open green extending almost to the road.

In the main street, beside the river, stands the Victorian schoolhouse, now a private residence, and 'The Dragon on the Wheel', the former inn. The dragon sign is still there, and the ridge-tiles at the ends of the rows are decorated with serpents, too. This is probably an allusion to the Somervilles who built the imposing pile of Dinder House: one of their northern branch killed the Dragon of Linton by rolling a carriage-mounted stake into its mouth which had been previously soaked in pitch to neutralize the monster's poisonous breath.

Dinder's church has a busy outline with its stair turret and

pinnacled parapet running all the way round. The
consecration date of the present building is unknown.
During the alterations of 1872, 'a strange dragon-like figure
was discovered in three pieces' lodged inside the chancel
walls. The ornament was late Norman and may have been
part of the tympanum depicting Michael, the church's
patron, dispatching the dragon of evil.

From Dinder, moving east through the rugged, ragged
Sheppey valley, strewn with bones of ancient industries, the
road climbs the watershed past Shepton, and then the
countryside broadens out in an expanse of sloping
meadowland flanked by tree-clad hills. Here the gaunt
Cranmore Tower pricks the skyline, but the village of East
Cranmore lies away from the tower, south of the
Shepton-Frome road. A turn to the right and a swoop round
a bend brings one up against the Strode Arms, facing a
capacious duckpond and the solid frontage of Manor Farm.
This is a delectable spot in sunny weather.

'Cranmore' derives from 'crane mere', 'lake of the cranes',
and shells have been recovered locally confirming the former
presence of a large pool. Originally it was one village, and
the east and west division might have resulted from the
feudal two-field system. From early times the church was a
mere chapelry governed by the larger foundation at
Doulting which was itself subordinate to the abbey of
Glastonbury. This factor may have been the foundation for
genial rivalries between the two villages. It is said that a
game of football was played with the kick-off line midway
between the places which acted as goals. A pig's head was
used for the ball, and what deputized for a whistle is truly
too awful to imagine.

East Cranmore is famous among railway enthusiasts as
the headquarters of the East Somerset Railway. The first
train ran through Cranmore in 1858 from Witham Friary to
Shepton Mallet. The line was extended to Wells in 1862 and
survived as a working railway, although never financially
successful, until 1967. The present line was founded in 1971
by David Shepherd, the wildlife artist, and a group of
railway enthusiasts who brought their locomotives from
Eastleigh to Cranmore. Cranmore Station preserves a rare

Victorian gents' dating from 1858 and a signal box which is now an art gallery selling David Shepherd's work. But the compelling attractions are the iron horses themselves.

Doulting, formerly the senior parish, stands on the high road to Shepton. The Abbey Barn Inn and Restaurant and a motley cluster of austere stone buildings, variegated by recent architecture, stand out from the main street, but it is the church that dominates the scene with its splendid spire which was rebuilt during the 1869 restoration and the height raised some eight-feet. It is attained by a side road where a row of estate-style cottages congregate, some bearing dates between 1881 and 1901 and the arms of Sir Richard Arthur Surtees Paget, a former lord of the manor. They are built of the attractive fine white freestone taking its name from the parish. (Local quarries supplied much of the material for Wells Cathedral.)

Associated with Doulting is St Aldhelm, patron saint of the parish church, former Bishop of Sherborne and Abbot of Malmesbury. In 709, while journeying from Sherborne to Malmesbury, he was taken sick at Doulting, where there was probably a crude wooden church, and died almost immediately. In the garden of Doulting's former vicarage can be seen Aldhelm's Well, a gushing spring enclosed by dressed stone and breached by a couple of arches. Aldhelm was said to have come here and meditated, reading and reciting the Psalms, and after his death it became a place of pilgrimage and healing. Although the exterior of Doulting church is arresting and dramatic, the interior is slightly sinister and chilling, but the modern reredos is a refreshing feature, carved with the figures of six saints, including Aldhelm and Dunstan with his tongs; near the former jets of hewn water gush forth from a spring.

South of Doulting and the Cranmores the Carboniferous limestone gives way to the Great and Inferior Oolite beds. Geologically a continuation of the Cotswolds, this attractive expanse of hilly country is similarly associated with sheep-rearing. Here are deep combes cleansed by energetic brooklets and hillsides clothed with ancient rookeries. Isolated villages perch on shelving hillsides or sequester themselves at the bottom of valleys.

Probably the finest village in this region is Batcombe. It lies on a feeder of the tiny River Alham and evolved linear-fashion – houses beaded along the roadway – apart from the nucleation at the crossroads east of the church. The name is plainly interpreted as 'Batta's Valley' but it could well derive from 'battable', 'good for the sustenance of flocks and herds'.

Impressions of Batcombe vary. The present writer found it a warm, cheerful village, with mullioned houses exuding a weathered warmth, and nearly all of them fronted or backed by gardens sweetened by shrubs or set ablaze by spring daffodil or crocus. But another scribe in the *Visitor* magazine (1984) found the village an altogether harsher, more ascetic spot, comparable with 'a Scottish townscape with stone holding back the fields and hills on one side and stone keeping hidden the gardens of houses on the other'.

Batcombe's church is justly famous for its dominant eighty-six-foot tower. A Will of 1540 refers to its construction, the last of the Great Towers of the East Somerset Group. Here are no notched pinnacles, only a pierced stone parapet with quatrefoiled tracery creating the effect of dignity and restraint. The dedication to St Lawrence is taken from the ancient chapel at Spargrove (a hamlet with a moated farm some two miles down the valley) which was demolished in 1560 when the chapelry was amalgamated with Batcombe.

The south porch (1629) bears the escalloped arms of James Bisse, who held the manor of Batcombe from 1606 to 1646. A very influential family of clothiers, also connected with Croscombe, the Bisses controlled the village during the seventeenth century. They were, to quote the catchy alliteration of Robert Dunning, 'rich, rigid and Roundhead'. Factions like these caused hostility between Batcombe and nearby Royalist Bruton; fights between the two places broke out, as the Bruton parish registers record in a 1642 entry:

All praise and thanks to God still give
For our deliverance Matthias Eve;
By his great power we put to flight
Our foes, the raging Batcombites.

On a lighter note, when, during the great storm of 1703, the battlements of the church tower were damaged, Hu Ash of Bruton relates, 'There was one widow Walter lived in a house by itself, the wind carried away the roof, and the woman's pair of bodice, that was never seen again ...'

Three miles to the east, looking across the Alham Valley to Creech Hill, Evercreech is the most populous village hereabouts. The name is Celtic, meaning 'hill of the boar', although 'creech' was a word latterly applied to a type of gravelly soil. Inns like the Shapway emphasize a formerly important wool village, and the various ponds, pathways, allotments and cattle grids enforce the still-dominant agricultural tradition. (At Prestleigh, a hamlet two miles north, the Royal Bath and West Show takes place during the summer.)

Endowed with a creamery, tile-making and engineering works, Evercreech has a brisker, more workaday routine than the surrounding residential villages. Street plans tend to be tangled and complex. Lanes and drangways (alleys) skirt cottages and backyards, providing odd angles and viewpoints. Discreet modern estates are implanted among a core of older buildings, and the main thoroughfares (Oxford Street, Weymouth Road, High Street) meet up beside St Peter's Church and the stepped village cross. There is delicacy and substantiality in the main square. The soaring church tower, with its set-back buttresses and audaciously extended window tracery, dwarfs the scene.

East of the church is a row of severely angular almshouses of the nineteenth century. To the north, Evercreech House provides a more stylish note, with its Venetian windows. Elsewhere red-tiled grey-stone houses are the keynote, occasionally varied – notably in Old Cottage (1639) – by Hamstone window dressing. But the main colour in Evercreech is definitely grey, the soft dove-grey of lias, rather murky in wet weather, but transformed in sunlight to the aerial floating shade of the sky.

Only one building can provide competition with the 110-foot tower of the church – the looming flues of the milk-processing plant. At the St Ivel factory, 420 people process 100,000 litres of milk from a hundred local farms every day, and produce almost eighty tons of cottage cheese every week.

Evercreech probably had a church as early as the eleventh century; it was demolished at the Dissolution. Two kinds of stone predominate in the present structure, Doulting and Hamstone, and the Perpendicular tower is of the type found at Wrington. The painted roof, featuring flocks of barbarically bright gold and blue angels, comes almost as a shock. Another curiosity is found on the south side of the church: a group of gargoyles featuring a grotesque monster, a monkey and two gossiping cats. A mason from Wells carved them in 1842, and they depict respectively the vicar, with whom he quarrelled, a publican and two women he disliked.

5

Around Frome

Situated in a valley high above the Frome basin, amid
running water, woodland and undramatic hills, Mells is
difficult to describe objectively because it has evinced so
many superlatives in the past. Leland began by praising the
village in the middle of the sixteenth century: 'Mells
stondith sumwhat clyving and hath bene a praty Townelet
of clothing. Selwood Abbete of Glessenbyri, seeing the
welthiness there of the People, had thought to have reedified
the Townelet with mene Houses of square stones to the
figure of an Antonie Cross, whereof yn deade he made but
one Streatelet.' The 'streatelet' comprising one arm of the
cross is called New Street and leads to the church – a severe
row of grey terraced houses with spiral staircases at the rears.

But that is only one minor feature of Mells. People arrive
in significant numbers to admire the hard-cut elegance of the
Perpendicular church, gaze at the H-shaped Elizabethan
manor of the Horners and wander the winding streets and
byways where they can observe such features as the old
village lock-up, the medieval tithe barn, a sixteenth-century
inn called 'The Talbot', and developments of more recent
times, such as the communal water-tap and Sir Edward
Lutyens' war memorial. The main road into the village climbs
past the church, inn and manor house, round a rambling
S-bend, then descends past the stately Clothier's Mansion
and stone cottages to the river valley. The grassy slopes
embanked against the stone thatched dwellings are yellow
with daffodils in spring, and the buildings themselves seem
rooted like ancient molluscs with dusky straw covers.

'Mells' means 'mills', and its architectural splendour, like
that of Nunney and Croscombe, was founded on the
medieval wool trade. The Mells stream was the artery
supplying water for fulling (thickening the cloth by beating
the fibres) and powering the heavy wooden hammers called
fulling-stocks. The cloth trade flourished from the
fourteenth to the nineteenth century, after which came a
marked decline.

Another industry centred at Mells was iron. Here the
Fussells established their first factory in 1744 'for grinding
edge-tools and forging iron-plates'. The business expanded
until there were six separate concerns, specializing in
scythes, spades, shovels, reaphooks, hay-knives and axes.
Agricultural implements from this region reached all parts of
the Empire: gold medals were awarded to James and Thomas
Fussell for their scythes and reap-hooks at the exhibition
held in Vienna in 1860.

The manor house and church of Mells lie alongside. The
age of the latter is uncertain but Leland stated in 1543 that it
was built 'in tyme of mynde', and the stone is local oolite.
The tower is tall, triple-windowed, with much rich and
intricate fenestration, and the south porch has all the taut
vigour and bejewelled detail one associates with the English
Decorated period. The interior is a veritable art gallery of the
early twentieth century, containing a large embroidery
worked by Lady Horner after a design by Burne Jones, a
memorial to Raymond Asquith, son of the liberal Prime
Minister (d. 1917) with lettering by Eric Gill, and a tablet by
Burne Jones erected to the memory of Laura Lyttleton,
showing a peacock perched above an empty tomb. The most
striking monument is found to the left of the chancel, inside
the Horner Chapel – an equestrian statue of Edward Horner,
Lieutenant in the 18th Hussars, killed in action at Fins, near
Etrecourt, who was the last direct male heir to the estate.

In the churchyard are the graves of Ronald Knox, the
Catholic priest and scholar, and Siegfried Sassoon, whose
wish it was to be buried near Knox. One gravestone in the
churchyard (no longer decipherable) bore the following
legend: 'All my inward friends abhorred me and they whom

Priddy church

Erecting hurdles for Priddy's summer fair

The Italianate chemists at Wedmore

The church and George Inn, Wedmore

Cheddar village: the market cross

The Fisherman's House at Meare

Rodney Stoke beneath the Mendips

Stone lions guard the entrance at Mark church

Painted fairground caravans at Wookey Hole

Stradling's Folly at Chilton Polden

Main Street, Dinder, runs alongside the River Sheppey

The dovecote at Doulting

The Somerset Railway at East Cranmore

I loved are turned against me. My kinsfolk have failed me and my familiar friends have forgotten me. William Leecox, husband of Rachell Leecox, who departed April ye 16, 1700.'

Close by is the Elizabethan manor house, which is H-shaped and not E-shaped as was most common. This was traditionally the seat of the Horners, who acquired the estate after the Dissolution. Charles I slept here in 1644 but not at the invitation of the-then owner, Sir John Horner. He was a Roundhead and had had his estates sequestered, but they were returned after the King's beheading. The family's supremacy and longevity gave rise to the suggestion that 'Little Jack Horner' of the nursery rhyme refers to their misappropriation of land. This is rather dubious, for they seem to have obtained their wealth by honest means. However they never suffered from an inadequacy of plums.

At the tiny, depopulated village of Cloford, several miles south of Mells, on the high road from Bruton to Frome, there is an old Perpendicular church dedicated to St Mary. An avenue of yews leads up to the door, and the site is windswept, faintly forlorn. The interior of the church has the plucked, tidied-up feel indicating Victorian restorers have been at work. The best interior feature is probably the elaborate wall monument to George Horner, knight, who died in 1676. He is shown with long hair over his collar and holding an open book – the Bible? Next to him is his wife, in black with a white collar and hood, and around them are gambolling cherubs and black marble columns.

Aside from the church there is little to compel the eye, apart from a Victorian post-box, scattered cottages, farms and Cloford House, visible from the churchyard, a handsome seventeenth-century building islanded among immense agricultural sheds and storage units. The date 1633 appears on the façade, which has transomed and mullioned windows and a round-arched porch.

The shallowest of valleys separates Cloford church from the house, and along it flows the Nunney brooke which has its source among the domelike hills around Wanstrow. Nunney itself is only two miles from here, as the stream flows, and is hidden in a delightful wooded combe. The village is charming and resilient in character and in no way self-consciously prettified. Since the Second World War and the creation of the extensive Flowerfield Estate, its population has doubled, spreading from the combe up to Berry Hill and the A361.

The castle-dominated centre of Nunney is rightly a conservation area – a memorable nucleus of Georgian manor, medieval church, cottages, orchards and gardens. There is a surging streamlet running down the street and replenishing the moat from where it flows on to Lower Whatley and the Frome basin. Four roads converge in the centre, which was the old market-place: Horn Street, Castle Road, High Street and the Frome Road. Horn Street is steep and picturesque with numerous old weavers' cottages; a few retain square holes in the ceilings made to take the increasing lengths of cloth as they were produced. The High Street blends with the Frome road and has the George Inn with its conspicuous signpost (by special permission) spanning the street. At the eastern end the parish church couches above the road. Inside there are memorials to the de la Mere family, including one of Sir John de la Mere wearing a helmet with a lion at his feet.

In 1373 King Edward III granted Sir John a licence 'that he may fortify and crenellate his house at Nunney in the county of Somerset with a wall of stone and lime ...'. This refers to the present-day castle. Unforgettable in its impact, this lofty, sheer-walled fortress has been compared with the Parisian Bastille and not incongruously, for Sir John, having campaigned in France, knew something of Gallic military architecture. The four angle towers command attention and compel inspection. The walls are nearly eight feet thick in places and served by passageways and staircases. The moat, twenty-two feet wide, is ten feet deep, and lifebelts are placed strategically around its perimeter just in case.

The castle did not see a great deal of action, except in the Civil War in the seventeenth century, when it was held for the King by Colonel Prater. Cromwell and Fairfax, believing it held a massive stock of munitions, despatched two regiments to subdue it, and they breached the thinnest part of the walls with cannon fire. Colonel Prater, putting self-preservation before pride, quickly negotiated a surrender and offered to change his allegiances. His army was ordered to disperse, and the castle was reduced to a ruin.

Stirring events such as these are not part of the integral life of Nunney. Originally it was a cloth village. The industry took root in the thirteenth century, and a mill was still operative at both Nunney and Whatley before the First World War. Rockfield House, a Regency mansion built for Thomas Dalimore in 1806, stands at the western extremity of the combe, and the name derives from 'Rack Field', the place where cloth was stretched and dried. A branch of the Fussells was also established here not long after the first workshop had been built at Mells. In 1828 the Reverend John Skinner visited it 'to purchase a scythe for mowing the garden, as the best in the county, perhaps in the Kingdom, are made by Fussells ...'. Skinner compared the servitude of the workers with that of West Indian slaves.

Apart from the thriving quarrying industry, Nunney provides few working outlets for its population. Houses are no longer cheap, and it has become a prestigious place in which to live. Locals are conscious of its exceptional heritage, and lorries have been re-routed to avoid the centre.

At the western edge of Nunney parish, about half a mile up a lane from the Frome road, one finds Sharpshaw Farm, the former abode of Squire Whitchurch who was buried at Nunney in 1752. The fabric is very old, deriving from Old English *scearp*, 'steep-wood', referring to the forest which once clothed the hillside. Squire Whitchurch preferred it to the immensely elegant manor house at Nunney (which he also owned) and liked to entertain friends there. His antics certainly spiced the social life of the area in the first half of the eighteenth century, and the farcical aspect of it is embalmed in the prose of Lord Orrery. Poor Squire Whitchurch. Orrery styles him as the eternal buffoon, a man who never bleeds, weeps or experiences soul-searching doubts. Instead he drinks, cavorts and plunges into ludicrous scrapes and japes. On one occasion he employs Lord Orrery's architect, James Scott, to build him a bridge at Sharpshaw. 'No parapet,' he ordered, hoping to save money.

And of course, coming back one night profoundly drunk, he rode over the edge and almost drowned. Dr Samuel Bowden of Frome was called. He revived the Squire by force-feeding him port and tickling his gullet fountain-wise.

A mile north of Nunney, sharing the same wooded combe and set amid gentle hills, the tall spire of Whatley church jabs the sky. It is quite a dramatic sight around these parts – a soaring sword of stone. Whatley is an ancient holding: Edmund, King of the West Saxons, gave the manor to the church of Glastonbury in 940, and the monks continued to hold it at the Conquest – until, in fact, the Dissolution. Today the village, with its rugged stone farmhouse grouped around the church, creates an impression of an unemphatic, prosperous unit. Manor Farm is entered through a medieval gatehouse and has a two-storeyed porch with mullioned windows. In the nearby rectory, Richard Church, a leader of the old High Church movement, lived for nineteen years, serving the small community, until he was made Dean of St Paul's Cathedral. A less exalted type of service, but more demotically convivial, is provided by the Rising Sun Inn with the cheery beams of its sign inviting the traveller.

The Church, when last visited, was not in a good state of repair, and roof-menders were at work. The interior was cold, vault-like and repelling. In one corner lay the crumbling effigy of the knight Oliver de Servington. He was the colour of rotting bones, and on his shield three stags were finely carved.

To the north of the village, at Whatley Bottom, the largest extractive quarrying operation in the Southern Region of ARC takes place. An awesome combination of aesthetic horror and economic necessity, Whatley Quarry employs over 150 people in the quarry and associated transport operations. Over two million tons of limestone are dispatched from here annually, over half of which is delivered by rail to south-east England. Other ARC Group activities in the area include the manufacture of concrete pipes and precast products at Mells and Mells Park Estate, which was purchased by the Group in 1976 and is currently used as a conference centre.

Whatley Brook rises in the village of West Cranmore and flows through the enormous dust-choked Merehead Quarry.

From there it runs by way of Asham Wood to Chantry, an ecclesiastical parish formed in 1846 out of the civil parishes of Whatley, Elm and Mells. Here ironmaster James Fussell built an Italianate villa in 1824 on land formerly belonging to the fourteenth-century chantry chapel in Whatley church. Combining utility and aesthetics, he dammed the brook, creating a 7½-acre lake that enhanced his mansion and provided power for his edge-tool works lower down the valley. Fortunately philanthropy is often the beneficent offspring of personal wealth, and later the Fussells were generous-spirited enough to endow the hamlet with a church and pioneer comprehensive school (1857), incorporating under one roof an infant school, a 'national' (elementary) school, an industrial school and a boarding-school for girls.

Chantry hardly presents an enlivening scene today. At Little Elm there are several old cottages, one heavily manned by plaster gnomes, and the White Horse Inn standing by a triangular green where three roads meet. Gilbert Scott's parish church is worth inspection with its jaunty, crocketed spire and carvings of angels holding scythes and other Fussell-made heavenly implements. The lake and mansion remain delightful. Unfortunately the former has pollution problems owing to quarries upstream. But more recently the water has been re-stocked with trout after a massive cleaning operation, and wildfowl have begun to return, yet one still comes across excrescences like floating plastic and metal containers, discarded vehicles and other objects unsuitable for the edification of local wildlife.

To the north and west of Chantry and Whatley, covering an area of some hundred square miles, and embracing the parishes of Mells, Kilmersdon, Holcombe, Coleford, Camerton, Stratton on the Fosse and Radstock, the Somerset coalfield formerly provided an important source of work. The last colliery to close was Haydon, in Kilmersdon, in 1973, not long after it had been opened. The coalfield was very much a local affair worked by small groups and companies until nationalization in 1947. The mines were confined mainly to the valley of the River Somer, the Wellow Brook and the Cam Brook. Around them spread sombre, terraced villages – almost replicas of their northern counterparts – such as Coleford, Camerton and the larger Radstock. The indomitable horsewoman Celia Fiennes observed in 1697 that Mendip coal was 'allmost as good as the sea-coale from New-Castle that is dugg out of the hills all about'.

Many of the veins, particularly in the Nettlebridge valley, near Ashwick, were buckled, heavily folded and difficult to mine. A colourful *argot* arose from this arduous mode of work and the varying conditions. Slyving, Peacock, Fern Bag and Dungy Drift were current names of seams in 1700, and collieries were similarly christened: Duck's Nest, Bilboa, Ringing Bell and Strap – the last being sited in the Nettlebridge valley. The tools of Somerset mining were the guss and the crook, rope and chain, by which means the carting boys hauled the putt, a wooden box with runners, to the surface. The seams were not very thick, usually twenty to thirty inches, which made the labour fairly frustrating. In summer, if the colliers happened to be on short time, they might vary the routine with haymaking or agricultural work.

One advantage of the collieries was that they were essentially rural – tiny industrial enclaves in green meadows or on lonely hillsides, and more sanitary than their northern counterparts. Only in the Norton-Radstock area was there anything like a density of workers in the industry. Having certain geological drawbacks, the profits were not excessive even for the coalmasters, and for the miners the reward was often miserly. After an effective strike, an agreement was reached at the Old Down Inn, Emborough, on 22 August 1792, that hewers were to be awarded 1s.8d. a day. By 1810 this had increased only to two shillings, so it is small wonder that history records a narrative of hunger, hardship and uprising. In 1757 the house of a Frome coal merchant was besieged by 200 colliers who had to be dispersed by soldiers. In 1766 a mob of several thousand colliers, together with sympathizers, attacked the flour-mill at Beckington. Similarly 500 hundred colliers stormed into Shepton Mallet and, enlisting the services of the cryer, demanded that foodstuffs should be sold at prices they could afford. They emphasized their anger and desperation by upturning stalls and kicking butter and cheese about in the street.

The Corn Laws of 1816 placed a heavy duty on foreign grain, making matters worse for the needy, and this was followed in 1817 by a ten per cent reduction in miners' wages. The outcome of this was anger and violence. Colliers armed themselves with huge bludgeons and stormed through the towns and villages chanting, 'Blood or bread – we're starving.' The underfed, badly housed mining communities soon acquired a fearful reputation, and burglaries and theft became commonplace. The gentry in the area were so worried that they actually formed a Society for Prosecuting Felons. The miners' one solace among all this oppression was the bottle. The Reverend John Skinner, the scholarly and luckless Vicar of Camerton, described them drinking and carousing after the discovery of a new seam: 'No work done at the pit,' he recorded, 'and the people more brutified than ever.' Similarly John Wesley once described the Coleford miners as 'darkness indeed', and such was the reputation of one spot that an advertiser seeking domestics in the columns of a Bath paper specified, 'No Radstock girl need apply.'

Certainly Radstock must rank low on any honeymooners' list of retreats but it does not deserve such a blanket condemnation. It lies in a basin in the hills, and black-snouted coal tips encircle it like Satanic carbuncles. There is a semblance of bustle and vitality around its centre, with its modern Co-op and the Victoria Hall, but on wet days the buildings exude a kind of exhausted grubbiness. An authentic existential gloom seeps from its very walls, which makes it a very refreshing place, particularly if one wants to escape from the beauty spots.

South of Radstock is Kilmersdon, also a former mining centre, but very open, salubrious and unindustrial. The name derives from 'Kunemersdon', 'down belonging to Cynemaer'. There are no drab terraced rows in this cool-looking, elegant village of hard grey lias warmed in places by pinkish stone from the same beds. Many buildings have a crisp, formalized appearance with their oolite dripstones and white and cream window-frames. Here is an artistic garage, formerly a stables, and the centre is tidy and spacious. The village lock-up, now a bus shelter, stands by the post office and a row of trim Georgian cottages. The Jollife Arms, where the courts of the local hundred were formerly held, faces the main road. So one is left with an impression of a bracing, well-kept estate village, framed by low green hills, with some demure council housing in tucked-away lanes and desirable thatched residences.

The church stands at the heart of the village and has a tower almost a hundred feet high, richly traceried and pinnacled. The stained glass window of the Mount of Olives is a copy of a sketch made by Thomas Jollife, who visited Jerusalem and paid for the glass. It was he who commissioned the fashionable architect, James Wyatt, to design the mansion amid parklike grounds – Ammerdown – above the village, dating from 1788 when the architect inspected the site and the project was begun. The result may be admired today: a regular and imposing classical mansion with Venetian windows at the ground floor, the upper ones square and encased by slightly projecting Doric pilasters. (Today Ammerdown House is a Centre for Study and Renewal, providing a setting for people to study, meditate, discuss or worship as they please.)

Thomas Jollife (1756-1824) distinguished himself as a soldier, politician, agricultural improver, local magistrate and landowner. Thomas Lawrence painted him in 1821 showing him firm-jawed, fastidious and consequential. He died at the age of seventy-eight and was succeeded by John Twyford Jollife, known as 'the Colonel', whose most enduring memorial is Ammerdown Column to the east of the house. This finely built obelisk was erected in 1855 and resembles a lighthouse with its austere lines and glass dome. Compared with the Wellington Monument, it is pleasant to ascend, being pierced by vertically equidistant portholes. Unfortunately the iron spiral staircase has come loose and is thickly clogged by jackdaws' nests that snap like small bones beneath the foot. The fine dust of bird-dropping pollinates the stale air, making it difficult to breathe. At the top the stonework is ruptured, cracked and poised to fall. Over-arching bands of iron, formerly paned with glass, make one feel as if inside an enormous battered parrot cage.

The wind blows through it, dislodging slivers of clinging glass, and the battlements seem to sway ever so slightly. The view is superb: all the countryside around rolls away below like a prairie, and one feels almost hawklike in the sense of utter detachment from the earth.

Over the hill to the south, occupying the upper reaches of Wadbury Vale or the Mells stream, stands the mining village of Coleford. Not in any way pretty or attractively situated, it has dour terraces and an air of being a discarded child of the Industrial Revolution, but locals firmly defend it and speak of 'the warm community feeling' engendered by its harsh streets and barren chapels. There are two main parts connected by a north-south bridging road. At Highbury one finds the curious Butlin-styled British Legion Club, the Eagle Inn, ostentatiously tasteless private estates and large-gabled colour-washed council homes at Merry Field Corner. The other part, to the south, descends the valley and curves up Bullock Hill toward Holcombe. There is a Gothic church on the slope of the hill with a window commemorating William Marchant Jones, that 'Jarge Balsh' whose charming Somerset dialect tales must have proven a great comfort to many in those early days before sleeping-pills had been invented.

Coleford borders on Holcombe, with which it shares points in common. They are both former coal towns whose livelihood now depends on quarrying. There is a cement works at Edford, the southernmost part of the parish, which draws on local workers to a limited extent. Commuting to Radstock and Midsomer Norton, towns relatively rich in light industries, has become the established pattern in a village which has been called 'prosperously residential'. This is not strictly accurate. A rambling hilly street of plain stone houses, interspersed with pale-grey 1970s-style homes, modern semis, drab Edwardian rows and the occasional civic building, the prospect is neither exhilarating nor exactly depressing. At the top of the hill, near the crossroads, is a recreation space with planted trees and an old people's estate called Scott's Close. Here also is the remains of an old brewery around which the community expanded.

Holcombe's name derives from 'hollow' or 'deep combe',

and the early settlement grew up around the wooded valley which is now partly private land used for fishing. The Georgian rectory and Moore's Farm, though which one approaches the old church, are what remains. The Black Death is claimed as the major factor determining the re-siting of the community, and the mound in the churchyard is said to contain a pile of its victims. Nevertheless, it is a strange, entrancing, but tiny Norman building, with neat horn-like pinnacles and shell-grey texture, outlined against shadowing woodland and gently dipping hills. The Norman doorway has an inscription recording that the church was consecrated by Wrotard, who was probably the Archbishop of York. It has been closed down for regular worship since the 1880s, when a new church in the centre of the village was opened, but its setting of serene and verdant desolation draws a steady trickle of visitors. They admire the faintly damp-smelling interior with the neat grey Georgian box pews, sparse white walls and few discreet memorials. The graffiti on the seats are legible and of some interest, varying from the mild remarks of a Victorian schoolboy to the avowed affections of an American GI who had formed an attachment to a local girl. Around the back of the church are the graves of the Scott family, the mother, father, brother and sister of the Arctic explorer 'who was translated into a glorious death' in a place as white and cold as this part of Somerset is mild and green.

About two miles north-west of Holcombe, on the stretch of road called the Broadway, a glum strip of ribbon development represents the overspill of Chilcompton. Here are a timberyard, indentations caused by the torn-up track of the old Somerset and Dorset line, and some less-than-lyrical modern homes. But this was the place which inspired Coleridge to write in 1794 'Lines Addressed to a Spring in the Village of Kirkhampton'. He got the name wrong but captured something of the ebullient liquidity of the setting:

Pride of the Vale! thy useful streams supply
The scattered cots and peaceful hamlet nigh.
The elfin tribe around they friendly banks
With infant uproar and soul-soothing pranks,

Releas'd from school, their little hearts at rest,
Launch paper navies on thy waveless breast.

To find the exact spot where the poet paused to
contemplate 'the milky waters cold and clear', it is necessary
to descend the hill down which the infant Somer dashes
Lodore-style. The stream sparkles over a waterfall, slips
under the road, then chases down the footpath called the
Pitchen where tight-packed cottages follow its course to the
church and manor house. All this unrestrained naturalness is
tempered by the Georgian façades of Shell House, trimly
escalloped, and Eagle House, with the winged predator
mounted above the entrance.

'Chilcompton' derives from 'Childecumpton', a child of
noble birth who may have part-owned the manor at an early
period in its history. Noble or not, the village has
experienced the baptism of industry, including edge tools,
clothmaking, the railway and coalmining. Collinson (1791)
noted it was situated on the turnpiked road to Wells and
Bridgwater. He alluded to the now-vanished manor of
Norton Hall, the seat of the Tookers, and the old house of
the Werrets, occupying the deep valley below the station and
looking out to the 'romantic shaggy rocks' clothed by a
narrow strip of woodland.

New Rock Colliery closed in 1968, marking the end of
large-scale mining in Somerset. The colliery was sunk in
1819 and employed around 210 men at its height. When the
National Coal Board acquired it in 1947, they installed an
electric winding-engine on the pumping-shaft. New
boreholes were sunk, and the old Strap Pit was drained with
the aid of a submersible electric pump, but the shaft turned
out to be only ten feet six inches in diameter and not fifteen
feet as had been expected. Although the colliery worked
effectively for a period, the combination of haulage
difficulties, labour shortage and remoteness from major
population centres, ensured its closure, and by 1969 all its
useful machinery had been salvaged and the shafts filled
with dirt from a waste tip.

The church and manor, in their remote meadowy setting
at the bottom of the hill, seem almost detached from village

life. The latter is a plain late Tudor structure with mullioned windows and the date 1612. This was the seat of the Stocker family whose initials AMS, or Antony and Margaret Stocker, can be discerned on the gable of the barn. The church was rebuilt in 1839 but retains its bold, handsome lines. A crenellated parapet runs all round it, and richer decorative flourishes are found in the honeycomb-like window tracery. The interior is light and spacious, with a mighty chancel arch, but there is a vacant feel, owing to the nineteenth-century renovation when all the decayed monuments were thrown out.

The streams that flow west from the coal valleys congregate in the Frome basin. Frome itself is an odd, underrated town, characterized by steep, narrow streets with rushing conduits, yellow-stoned weavers' cottages, rambling Georgian rows, plunging cobbled ways furnished with second-hand shops, bookstores, estate agents and antique-dealers. Property is relatively cheap: fine old clothiers' cottages can still be had reasonably, and many Londoners have become aware of the town's charm and potential. Frome has weathered through booms and slumps, depressions and elations of trade, yet still maintains a kind of blunt vivacity.

To the west of the town lies the Wiltshire border, outside the limits of this survey, but to the north, where the fuller's earth bed overlies the Inferior Oolite, there is a string of ancient wool villages, notably Norton St Philip, Rode, Beckington, Woolverton and, most remote and compelling of all, Lullington, whose very name suggests the deep peace experienced before relapsing into oblivion.

Norton St Philip climbs a hill which narrows and culminates in the famous George, one of England's oldest inns and definitely Somerset's most renowned hostelry. The village centre is not sunny and glowing as the Hamstone places are, nor is it exactly dark and grim, but it does have a sombre aspect despite its many attractive features, including a large, open green known as 'the Mead' (where the archery butts were set up in medieval times) which backs onto the George and provides a perfect play area for children and sportsmen. On a bluff overlooking this expanse is Hinton

Poultry, a frozen-chicken factory providing the only local industry. The village has spread out and expanded during recent years: new estates, such as the council-owned Wringwell and the private Springfield, have boosted the population considerably, yet there are only two small grocery shops and a post office. A well-kept village, with a large middle-class commuting population, it retains its essential character admirably. The High Street is dark, narrow, intriguing with its profusion of gables, mullions, dripstones and doorways abutting on the road. Traffic bolting towards Beckington and Frome has begrimed the natural whitish-brown limestone, and this dark, murky look emphasizes its great antiquity. There is a whitewashed Tudor-gabled house with a fish doorknocker, a Baptist chapel (1814) and the Fleur de Lis Inn, a hostelry little invoked on account of its immensely distinguished neighbour, the George, a sixteenth-century building, lofty and rambling, with a stone-built lower storey and a large timber-framed upper part projecting above the road.

The story of the George Inn is a kind of tapestry of old England. William Longspée (Longsword) was the half-brother of Richard the Lionheart, his mother being the Fair Rosamond, mistress of Henry II. He married the daughter of the Earl of Salisbury, Ela d'Evreux, who possessed the estates of Norton St Philip and Hinton Charterhouse, and thus became a wealthy, powerful landowner. When he died, he left a generous bequest to the Carthusians. Ela continued the tradition of patronage inaugurated by her husband and offered to exchange her lands at Hinton and Norton St Philip for the Carthusian lands at Hatherop, Gloucestershire, which William had granted the order earlier. They agreed to establish a new priory in Somerset, and the first of the complex of buildings was the monks' guest house, where ale may have been brewed from the start and where the present George Inn is now sited. This would date the George from around 1227, a highly contestable claim, yet Collinson (1791) acknowledged in the main street of Norton 'a large and very ancient building formerly a grange of the abbots of Hinton'.

The Dissolution ended the rule of the monasteries and their brewhouse, now the George, became a popular roadside inn.

The Duke of Monmouth made his headquarters there in 1685 after he had abandoned his attack on Bristol. There was a bloody skirmish at Norton during the Rebellion between the King's men and the rebels, who had barricaded the main road. One local builder, Geoffrey Coombes, claims that his ancestor Thomas Coombes was bound to the stake and burned alive for his allegiance to Monmouth. He claims that eight other local men shared that fate and cites the parish records of the period which reveal that the sum of 12s. was paid for a hundred bundles of faggots 'for ye execution'. Geoffrey Coombes owns a cannonball picked up from the scene of the fighting.

The parish church of SS Philip and James was originally built of limestone rubble, and traces of early windows are visible in the south wall. The seventy-foot tower is suitably imposing and looms dramatically when viewed from the Mead. Inside are memorials to the Rundell family, Somerset clockmakers who lived at Norton, one of whom, Edward, made a fortune as Court jeweller in London. He left the money to Joseph Neeld of Norton who used the bequest to build and endow the adjoining village school (1827), a Gothic building with high, narrow windows.

Samuel Pepys stayed at the George and visited the parish church in 1668. What appealed to him was 'a very fine ring of bells, and they mighty tuneable' and the grave of the Siamese twins, 'the tombstone whereon there were only two heads cut, which the story goes and creditably, were two sisters called the fair maids of Foscott, that had two bodies joined at the stomache and there lie buried'.

Norton St Philip lies on the border of Avon county which hereabouts follows the A366. To the west it climbs past Norwood Farm to descend the Frome valley, and in the opposite direction it skirts the edge of Hemington parish. Over a mile from the village, near the junction with the B3139, stands Ammerdown Terrace. This brooding row of early nineteenth-century houses was built by the Jollifes for their employees. A less austere note is struck by the village, which has several attractive farmhouses – again with darkish limestone predominating – and a church tower that makes another swagger display of pinnacled intricacy.

A fascinating hamlet, only 1¼ miles distant, is Faulkland, with a Wesleyan chapel (1842) and a village green famous for its old wooden stocks. A dashing note is introduced here by Thomas Turner's house, with its neat square dormers and arched pediment. This show of Georgian architecture formerly claimed the garden that ingeniously or eccentrically annexes the village green. Here are a rockery, ornamental willows, shrubbery, little bridges and, of course, running water to add glitter and movement.

Faulkland was a nineteenth-century mining settlement which became run down when Somerset coal slumped. It lost some of its population but revived when commuting incomers changed its character. Dapper conversions were effected on several houses, local village groups were revived and a new community spirit arose.

The spectacular feature around these parts used to be Turner's Tower, a 180-foot folly with narrow arched windows and three distinct stages, the last being made of wood to peg up another twenty feet of boastful altitude. This Arabian Nights three-dimensional fantasy was intended to provide competition with the nearby Ammerdown Tower. It is pleasant to contrast the ludicrously large sums involved in such projects with the mere whimsy of their purpose. But perhaps Thomas Turner, who was a wealthy businessman, had another reason – namely to provide work for the unemployed.

Situated in traditional sheep-rearing country, about three miles north-east of Frome, Beckington prospered during the Middle Ages, and the principal inn, the Woolpack, provides the familiar clue. Today there is some agriculture and some light industry but its nature is primarily residential. There is controlled estate development, fairly unobtrusive, and a complex of bungalows for the elderly at Sandy View. The community remains alert and sedate in its sheltered setting, on a green rise above the valley floor, and its buildings – a vista of mullioned windows and Tudor-style gables – exude the nostalgia of well-preserved patricians. The so-called abbey was probably a hospital founded in 1502 by Augustinian canons, and the larger sixteenth-century 'castle' is another eye-catcher with its castellated porch.

The parish church of St George, standing opposite the primary school on the hilltop, has a vigorous Norman tower, four-square and commanding, with massive diagonal buttresses. Inside there is a bust of the Taunton-born poet Samuel Daniel, who spent the last sixteen years of his life in a farm at Rudge, near Beckington.

Two miles south of Beckington, sheltering under Black Dog Hill and nudging the Wiltshire border, Berkley presents a typical trio of church, manor and old schoolhouse. Viewing the complex from the surrounding lanes, the effect is entrancing: flocks of gables, stalky chimneys and broad-leafed trees crowding up to the demure little church – creating an excitingly broken effect. Berkley House was built by Thomas Prowse in the reign of William III and Mary II but what remains is a dignified building of the 1750s with Ionic pilasters at the angles and Tuscan columns at the entrance. The church (1751) is said to be a copy of Wren's St Stephen's Walbrook, in London. The interior is famous for its dome, with 'lacelike swirls of rococo' creating the atmosphere of a ballroom.

Looking across to Beckington, set high above the west bank of the River Frome, Lullington couches in its habitual quietude. It comprises a green encircled by prim grey-stoned Tudor-type cottages, an old-fashioned water-pump, a converted Victorian schoolhouse and a church with a yew tree beside it. Initials are recognizable above some doorways, such as W.D. (William Duckworth, an early nineteenth-century lord of the manor), and all the gardens seem moist, colourful and lovingly tended. This is not a place wherein one can think evil thoughts but, according to dear old Arthur Mee, 'a jewel in the crown of Somerset, an enchanting gem of the delicate beauty of the countryside'.

Lullington was part of the domain granted by the Conqueror to Geoffrey, Bishop of Coustances (in Normandy), and the original church was built between 1070 and 1100. The Norman doorway in particular is rich, magical, primitive, a medley of chevrons, billets and nail-heads, crowned by a carving of God on His throne that recalls the Coventry Cathedral tapestry by Graham Sutherland. The tympanum, although weathered, shows the tree of life being devoured by wolves and may have been the work of master masons imported from Normandy, because the doorway echoes many of the details to be seen at Caen. Inside there is a Norman font, a rugged tub of stone vigorously decorated with human faces, animal heads, flowers and a Latin couplet, 'Hoc Fontis sacro pereunt delicta lavacro' – 'In this holy font sins perish and are washed away.'

Nearby Orchardleigh is an 800-acre estate approached through an imposing fake Tudor archway. There is a beautiful wooded lake with a romantic boathouse and rotunda attached to a big, turreted pile with oriel windows and a fat, heavily corseted look, resulting from the merger of Victorian and Scottish Baronial styles. This mansion in Orchardleigh Park replaced the old house pulled down in 1856, but the follies in the grounds are earlier (c. 1760). The island church of St Mary, a small fifteenth-century shrine reached by means of a footbridge, is in an idyllic setting, amid swaying beech boughs and shivering copper leaves. It has a Jacobean pulpit, a chapel of the Champney family and a medieval glass window showing a white-robed saint surrounded by angels rising from clouds and playing lutes, harps, bagpipes and psaltery.

The grave of the intensely patriotic poet Henry Newbolt is here. Orchardleigh featured in his story 'The Old Country' under the guise of 'Gardenleigh'.

Buckland Dinham lies west of Lullington and Orchardleigh Park. It is a somewhat austere wool village framed by low, wooded hills and fields studded with oak and ash. After weathering a period of neglect, it has re-established itself as a desirable place for those commuting to Frome, Bath and Radstock. Formerly it was a quite important place: a charter was granted in the reign of Henry III for holding a weekly market on Tuesday and a fair at Michaelmas, but these gradually expired along with the textile trade and teazel growing. Shafts were sunk here in the nineteenth century, in hope of finding coal, but the venture failed. Most of the buildings are concentrated around the A361 which climbs a hill overlooking the Frome valley. Near the top is the Bell Inn, some yellowish loudly apparelled new houses, and the Ebenezer Chapel, an attractive Methodist

church with a curved pediment over the doorway and an urn
on top. It is dated 1811 but was put up earlier – Pevsner,
quoting the architectural historian Bryan Little, gives the
date 1730. Notable is the stone of Buckland, a slightly harder
variety of oolite producing yellowy-brown houses with
mullions and a rugged, weather-resistant look. Some of them
have been 'improved' by the addition of sham leaded panes
and Bradstone facing.

Halfway down the hill, at St Michael's Close, the
pinnacled tower of the church overlooks meadowland grazed
by Friesians and sheep. A small village lock-up with a barred
porthole window is set nearby, and an old, delightfully
battered-looking farmhouse sidles up to it. Inside the church
is the chantry chapel of the Dinhams. Embedded in the floor,
trampled-on and rubbed-smooth, are the lias figures of Sir
John Dinham (d. 1332) and his lady. He is armoured and she
is clad in scarf and wimple. The pair of them look faded,
forlorn, yet not without a wistful dignity.

The River Frome flows north from Rode through a
steep-sided wooded ravine at Farleigh Hungerford. A
trout-farm hides among the beeches, and several houses,
including the post office, stand in clumps around the river
bank. Seen from the towering castle ramparts, they appear
like toytown blocks, inessential oddments, with their gay,
red-tiled roofs and glowing Bath-stone walls. The fortress is
set high above the verdant gorge, bounded by the dramatic
plunge of Dane's Dyke, and its broken towers and arrogant
gatehouse exude the shattered majesty of the past. The castle
annexed a fourteenth-century chapel, formerly the parish
church of Farleigh, where one may inspect life-size effigies
of long-dead lords of the manor, the Hungerfords, and items
such as medieval armour, Saracen mail, a scimitar and a
crusader's sword.

Farleigh's parish church perches on a hillside opposite a
row of houses called White Horse View, an allusion to the
hill-figure at Westbury, Wiltshire. It was erected by Walter
Hungerford in the reign of Henry VI and consecrated on 6
November (St Leonard's Day) 1443 by James Blakedom,
Bishop of Achonry. The tower is fifty-four feet high with a
short pyramidal tiled spire.

To many people Rode signifies the extremely popular tropical bird garden haunted by penguins, macaws, pheasants and various other ornithological importations. About a hundred years ago it was associated with a brutal and intriguing murder.

The parish church of St Lawrence is situated about half a mile from the village centre on a tricky bend of the A361. Lorries *en route* to Trowbridge and beyond grind and shove up the gradual slope. In a field to the east are the Devil's Bed and Bolster – 'a collection of brimstone stones in a dip', so an old man told S.P.B. Mais. Mainly of the fourteenth and fifteenth centuries, the church is solidly reassuring, a friendly, unfussy building rather than a show of Gothic spikiness. The tower is sturdy and crenellated and has a fan-like stone vault ceiling which was restored in 1874. At one corner is a railed battlement called 'the King's Chair'; a tradition was current in the parish that Charles II, after the Battle of Worcester, in 1651, climbed the tower for the purpose of reconnoitring the surrounding country. There is also a brass to a pair of parish clerks 'who lived in friendship during their long service for Rode and Woolverton' and died so that they were buried on the same summer's day in 1799.

From the church, the village is reached by way of Church Lane which twists among estates and farms before penetrating the centre of Rode, where it joins the High Street by a small triangular patch of grass occupied by the war memorial. Quiet traditional exteriors are retained here, but to the north, stretching down to Farthing Memorial Hall, are modern estates pegged out in rigid rows, with pale bricks and interlocked tiles glittering in sunlight and creating an effect of raw newness. In the other direction, to the south-west, one enters the High Street, dark, with a cosy, hemmed-in feel. There are the Cross Keys and the Red Lion, rivalling hostelries, and an elegant white Georgian townhouse, adding a dash of classicism to the irregular terraces, attic gables and stone mullions that predominate. The eye-catcher is the towering brewery of the Fussells (used solely for dispatch purposes) with its tall chimneys and cheerful sunset colouring.

Rode's second church is a fantastic Gothic structure which has evinced some derogatory comment. Its notched twin spires, 'big, gaunt and lacking in grace', offend certain eyes, but they add a touch of exoticism, a dash of Gaudi's Barcelona to Somerset, and visual relief is always welcome in an increasingly standardized world. One curious point is that the finials are not attached but balanced, held down by stone weights suspended on iron chains hidden inside. The interior of the church is elegant, grey, very tasteful, with big modern glass doors sealing off the back.

Further down the road is Langham House, a big, four-square Victorian mansion which has a tragic history. Constance Kent lived here with her father, stepmother and stepbrother, Francis, ostensibly in harmony and friendship but secretly nurturing resentment against her stepmother for her attitude towards her own mother. Constance killed Francis, aged three, and hid his mutilated body in a cesspool in the garden. The body was discovered soon after the murder but, despite the most exhaustive investigation, no satisfactory explanation could be found. Five years later, in 1865, Constance confessed to the murder in the most poignant and heart-rending way – allegedly the court was in tears. She served twenty years in Portland Prison, then was set free, and several locals, no longer living, recalled her returning to Rode Hill House dressed in black and looking pathetic.

6

The Brue Meadows

It has been stated that the road from Glastonbury to Shepton Mallet is paved with stones of the ruined abbey. How true this is cannot be established without the co-operation of an earthquake, but along various moorland roads there are buildings with the paschal lamb inset as decoration in the walls. Also, more suspiciously, there are numerous houses with names like Abbot's Rest, Priest House, Friar's Cot, as if wishing to boost their appeal by spurious ecclesiastical connection.

This is not true of West Pennard, a sturdy, unpretentious place, socially active, with an old coaching pub called the Red Lion (reputedly haunted by the ghost of a young girl who glides noiselessly among the pump handles), some stylish chapel conversions along the A361, and a café called the Chequered Flag. From the main road marvellous views can be had of Glastonbury Tor, that mysterious implant from elfland, crowned by a solitary tower, looking mist-wreathed and magical on dull days and a violent burnished green in bright weather when its terraces stand out like serpents' coils and sheep graze its slopes.

The church of St Nicholas is some distance from the pub, tucked at the foot of the hill, a little way above a nucleus of older houses. Erected in the reign of Edward IV, it has a western tower ending in a short octagonal spire. There is much forceful buttressing and crocketing, the parapet is embattled, and the frieze above the west door has busts of angels – an elaborate, effective church.

The breath of fame touched West Pennard in 1838, when

local folk produced the largest Cheddar Cheese ever – weighing eleven hundredweight and made from the milk of 700 cows in a vat specially assembled for the purpose. Throughout its slow maturing it was exhibited, first at the Egyptian Hall, Piccadilly, then in various towns, until it was time to return to its birthplace. When it was tasted, it was found to be lacking the rich, pungent tang befitting its massive girth, and it was broken up and fed to pigs. Charles Dickens alludes to this in *All the Year Round* (1860).

East Pennard has a more remote and hillier situation, about three miles to the east, in a fold just below King's Hill. Here is the sober-looking Jacobean Pennard House, drastically rehabilitated in 1815 and standing in a private park. The village lies to the south. A stream trickles through, along by a narrow strip of woodland and snail-grey cottages which, with red-tiled roofs and thick hedges, survey the yawning quietude. The church has a tower which has been called 'plain and dignified' (Hutchings) and 'refreshingly blunt' (Pevsner). The carved Norman font is powerfully decorated: four sphinxes with birds' claws are shown crushing the heads of four demons – a throwback to atavistic horrors.

North of East Pennard is an area still called Pilton Park after the medieval deer park owned by Glastonbury Abbey. Pilton is an extensive parish incorporating Westholme and East and West Compton. The main village has become expensively residential and most cottages have a renovated sheen; dormer gables wink from new red roofs, and double-glazed frames gleam self-satisfiedly. Motorists tend to see the dullest part of Pilton along the Glastonbury-Shepton road, a staid gathering of stone houses, inn and post office, but to the south is a place of different character, a settlement drained by a fresh streamlet crossed by fords and footbridges and interconnected by plunging lanes. Bread Street is memorable. It hooks round a bend and steeply descends to a bridge above which the church rises like a gaunt stone symphony. Traceried windows light every section of the aisle, and pinnacles and crenellations repeat themselves exuberantly. Below, the little river slips by, enhancing the broad-leafed trees and easeful meadows which thousands of years ago lay under water. In fact, 'Pilton' is said to be derived from 'Pool-town', a harbour village where Joseph of Arimathea traded and where Mendip lead was dispatched by barge. There is some truth in this assertion. A fourteenth-century lease of an abbey holding mentions William Arviragus who had to look after the fishing and provide a large boat with eight rowers to carry the lord abbot, his horses and dogs, to Butleigh, Godney and Steenbow. The latter was the causeway between Pilton and West Pennard and indicates that only 600 years ago the water-levels were dramatically higher than today.

The parish church of St John has a Norman arch and a star-shaped east window. There is a lovely embroidered cope, in white, silver and blue, portraying the Madonna, which was partly eaten away by spiders, then restored by some kindly ladies from Wantage. A curious point concerning the church is that the parish boundary line bisected it, so during a formal perambulation, or beating of the bounds, the monks, abbey officials and tenants wandered through it and around the graveyard to impress the divide firmly in their minds. This oddity accounts for the name of the village, which derives from the Saxon 'lang Pillis', 'boundary marker'.

Near the church, set slightly lower, is the old manor house, sedately Georgian in appearance with a Venetian window, crenellations and an approach dominated by tall trees lumpy with rooks' nests. The Gothic flourishes were provided by Edward Andrews, a Bristol merchant who bought it in 1754. The manor did not remain long in the family, for his son gambled it away during the course of an evening. Nowadays it is locally famed as the home of Pilton Riesling. This is entirely in keeping, for vines were first planted on the slopes flanking the manor in the middle of the twelfth century, when it served as a residence for the abbots of Glastonbury. Today's vineyard is a novel tourist attraction.

Pilton has two converted chapels and a former working men's club which has been adapted as a parish room, a rather raw-looking pretender compared with the grand tithe barn surmounting the hill, carved with the symbols of the four evangelists. Seen from the road above the church, a superb view is had of vine-terraced slopes enclosing the formal manor and squat dovecotes; then the barn itself, crowning the other side of the valley, with the triangles of its gaunt gables stabbing the sky. It is ruined and roofless owing to a fire which destroyed its fine arch-braced interior in 1963.

On a south-eastern spur of Pennard Hill, approached by ragged, wandering lanes, Ditcheat looks out over pasture land, arable and orchard. The tiny River Alham separates it from the hamlet of Alhampton and the imperious Fosse Way from East Pennard.

The name 'Ditch-eat' derives not from an unhygienic local custom but from 'Dices-yat', 'Dyke-gate' – indicating the presence of a lock-gate to regulate rising water. An ancient settlement, in which agriculture has traditionally provided the chief livelihood, today it has its full quota of modern buildings, and the original nucleus around the church has grown arms and extensions. But despite the convulsions of change, a cheerful communal atmosphere prevails. The stoic acceptance of everything bar immediate personal extinction is one of the more endearing Somerset traits. Only a tiny percentage work the land today; others look elsewhere, to the local industries of Glastonbury, Street and Wells, for employment, and the commuter element by far exceeds the village-based faction.

Physically Ditcheat offers few scenic nooks and corners but a number of individually interesting buildings. The high street curves round by King Alfred's Inn, a picturesque Gothic Revival structure in red brick with fancy lancet windows. Not far away, on the same road, is the church, almost awe-inspiring in its cathedral-like dimensions. Pinnacled and embattled, massive and sprawling, it is sunk in Norman foundations and arises from the heart of the nonesuch village like a gigantic carved stone treasure-chest. An unusual interior decoration is the wall painting of a giant St Christopher carrying the infant Christ; he holds a staff and wades among fishes and watersnakes; behind him is a little yellow windmill, and before him a white church with a belltower. It was probably done around 1500 and later whitewashed over, until 1931, when it was uncovered.

Hard by the church is the manor house. This long, two-storeyed building with attic gables bears the date 1603 and creates an impression of symmetrical severity. The interior is pleasing, and the entrance hall has a window bearing the arms and crest of Dawes, a Dorset family who acquired the manor from Lord Hopton (whose escutcheon stands in the church) in 1669.

What is called the Priory at Ditcheat, a capacious Victorian building, was formerly the rectory of the versatile and brilliant Dean Gunthorpe dating from 1475. A window was unblocked in 1912 and there was found a piece of glass painted with the initials I.G. in yellow stain. This was the Gunthorpe monogram, less fantastic than the gun motifs adorning his Wells deanery: great stone cannons sprout from the exterior of the bay window, and there are long guns with straps and small hand-grenades forming centres of roses.

Less intellectually gifted than Dean Gunthorpe, but more vulgarly appealing, was a farmer named Kingston who was born at Ditcheat without arms. His remarkable ability 'to remedy the defects of nature' was reported in the *Bristol Mercury* (1826): 'He shaves himself and writes with a bold legible character, and performs all the manual labour of the farm.' All these skills were accomplished with his feet; other, less utilitarian skills included being an admirable bowler and adept at 'throwing sticks at the snuff boxes, as practised at country fairs' – an odd one that. Kingston was married twice and each time the congregation were delighted at the way he took his wife's hand, placed the ring on her finger, and signed the register – with his foot! Kingston had twelve children, all normal in appearance.

Even more odd is a slightly sinister document relating a case of possession which took place at Ditcheat in 1584. It concerned one Margaret Cooper, wife of a yeoman, who was suddenly taken ill after a journey. Her husband observed her early symptoms – she was talking constantly 'as if were one that had been bewitched or haunted by an evil spirit' – and then apparitions began appearing, one resembling 'a bear, but it had no head, nor no tale' and was as broad as it was long. This creature 'thrust the woman's hed betwixt her

legges, and so roulled her in a rounde compasse like an
Hoope through three other chambers downe an highe paire
of stairs in the Hall, where he kept her the space of a quarter
of an hower'.

South of Ditcheat the Alham wriggles along to join the
Brue. Unkempt but spacious meadows stretch away from its
banks, broken by patchy copses and the purposive Fosse
Way. Hornblottom lies a quarter of a mile east of the Roman
road. Formerly it was called 'Hornblawerton', evoking the
blower of a hunting-horn, who may have lived there once,
perhaps before the time of King Ethelwulf when the holding
was given to the abbey of Glastonbury. It has thatched grey
lias cottages and some worthy farm buildings, but the hub of
the hamlet is the church and manor house. The latter, built
as a rectory in 1867, is as sober-looking as a Unitarian
chapel. Grave, uncluttered gables overlook a tidy lawn by a
charming tree-shaded lake with ducks. Next to it stands the
church (1872–3), an intriguing gaudy building of orange
oolite with Doulting dressing. The wooden spire is covered
with oak shingles and contains an electric clock and three
bells. Looking quaint and faintly Swiss in appearance, the
bell-cote and spire of the earlier building stand next to it.

The Fosse Way cuts diagonally across the Brue at
Lydford. The houses lie on a slight rise to the south of the
river. A seventeenth-century bridge connects them with the
church – five-arched with a specially pierced parapet to take
any flood overflow. The church, rebuilt in 1844, is the work
of Benjamin Ferrey, a pupil of Pugin's, and stands strikingly
beside the river. This is a favourite photographic
composition, especially when the fabric is mirrored by the
still water. Pevsner called attention to the 'antiquarian
exactitude of the reconstruction', a feature found only in
structures commenced after 1840. East Lydford (1866) is by
the same architect but has a tower and spire rising ninety
feet. The alabaster relief of St George assailing a dragon
provides a pleasant, if conventional, decoration.

A lane forks off the Fosse Way (A37) south of West
Lydford and leads to Babcary, a modest knot of farm
dwellings, post office, telephone booth and Red Lion Inn – a
pleasant place, inconsequential as a daisy. The diminutive

Cary stream flows by the west end of the village and round by Wimble Toot, an isolated burial mound, and then on to Cary Fitzpaine and Kingdon. The local inn is thatched, and there are several substantial lias houses as well as an austere Wesleyan chapel. Formerly this was an elm-rich area but disease has ravaged them and they lie chopped, blighted and blasted. Limes, however, are plentiful in the churchyard of the Holy Cross – a Norman-styled fabric with an embattled tower and a carved oak pulpit dated 1632.

South of the Pennards lie the hamlets of West Bradley, Parbrook and Lottisham, all with their points of interest, and the meadows of the sluggish Brue. This is deep in dairy-farming country, and one cannot travel far along a road without being held up by the apparition of thirty or so Friesian rumps in stately procession to the next field. Visual titillation aside, the country is passing fair. Apple orchards abound, there are many fine stone barns and cobbled-together bridges, plus sufficient trees and hedgerows to hold monotony at bay. Undramatic country, tamed by thousands of years of tree-felling, pasturing and ploughing, its charm becomes apparent in summer when all the grasses, nettle patches and hedgerow life is astir and burgeoning.

Baltonsborough is in the midst of this countryside, south of Kennard Moor. An intricate network of droves leads into the village which has several centres. The main part clusters around the old church, which is thrust out into a meadow and beckons from the ragged, willowy lanes. Southwood, with its stream and plantation, maintains its separateness; adjoining Catsham stands at the junction of Muchelney and Honeymead Lanes. Ham Street is expanding with light-coloured new estate homes. Westown, out on a limb by Butt Moor, remains much the same. But in Baltonsborough, as in the surrounding villages, the pattern of life has altered. Little or no arable farming is carried out, and the old cider orchards are fast disappearing. Dairy farming is increasingly important, and 'factory units' housing chickens, pigs and calves are being adopted. Tractors and milking-machines have replaced human labour, and most locals commute to Glastonbury and Street.

Although marred by casual estate building and unsightly

development, Baltonsborough remains attractive in com-
ponent parts. The village crowds one with a series of isolated
impressions: the Greyhound Inn near the crossroads;
clustered cottages by the food store; St Dunstan's with its
iron entrance gates; the Clerk's House mentioned in 1552;
the old hump-backed bridge in a field west of the church; the
ancient flour-mill (said to have been owned by Dunstan's
father); the cider-mill seen from Mill Pond; Plumley's
cider-apple orchard; the thatched gatehouse with its
seventeenth-century porch – all combine to create an image
of historic continuity of unusual depth and richness.

Baltonsborough was one of the twelve hides, or manors,
of Glastonbury Abbey, and the lives of its tenants were
strictly controlled. If they wished to marry off a daughter,
the permission of the abbey had to be sought, and when they
died, their beasts and chattels reverted to the monastery. A
feature of the parish was the great Baltonsborough Wood
which was liberally plundered to bank up the fires of the
abbey and warm the hearths of the locals. There were four
miles of it in Norman times, stretching from West Lydford,
through Baltonsborough, Bradley and West Pennard, but by
the thirteenth century a good deal of it had been felled, the
main concentration of trees being at Northwood, Southwood
and Bradley.

Legend attests that St Dunstan was born at Baltonsborough, between 909 and 925, in an old cob cottage in Ham
Street, presently the site of the Legion hut. As a young man
he found favour at the court of King Athelstan but soon
renounced the pleasures of life and entered Glastonbury
Abbey, where he imposed upon himself a stern regime:
fasting, praying, scourging the flesh and developing
pronounced spiritual authority. This set him apart from the
others, and he quickly rose to become abbot. His rule was
distinguished by vastly increased efficiency and reforming
zeal. No longer were monks allowed to enjoy wives and
concubines, and the strict rule of the Benedictines was
imposed. The fame and wealth of Glastonbury increased
under Dunstan's control. He presided over the stocktaking,
ensuring the abbey received its full quota of revenues from
the various estates, and he encouraged pilgrims to visit the

abbey and inspect the holy relics. Both entrepreneur and mystic, an unusual combination, he eventually became Archbishop of Canterbury. In such a position of monolithic authority, he tried to institute his reforms throughout the land.

The practical side of Dunstan's character is demonstrated by his prowess as a drainage engineer. The Brue used to sprawl over the marshy meadows around Baltonsborough until Dunstan intervened by digging a deep ditch from Tootles Bridge to a point beyond Catsham; also, he is credited with making a series of weirs and diverting the flow of water to ensure the mill received a constant supply. The trench is still known as Dunstan's Dyke, and Tootles Bridge, with its unequal arches and humped outline, has a built-in font (where Dunstan is said to have been christened) which featured in a tragedy about a century ago when a drunk 'overspilled himself' into the Brue, wedged his head inside and drowned.

Butleigh village perches comfortably above the floodplain of the Brue. Although it radiates serenity and slow-paced rural repose, it is actually a vigorous and well-equipped community with a hospital founded by Sir George Bowles in 1882, a pub called the Horse and Lion, several shops, a school and village hall. There is modern development pushing out here and there in scattered pockets: ash-grey estate houses, ranch-style bungalows, austere 1980s homes, but nothing overtly offensive. Given over principally to mixed farming (sheep, dairying, some arable), Butleigh's quiet ways are shaded by a profusion of cedars, oak and chestnuts which enhance the lias cottages with their red-tiled roofs and stolid walls. Outstanding among older buildings are two farms, Lower Rocke's and Higher Rocke's, once owned by the sons of Thomas Rocke, who was made vicar in 1577 and whose elegant handwritten registers still survive. Higher Rocke's Farm has a handsome Tudor façade with close-set mullioned windows and a broadly moulded entrance porch. Lower Rocke's is similar, with high-pitched gables, and bears the date 1671. The latter abuts on Compton Street facing Parsonage Farm, a relic of the ancient monastic estates scuppered by Henry VIII's drastic policies.

In 1539, after Abbot Whiting had been murdered, Butleigh Manor was granted to Edward Seymour, brother of the late Jane Seymour, Henry's third queen.

Contrasting with the agricultural sobriety of the cottages, the court at Butleigh is all pseudo-Elizabethan fantastication. Set back from the village, adjoining the church and swathed in ample parkland, here is a medley of sky-defying pepperpot chimneys, florid oriel windows, battlements, turrets and lacy traceries. The moving light behind this paragon of architectural restraint was George Neville Grenville, Dean of Windsor, who employed Buckler, a renowned architect of the day, to transform his ploddingly functional Georgian house to a dwelling suitable for one who hobnobbed with the highest. This was around 1850, when dwellings of the rich became very pinnacle-prone and crenellation-conscious.

The church is squat and solid-looking, with a dedication to St Leonard, indicating a likely Norman origin. The fourteenth-century windows with unique stained glass figures are set against a red and blue background: St Thomas with a lance, St Bartholomew with a big knife, St James with a staff, yet another apostle brandishing a scimitar – spiritual weaponry one hopes.

A narrow road from Butleigh runs by Broadmoor Farm and turns into Barton St David. Not a cohesive village but consisting of blunt blocks and rows set amidst orchards and farms, it has the old and new post office in what could be termed its main street. There are many solid stone houses and many farms with highly modernized outbuildings and equipment. Few planning restrictions here: utility reigns unchallenged. Estate development is prominent, and there is a well-established commuter population living in substantial modern houses with garages and luxuriant gardens. The Barton Inn caters for their liquid desires. Other buildings include an ancient buttressed cottage, slightly dilapidated, Broadstone Farm in Silver Street with gabled dormers and worn mullions, and the Gothic church, which stands at the highest point in Barton, which is exceedingly low. A memorial plaque inside honours the birth of Henry Adams, formerly a farmer of this district, who emigrated to New England in 1638. The Adams family propagated an illustrious line, literary and political, including the presidents John Adams and John Quincy Adams.

Barton St David has a detached residential air compared with its southern neighbour, Keinton Mandeville, situated on the busy B3153 linking Somerton and Castle Cary. There is a fair amount of through traffic, spurring on ribbons development, and a density of small businesses. Aside from the dark Norman past, when William the Conqueror granted the manor to Geoffrey de Magnaville for his services at the Battle of Hastings, the historical character of the village is best summed up by its characteristic pub, the Quarryman, showing a moustachioed practitioner of this trade looking pugnacious yet self-satisfied.

For stone was formerly the bread and butter of Keinton, the notable blue lias called Keinton marble, a greyish-blue shaly rock used in pavements, doorsteps and kerbstones. Immediately recognizable by its colour, and also by the irregularly spaced bivalve shells of which it is partly composed, it was used on the shafts of the west front of Wells Cathedral and on the basal platform of the tombs of Bishop Drokensford (1329) and Dean Godelee (1332). The past, however, is the past, the quarries are worked out, but vestiges may be seen around the gardens of a few houses which are enclosed by hefty rectangular slabs of Keinton marble instead of fencing or hedging. This once-common custom has declined.

The two adjoining parishes, Charlton Mackrell and Charlton Adam, lie south of Keinton on the old Fosse Way to Ilchester. They have much in common, although Charlton Adam is a more nucleated settlement with houses forming a definite rectangle east of the church. The latter is a fourteenth-century building with a Norman font and a memorial (1638) to Anne Strangways, mother of sixteen children. East of the church, almost overshadowing it, is the late-Elizabethan abbey, a gabled and mullioned mansion with tell-tale sags and kinks in its roof.

The road running south from the centre of Keinton passes old stone cottages, Tudor-suburban essays sweetened by petal and shrub, and the rather dull parish church of St Mary Magdalene which was largely rebuilt in 1800. Taking the right-hand turn across the meadows and over the railway bridge, one enters Charlton Mackrell: a higgledy-piggledy string of houses faithfully following the twists and uncertainties of its main street, which slips under the railway track and ends up near the church of St Mary the Virgin, established in 1217 and renovated during the nineteenth century with almost savage thoroughness.

South of Charlton Mackrell and Charlton Adam the Cary Brook winds across the meadows. It merges with the boundaries of Kingdon, a village built on the lower slopes of a hill of the same name, situated slightly to the east of the Somerton-Ilchester road. Kingdon is a little-mentioned, little-visited place of distinctive character; fine thatched houses, such as Stoneleigh Farm and Old Rectory Cottage, occupy its corners and byways. Street names are picturesque and instructive: Frog Lane, Pound Street, Nuthill Lane, Quarry Lane, Lime Pit Lane, Pike Corner (after the turnpiked section of the Langport-Wincanton road) and Mill Lane – all telling us something of Kingdon's past and its physical features.

7

Sowy Island and Burrowbridge

Bridgwater has tended over the years to extend red-brick
tentacles and colonize any suitable parish. This has
happened to some extent at Weston Zoyland, the largest of
the *zoy** parishes, occupying the lower slopes of that gentle
uplift Sowy Island which reaches its greatest height at
Middlezoy church. Not precisely a dispersed settlement, the
original layout seems to have been determined by the
trackways connecting farms and smallholdings just above
the marsh floodline. The dwellings are strung around two
broad open spaces of common which are being rapidly
infilled. The main A372 from Bridgwater, slicing by estates,
reservoirs and electricity stations, penetrates the village from
the west, takes an abrupt northerly turn almost at the gate of
the church and then sweeps eastward past the bleak ruins of
the aerodrome and on to Middlezoy and Othery.

Weston Zoyland has character. Old cottages huddle and
squeeze up together round the back of the church, and the
main street exudes the blunt functionalism typical of an
agricultural community. There are red-brick houses and
stone houses with painted quoins, and houses faced with
pebbledash. Two pubs stand out: the Shoulder of Mutton
and the more tradition-conscious Sedgemoor Inn, the latter
having a sign showing a sword-slashing cavalryman bearing
down upon peasants armed with scythes and pitchforks. A
shock-white Methodist chapel shouts its contrast loud and

---

* Deriving from 'eye or island. Westhay (West*ere*) is a similar
corruption.

clear, and the modern Spar supermarket is similarly flamboyant. On the garage of a modern brick house is an enormous green snail with an orange shell and wearing a red top hat. Less frivolous is the five-foot silver shell in an alcove by the post office, erected by the Stacey brothers to commemorate the fallen of 1914–18 and a sober reminder of a far bloodier, quantitatively speaking, massacre than was enacted here in 1685. For the Battle of Sedgemoor has not been exhumed around these parts. The very names keep it green: Monmouth House, Standards Road, King's Drive – when, as the song goes, will they ever learn? A slab of Cornish granite commemorates the slain of both sides. It was erected in 1928 after, so the story goes, a Chedzoy woman named Elizabeth Winter heard an unearthly voice lamenting all those lost, desolate souls lying unremembered in a careless heap as a result of the Western Rebellion.

Here is a brief summary of that event. King Charles II died in 1685 and was succeeded by his brother James – an unpopular Roman Catholic whose supremacy was challenged by his nephew, the Duke of Monmouth. He was the illegitimate son of Charles II and was in Holland at the time of the accession. Setting sail, he landed at Lyme Regis and picking up supporters on the way led the Western Rebellion (which numbered 7,000 men at its height) through Taunton, Bridgwater, Greinton, Glastonbury, Shepton Mallet and Norton St Philip towards Bristol. He intended to march through Bristol to London but was thwarted by the Royal Army commanded by Lord Faversham and retreated to Bridgwater. There he was cornered, in a position of hopeless vulnerability, with an army of ill-equipped peasants. As a final ploy, he decided to march across the moor at night and surprise the King's men encamped behind the Bussex Rhyne. Aided by a Chedzoy man who was familiar with the marshes, he took his army across two deep dykes. At a place called Langmoor Rhyne, the guide missed his way in the dark. There was confusion after which he found the crossing, whereupon a pistol was fired, raising the alarm. Alerted, Sir Francis Compton and his Horse Guards Blue attacked the rebels and stemmed their advance. Later Faversham rallied his Life Guards, Horse Guards and

Dragoons, together with artillery and the Royal Foot, and unleashed them upon the peasant army. Indiscriminate slaughter followed. The rebels were shot, hung and hacked down without mercy. Those who remained alive were herded cattle-wise into Weston Zoyland Church – about five hundred in all – where they were kept until the Bloody Assize. Five of them died in the church and an account of the battle is recorded in the parish register.

East of Weston Zoyland, along the main road, there are broad fields littered with red cowshed-like buildings that glow bloodily in the evening light. Around those former barracks are long strips of weedy tarmac runways on which apprentice drivers are tested before acquiring their heavy goods licence. Markets also take place here on Saturdays. Originally a World War II base for Army Co-operation Aircraft, once this ravaged, plundered site paid host to big, blotchily camouflaged Lysanders, Martinets, Mustangs and Blenheims, but now it lies abandoned to the caprices of the wind and rain.

Across the moor, to the north-west, and bounded to the east by King's Sedgemoor Drain, Chedzoy plies its quiet affairs. Smaller and less developed than Weston Zoyland, it is not unsimilar. Aside from the longish main street, there is not a lot to hold the eye, except the church with its strong, square tower with set-back buttresses; on the lower sections of one of them are marks allegedly made when the walls were used by the rebels of the village to sharpen their scythes before the engagement at Sedgemoor.

Across the fields is West Moor. There overweight Friesians browse among buttercups alongside the Sedgemoor Drain, a broadsword of water slicing clean to the muddy Parrett. The flat, receding fields, intersected by innumerable waterways, often lined by the spiky head-dresses of pollarded willows, provide an image of cultivated quietness. In the morning mist, when outlines are silvered to insubstantiality, and the isolated red-brick farms glimmer faintly like flames seen through thick smoke, the scene might have tempted Corot or Constable.

Two miles south-east of Weston Zoyland, standing back from the road, Middlezoy is the most unspoilt of the *zoy* parishes. Its church commands a good view across North Moor to High Ham. Beside it, separated by the road, is a row of stark-angled red-brick dwellings. The tower is tall and finely moulded, with a stair turret and pierced parapet. The interior has a small brass in the nave recording the exploits of a Frenchman, 'Louis Chevalier de Misièr', slain fighting 'against ye king's enemies, commanded by ye Rebel Duke of Monmouth'.

Othery St Mary has been described 'as the most interesting of the *zoy* villages' – a contestable description. Writers have alluded to the quaint old houses clinging limpet-like to the hard, high shoulder of land by the church, the only place safe from the sprawling floodwater – this may have once been so. Unfortunately the main Taunton road rushes through its centre, and this gives it a tired, traffic-trampled air. The church has an imposing stone tower with angle buttresses. Inside there is a fifteenth-century cope of great richness and delicacy, 'showing the Madonna rising to Heaven, the whole shimmering with silver threads and rays of glory', and vigorous medieval bench-ends carved with flowers, birds, butterflies, saints, knights and kings.

Othery is the closest of the *zoy* villages to that mysterious monadnock called Burrow Mump, a dramatic knoll that rises abruptly from the wetlands. Situated at a fording-point of the Parrett, on its crest is a ruined church dedicated to St Michael. Its odd appearance and powerful aura have provoked speculations similar in their wildness and fantasy to those surrounding Glastonbury Tor. Katherine Maltwood included the Mump in her *Glastonbury Zodiac*, wherein she perceived the features around the town as a huge landscape sculpture representing an ancient Babylonian or Sumerian zodiac. The Mump was the snout of the Girt Dog of Langport, the guardian of the Temple of the Stars. This theory has not been enthusiastically taken up by archaeologists.

Burrowbridge is a traditional refuge of King Alfred, who is said to have established his fort on the Mump in 877-8. The King Alfred Inn, below the hill, displays him crowned and red-robed holding his flag and sceptre. Alfred, were he alive, might be intrigued to learn that his popular reputation rests not upon his piety, foresight or military genius – all these are dwarfed by that towering culinary mishap that is lodged deep in the minds of every Englishman. Yes, he burnt the cakes, and by fortuitous coincidence the actual table upon which he spread the charred articles is preserved in his very own public house. In the skittle alley it stands, solid as Gibraltar, and in the 1930s it featured as 'A Table 1000 years old', and advertisements ran 'Call and see the original King Alfred's Table'. Despite this incontrovertible evidence, further backed up by the fact that a skittle team is named the Burnt Cakes Team, sceptics have described it as 'a piece of knotty elm rescued from a flooded cottage' but some people would describe the Grail as a 'liquid container' or the immortal Helen as 'a female of pleasant aspect'.

Two miles from Burrowbridge, situated on a low rise above the floodplain, Lyng is a trim march of Georgian red-brick cottages and renovated traditional dwellings, a former centre of withy-growing and basket-making. The church tower beckons from its mild elevation, jauntily dramatic, with blue lias and Hamstone dressing combining attractively around the quatrefoiled battlements. Summertime endows the surrounding orchards with a kind of lustre which lightens the mood of its inhabitants during their daily commuting to Taunton. Until recently it had a railway halt which inspired S.W.B. Harbin to write a poem recalling Edward Thomas's 'Adlesdrop':

In Lyng upon Sedgemoor
The branches bend low
Neath weight of ripe apples –
Oh, would I might go

To Lyng of the orchards
And see there again
The lines of green willows,
The slow pufing train.

The tall church stand up
O'er the old apple trees
As a reaper in harvest

With sheaves to his knees,

And pinnacles and parapet
And gargoyle of stone
Are yellow as the corn
On the banks of the Tone.

Originally Lyng's church of St Bartholomew was a chapelry of Alfred's monastery at Athelney; the King sheltered here in 879, when he was planning the overthrow of the Danes. His biographer Asser described it as surrounded 'by water and vast impassable peat bogs'. At a later date William of Malmesbury evoked it as 'an island surrounded not by sea, but fens and overflowing marshes ... On this island is a forest of alders of vast extent, giving shelter to stags and roebucks, and many other kinds of game ... There is a small monastery, with offices for the monks'.

About three miles from Lyng, moving north-west, North Newton stands at a crossing-point of routes on a bend of the Bridgwater-Taunton canal east of the M5. Its parish church, St Peter's, was largely rebuilt in 1884 but is of primitive origin. Parts are alleged to be Saxon, and the setting is charming. A rill trickles down one side of the churchyard, which has daffodils crowding its banks in spring, and old cottages nearby that add a dash of homely primitivism. The curious red sandstone tower has narrow slits for windows, creating a general effect of stump asymmetry, inelegant but interesting.

Another village saturated in the lore of Alfred is Aller, about three miles south-west of Burrowbridge, at the foot of High Ham escarpment. Asser, King Alfred's chaplain and biographer, wrote: 'After seven weeks Guthrum the Pagan King with 30 of the principal men of his army redeemed their promise and came to Alfred at the place called Alre, and King Alfred adopting him as his son stood sponsor for him at the sacred font of Baptism.'

Aller is not a romantic place but very much a mixed village straddling the A372 and dominated by the steep wooded slopes which beckon hauntingly. No square or focal-point stands out; the village rambles along the main road in

random, indeterminate fashion, but good buildings catch the
eye, such as the red-brick Georgian Chantry House, and
there is evidence of a burgeoning community spirit in the
fine new village hall. A seed-development factory provides
some local employment, supplemented by private enterprises such as the pottery. The village inn is called The
Pound and appears to have had a recent facelift. The church
lies almost a mile to the south, beside the cement-rendered
(and rather drab-looking) Victorian pile of Aller Court. The
churchyard is of round shape, allegedly denoting a Saxon
origin, and the zigzag doorway survives from the Norman
building. The Saxon font is a capacious, strongly moulded
block of Hamstone with a large basin and rimmed base. It
was discovered among rubble in the rectory garden in 1862,
draped in ivy; in the belfry were a discarded plinth and shaft
which fitted the bowl perfectly. Guthrum must have knelt at
this spot and received his Christian name, Athelstan; then
holy oil was poured on his forehead, which was bound with
white fillets (chrism cloths) to preserve the blessed substance
for seven days until the ceremony of chrism-loosing
(untying the sacred bandages) took place at Wedmore.

East of Othery the main A361 crosses the parallel rhynes
of North Moor and curves south along the gentle
escarpment below Aller Wood. This is a military area which
the army has cordoned off in order to test how effectively
they can fire things at each other. Still there is much of the
remaining Ham plateau which is unspoilt, intriguing and
beautiful. Formerly the whole ridge, from Aller to Somerton,
was dotted with windmills, for its relative elevation caught
the strong winds as they planed across the surrounding flats.
High Ham stands very much in the centre of the uplift. The
church dominates a green shaded by shaggy chestnuts and
adorned with an iron bench and postbox. Pevsner found the
church 'not up to much' but in fact its gargoyles are up to
quite a bit: one of them plays a trumpet; another pipes,
another strains to listen, another fiddles, while a fifth casts a
stone at them to try to make them cease the racket.

The church at Low Ham is famous because it stands alone
in a field and was formerly the chapel to a great, unfinished
manor house. It replaced an earlier fabric built by a man

named Bartlett, of Bursi's Court, Low Ham, which was described by Adrian Schaell (1598) as 'narrow, obscure and renowned with no ancient monuments'. Pevsner thought it 'one of the most instructive examples of early Gothic in England'. The interior is light and inspiring: Hamstone window tracery contrasts with white walls and dark and pale marble.

Low Ham overlooks the gentlest of valleys through which trickles a tiny feeder of the River Yeo. On the other side of this depression, about one mile south-west, just north of the B3153 to Somerton, stands Pitney, a medieval village which gave its name to the local hundred. A joke was once current which referred to Pitney Harbour – and indeed the concept does seem fantastic – but water-levels were far higher hundreds of years ago, before Sedgemoor had been entirely drained, and there is a very low point to the west of the church where boats might have been able to tie up and receive butter, cheese and milk, dairy produce being the main Somerset export. Pitney village is quiet, emphatically agricultural, with its several thatched farmhouses of blue lias, and tiny brook flowing down the centre with a road on either side.

8

Curry Country and the Blackdowns

Two prominent ridges extend from Aller Moor running in an approximately north-east to south-west direction and joining together at the hamlet of Newport. They enclose a flat wedge of moorland drained by the West Sedgemoor Rhyne that reaches the Parrett at Stathe. The ridges are gently undulating and fertile and support a string of intriguing villages, notably North Curry, Curry Rivel and Drayton.

The latter is as quietly inconspicuous as a hermit could wish for, islanded among the orchards and reposeful meadows. The soil is partly alluvial and in places peaty, deep and rich, capable of producing good crops of corn, pulse, potatoes and mangold-wurzel. Formerly there was a fair amount of quarrying of white and blue lias around these parts, but that has declined of late. The village offers vistas of tile, thatch and twining roses to divert the eye. One sees grey stone houses with wooden-framed windows contrasting with the golden dripstones of earlier times; the pink Crown Inn advertising snacks and grills; a noticeboard informing of the Jubilee Celebrations of the Drayton and Muchelney Wives Group – members and husbands cordially invited; St Catherine's Church, a stubby, resilient lias fabric with a Perpendicular tower and a churchyard cross bearing a carving of St Michael and the dragon, and, about two miles south, past Whitecross and over the Isle bridge, the two-storeyed Elizabethan manor of Midelney, built for the brothers Trevillian, one to use the left, the other the right half, with gabled dormers and a falcons' mews around the back.

Although fair in parts, the adjoining village of Curry Rivel strikes an altogether harsher note. Here the hammer blows of change sound loud and discordant. The A378 forms the high street along which gaudy kiln-baked houses are springing and spreading. Large, brash and architecturally hideous, they emphasize how Curry is being transformed into a dormitory for Langport, Somerton and Ilminster. Older buildings vary from traditional stone cottages to late-Victorian red-brick and tile. The road rambles, climbs and descends past the fancy Victorian frontage of Curry Rivel Gallery, where the artist E.R. Sturgeon, the son of the village shoemaker, recreates the background of his youth. His paintings evoke the dim nostalgia of weedy stream flowing past tree-shadowed mills, of quiet streets with pipe-smoking gaffers and lace-bonneted women, of tritt-trotting gigs idling down country roads where everything seems silent, poised. They are the past as we like to see it today.

The parish church of St Andrew's is fifteenth-century Perpendicular and built of blue lias with Hamstone dressing, overlooking the square, perhaps the most attractive part of the village. Its north chapel has a large tomb thought to contain the bones of Sabina Revel (d. 1254), wife of Henry de Lorty. She was the last of the great family from whom the village takes its name and the likely builder of the chapel. There is also a cross-legged knight, probably her son Henry de Lorty II, and the shield bears the family arms.

If Rivel has a clear-cut explanation, what of the prefix Curry? The Domesday Book states that 'the King holds Curri', and the derivation appears to be Celtic, allegedly from a hermit who lived and did good work hereabouts, St Currig.

To the west of Curry Rivel, on Troy Hill, stands Burton Steeple. This 150-foot column, built of local lias with an outer casing of Portland stone, is surmounted by four arched windows and a domed cupola. 'Capability' Brown designed it in 1767 for William Pitt, Earl of Chatham, who wished to honour his elderly benefactor, Sir William Pynsent, who had bequeathed him his rambling Elizabethan manor and estate.

The column still excites curiosity and interest. There is the sad story of the cow which got stuck inside the spiral stairway and was found to be inextricable. Eventually the local butcher had to be called in to reduce her to tradeable sections. In consequence of such incidents, the column was bricked up, the old iron railings having been removed by zealous residents wishing to assist the war effort, and nowadays it can be approached only by special permission.

North Curry has a placid, sedate, civilized aspect recalling somewhere pretty in Kent or Sussex. There is a hint of self-consciousness befitting a place that is highly desirable to live in, especially nowadays, when fewer and fewer people work on the land and increasing numbers commute. Local industries include van Heusen shirts (Taunton), the cellophane factory (Bridgwater) and cider-making (Norton Fitzwarren) plus the sundry shops and offices common to all large towns.

Queen's Square is the kernel of North Curry, where several roads converge around walled 'garden' space with a flagpole and slender fluted cross standing on five hexagonal steps, erected to commemorate twenty-four men of the parish who died in the Great War. A highly attractive centre, it has a freshly planted limewalk leading to the church, mainly of the fourteenth and fifteenth centuries, with a central octagonal tower. There are some good carvings on the exterior, the best being of the devil in chains; the collared and stonebound demon juts out angrily pointing in the direction of the vicarage.

The ambling streams watering the moors around the Curry villages have their source in the Blackdowns which loom steeply on the southern side of Taunton Deane. East of the Blackdowns, between Taunton and Ilminster, is a distinctive stretch of off-the-tourist-route country characterized by undulating panoramic hills, not high but broad, sweeping, amply coppiced and rich with orchards, nurseries and fruit farms. Hatch Beauchamp is situated squarely in this region and dominated by the Palladian Hatch Court (1755).

The village comprises a string of farms, cottages, modern

bungalows and sundry businesses loosely beaded along the main road and older droves around Hatch Green. Since it lost its railway station, lorries nose through like mad mechanical hounds. But despite this onslaught, Hatch is intensely rural and well served by most inviting walks that break away at all angles from the road to penetrate park and open meadow, a most agreeable spot to savour the burgeoning summer countryside. The amble is varied at every turn by vistas of thatch and stone, slate and brick, tree and hedgerow – a peregrination of gentle interest rather than heart-stopping excitement.

Hatch was called 'Hache' in Saxon times, before it gained its suffix from the illustrious Norman family who also held the manors of Marston Magna, Shepton and Stoke-sub-Hamdon. 'Hache' denotes a gateway, referring to the ancient forest of Neroche, whose boundary was marked by the little River Rag flowing through West Hatch. The Beauchamps' manor lay somewhere in the vicinity of the present-day Palladian mansion. Thomas Gerard inspected it in 1633 when it was in a state of dereliction: 'The mansion house in which these noblemen lived,' he observed, 'is so ruined that were it not called Hach Court you would not believe that it were any of the remaynes of a Baron's house.' Hatch Court exudes aplomb with its civilized Palladian lines and four angle towers with pyramidal roofs. The arcaded loggia approached by a broad flight of steps creates an Italianate feel. A rich clothier, John Collins, commissioned the architect Thomas Prowse of Axbridge to design the house which was completed in 1755.

The church at Hatch is attractively situated within the park, and its tower was put up during the period of the master masons which began with the tower of St James at Taunton and ended with St Mary's at Huish Episcopi. Clusters of five pinnacles are set at the corners, and the parapet has pierce quatrefoils. The interior bears witness to the thoroughness or ruthlessness of the 1867 restoration when the roughcast coat covering the walls was removed and repairs were effected with Langport stone. The buttresses of the tower were built and the parapets and pinnacles dismantled and re-fixed. One sad loss was the old Norman chancel arch with zigzag work which was replaced by the present arch erected slightly to the east of the original.

On the same main road as Hatch but not actually penetrated by it, Ashill provides an agreeable halt. The village centre blends brick houses with Victorian Gothic and sturdy stone cottages: a tight, sociable combination of dwellings served by a primary school and post office. The organizers of the Best Kept Village Competition (June 1984) commented on the 'tidy litter-free streets' but were less impressed by the ivy growing inside the bus shelter and the 'weedy' telephone kiosk at Windmill Hill.

Ashill's church durably combines Norman, Early English, Decorated and Perpendicular work. Inside snowy whitewash blends with honey Hamstone, creating an effect of delicate austerity.

To the west of Hatch the land becomes hillier and woodier as it enters the domain of the ancient Forest of Neroche. A half-brother of William the Conqueror, Robert of Mortain, subjugated the primitive Saxon fortress near Staple Fitzpaine in 1067 and converted it to a residential castle: 'Castle of Raehich in the Forest of Neracchich' as it was known in 1298 before dilapidation set in. Robert of Mortain was not entirely satisfied with the stronghold he had created, for he stayed there only twenty years, afterwards moving to Montacute, a spot he probably found pleasanter and infinitely more civilized. Not a stone remains of his castle but there is an immense ditch, consolidated by four inner concentric ramparts, and the whole plan is broken and overshadowed by gargantuan beeches.

Staple Fitzpaine, the nearest settlement to Castle Neroche, grew up at a crossroads on the Taunton-Chard route and the minor droves linking the village with the watery meadows of southern Sedgemoor. The suffix alludes to the Fitzpaine family, who built the manor house, a dwelling that suffered hard times, changing hands and becoming a poorhouse at the end of the eighteenth century. The Portman family, who were granted it by the Crown around 1600, sold off almost the whole parish to pay death duties in 1944, retaining only the manor itself and forty acres of land. They had proved benefactors in the past, donating the almshouses in 1643, which were restored in 1970 and stand today, with a bright red Victorian letterbox shouting cheerfully in the garden, bearing the inscription: 'These poor to have two-pence per week and a black cloth gown once in two years, which they are obliged to wear (if well) at church every Sunday, or forfeit sixpence to the clerk.'

By the road stands the popular Greyhound Inn, advertising itself as 'An Inn of distinction in rural England', but more spiritually fortifying is the church of St Peter, with a west tower of magical intricacy. Hamstone and blended lias contribute to the effect which Edward Hutton likened to 'a cluster of tufted spears, brave and graceful'. Near the churchyard, almost concealed in the undergrowth, is an anonymous-looking sarsen, said to be the 'stapol', an Old English word meaning 'pillar' or 'post' – after which the village is named. This is debatable. 'Staple' can also mean a place where a market was held; another Latin derivation, 'stabula', denoted proximity to a Roman cavalry station. The rather forlorn stone is said to bleed when pricked with a pin.

Staple Fitzpaine is in the depths of the Blackdowns, those remote and relatively unvisited hills, covered mainly by Upper Greensand, that form a high borderland between south-west Somerset and north-east Devon. They lack the plunging wooded combes of the Quantocks and northern Exmoor and tend to be opened and exposed. The highest point, Staple Hill, is 1,035 feet above sea-level, overlooking the lush alluvial pastures of the Tone and Otter, and around there are plantations of tall beech hedges, coppiced oak, sycamore, hawthorn and birch.

Historically the reputation of the hills is unattractive. A pinched miserliness of outlook is associated with Blackdown folk, attitudes engendered by poverty and privation. Faintly malicious stories exist of local farmers licking the remains of broken eggs off the road rather than let the nourishment go to waste, and of the old lady who, on being taken out of her hamlet to view the expanse of Taunton Deane below the Wellington Monument, exclaimed, 'Lordy, Lordy, I never knew the world was so large.' Neither religion nor education achieved much impact here until the nineteenth century when John Brealey, a Devonshire evangelist, abandoned his plan to emigrate to the West Indies and decided to take the gospel to the natives of the Blackdowns. He set up the Blackdown Hills Mission chapel at Clayhidon in 1865, acquiring the stone from a deserted quarry, and set about contacting the under-privileged heathens of the hills. He discovered an old woman of 87 who lived in a cottage with glassless windows; the wind roared through and snow feathered the hearth in bad weather. Another old woman, who cohabited with dozens of cats, danced a hornpipe before him, demonstrating her gleeful emancipation from her Creator. Then there was the man of ninety-seven who lived in a loft attainable only by a rickety ladder; but even he was outclassed by the gaffer who lived alone in a terrible stench, having not washed or removed his clothes for seven years, his sole companions being the rats with whom he shared his food lest they start to eat him.

The largest of the Blackdown settlements, approached from the west by the high beech hedges that sweep imperiously over the domed summits, Combe St Nicholas is technically set in a valley but not in any sheltered protected sense. It sits open and exposed on a broad slope through which the road winds in and out and on to Chard. There is a brush factory here but little other industry except agriculture. Commuting to Chard is central to its livelihood, for the town annexes the world's largest milk factory as well as producing animal feedstuffs, fans and air-blowers, surgical appliances, agricultural machinery, nets and lace.

Combe St Nicholas stands above such industrial pressures as yet. It is not an austere village but the breath of cold hill winds blows through it, and it has that bare, bony look of a place that has weathered the hard centuries and emerged clean-cut and self-contained. It has no nucleus proper but there is a modest civic grouping of stores and post office around a green with a tall ash tree and a tubby black Victorian lamp-post commemorating sixty years (1837–97) of the Queen's reign.

Exploring the church is a delight because it has the most helpful and well-informed caretaker imaginable, one of those genial polymaths occasionally encountered in unlikely places. Predominantly in the Perpendicular style, it has a fragment of a Norman doorway and a rood screen (restored 1921) carved around 1480; the wooden knights are depicted with spear-holds in their shields. Making the church doubly quaint, its miniature museum in one corner exhibits a statuette of Osiris, an Ushabati figure, mummy wheat, a Roman lamp, flint flakes, early Iron Age pottery and a plan of the cutting across Combe Beacon long barrow.

Beyond Combe St Nicholas, the main road passes the Haymaker Inn, with its floridly painted mural, and the severe but tasteful Chardley Green House set in its tidy grounds. Eventually Wadeford is reached, supposedly named after woad but more likely the literalistic interpretation is correct — the *wading* ford. On top of a small hill, among badger setts and tall trees, is a curious little sandstone temple which came from Burton Pynsent, the house bequeathed to William Pitt. It is a modest rotunda, a little worse for wear nowadays, but perhaps that is how follies should be — exploiting the stealthy poetry of decay and desolation.

East of Wadeford, fitting tightly into a deep combe, Whitestaunton ('white-stone-tun' — alluding to the local chalk outcrop) stands by the source of a tiny stream that issues from St Agnes' Well (alleged to have medicinal properties) and the remains of a Roman villa discovered by Charles Elton in 1882. Excavation revealed hypocaust heating, frescoed walls and mosaic floors.

A hermetic spot if ever there was one, where birdsong still dominates traffic noise, close to the villa is the old manor house of the Bretts and Eltons. Parts date from 1493, and it has a most distinctive hall roof of 'collar beams on arched braces and cusped wind-braces of very unusual design'. It slumbers mellowly in the sunshine, or broods in the shade, its arched Elizabethan windows glinting secretively.

A road runs from Combe St Nicholas to Buckland St Mary, another village with a hilltop situation. It perches east of Dommett Moor above the Devonshire hamlet of Bishopswood, and, as Collinson (1791) observed, 'The situation is pleasant, being under the north ridge of the Blackdown Hills and agreeably varied with eminences and vales.' 'Buckland' means 'land granted to the thanes by the

The St Ivel Factory at Evercreech

The village cross at Evercreech

Quarry near Nunney

Nunney Castle

Croscombe

Mells church: the south porch

The boathouse at
Orchardleigh Park

Ammerdown Column

Ammerdown House

Holcombe church

Holcombe church:
the Norman porch

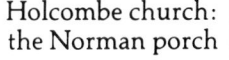

The Redan at Chilcompton,
named after a simple type of field
fort consisting of two parapets of
earth making a V pointing
towards the enemy

The George Inn, Norton St Philip

The entrance gate to Pylle church. The hamlet lies on the route from Ilchester to Cannard's Grave, three-quarters of a mile from the Fosse Way

Hornblottom church

Glastonbury Tor

Tootles Bridge, Baltonsborough

Saxon kings', although the earliest recorded owners of the manor, named Meriet, were of Norman stock. The village winds around a network of lanes, taking in many points of interest such as the Lamb and Flag and Eagle Inns, Ye Post Office, Keats Mill and the portentous gesture of St Mary's Church.

Keats Mill is working no longer. It is over 200 years old and ground corn for animal feeds until steam-powered grinders obviated such structures. A notice once advertised:

If you want cakes or corn or meal,

Come to Jenkins at the mill,
And all kinds of poultry food.
Prices are right and quality good.

In 1830 an inquest was held at the Eagle Inn on the death of a twelve-year-old boy, John Lane. He was maltreated by his father, who was seen striking him and throwing him into a ditch. Then the man dragged him from the ditch and took him back home, placing him in bed beside his other two children – but he was already dead. This happened at a farm called Deadman's Post.

The parish church (1853–63) stands on the same eminence as the old church it replaced. Built of flint with Hamstone facings, after a design by Benjamin Ferrey, an architect from London, the cost was borne by John Edwin Lance, rector 1830–85, who wished to honour his dead wife Louisa by this 'elaborate, totally alien building in High Gothic'. It has been called charitably a 'noble incongruity' – a fairer estimate in that incongruities are a pleasure to come across in deserted districts and sharpen the observer's responses.

A notable seventeenth-century rector of Buckland was William Piers, son of the Bishop of Bath and Wells, whose income was taken away as a result of the Civil War. After the Parliamentary forces had gained control, committees were set up in Somerset to deal with the clergy who were loyal to the King and the Prayer Book. Piers suffered a period of imprisonment followed by years of penury in which he was 'forced to marry'. He travelled around the countryside, selling cheese and tobacco at the fairs and markets, and became one of a conclave of sequestered clergymen 'who sometimes meeting together had no repast but a piece of bread which they ate with salt, and a little water for drink'.

A narrow road from Churchstanton goes past Stapley Cross and over the hill to Churchinford. Set at the head of a combe on a feeder of the Otter, it is the Piccadilly Circus of the Blackdowns, where six roads converge around a nucleus of fifteenth and sixteenth-century cottages. There is not a great deal of through traffic, however, save for farm vehicles and cars of wayfaring sightseers. In Roman times the settlement marked the crossing of branch lines that joined the Fosse and Icknield Ways, two important military and trading routes, and a small garrison was stationed here. In later days it marked the Honiton-Taunton route over the hills and was the scene of a regular fair described by Thomas Westcote in 1845: 'At Churcheon-ford,' he wrote, '(where stands not above a house or two) is kept a great yearly fair, on the feast-day of St Paul. It was the inheritance of the Tudenhams in the reign of Henry III, and after some descents has now been sold to the Damarels of Woodbury.'

'Churchinford' obviously meant 'church by the ford' (which has now been uprooted and replaced by a concrete bridge), and the prefix referred to a chapel of ease (dedicated to St Paul?) whose remains are near Fairhouse Farm.

Some two miles distant, Churchstanton is a big parish of some 4,000 acres formerly called Estanton, Cheristanton and Stanton Tudenham – after the landowning Tudenham family. It has the spiritual and secular standbys of a church and pub but no solid architectural core. The flint-dressed church has a lonely setting and its most famous rector was the learned Jesuit John Salkeld who enjoyed a dialogue with James I and afterwards became a Protestant. He was made vicar of Wellington and moved to Churchstanton in 1635, but was dismissed in 1646 when the Parliamentary forces gained control of Somerset. The church tower has several gargoyles, one with buttocks protruding over the parapet and serving none too decorously as a waterspout.

9

Taunton Deane

The Borough of Taunton Deane is the area predominantly occupied by the Tone valley and lying between the Quantocks, Brendons and Blackdowns. It measures some twenty miles long by fifteen miles wide and extends far east into the Somerset wetlands around the Curry villages. The area was owned by the Saxon royal House at the beginning of the eighth century and afterwards by the bishops of Winchester, who held Taunton Castle. It is a fertile area of small fields with precise hedgerows, rich pastures, grazing cattle, cornland and cider orchards. Such attributes attracted early settlement, and place-names testify to Celtic, Saxon and Norman infusions. A Saxon charter of 682 refers to 'Cructan', a hill of fire where beacons were lit – an instance of Celtic usage being preserved by incomers. The Saxons re-named it 'Creechbarrow' – 'Crychbeorh' in the original form. The latter established the 'tuns' (farmsteads) and the 'stocks' and 'combes' of valleys. Their names are often graphic and informative: 'Milverton' refers to the farm by the mill, and 'Ruishton' to the farm by the rushes. The Normans further complexified the pattern, adding their names to the parishes they were granted by the Conqueror: Staple Fitzpaine, Norton Fitzwarren, Sampford Arundel. The lands owned by the wealthy monastic foundations are also recorded at places like Ash Priors, meaning the priors of Taunton, Bishops Lydeard, once owned by the Bishops of Winchester, and Bishops Hull, the place on the hill formerly belonging to the Bishops of Bath and Wells.

The heart of the region is the administrative centre of

Taunton, serving a catchment area of about 170,000 people
and embracing within its boundaries some forty parishes.
Among the suburbanized villages around the county town
are Creech St Michael and Ruishton to the east, Trull to the
south, and Bishops Hull and Norton Fitzwarren to the west.

The unifying physical feature is provided by the River
Tone, named after the Welsh word for fire, an allusion to the
bright red subsoil staining the river in spate. The stream rises
in the Brendon Hills, near Wiveliscombe, and, flowing
northwards to the Devon border, takes an easterly course to
Taunton (where it was deemed navigable) and finally joins
the Parrett at Boroughbridge.

The capital of the Tone villages is Bradford, occupying a
formerly important position. In Saxon times it was the
'broad ford' across the river, and its fifteenth century bridge,
with chamfered ribs and pointed arches, is a robust relic
which has resisted the onslaught of heavy vehicles. It crosses
an agreeable sludgy part of the river, overhung by willows
and alders, and in summer the uproarious greenery almost
camouflages it.

In Saxon times Bradford lay on the border of the great
Taunton estate of the Bishop of Winchester; the present
parish boundary between Bradford and West Buckland
began as the dividing line between the lands of the Bishop of
Winchester (as defined in a charter 854) and those of the
Wellington estate, held by Bishop Asser of Sherborne in the
tenth century. Two landmarks from that early boundary
survive: the 'Stone Ford', now Stoford, and the 'Alder trees
of the Hawks,' now Hawkaller.

Luxurious bungalows line the southern approach to
Bradford exaggerating a natural tendency towards ribbon
growth. The body of the village perches on a hard shoulder
of land above the river and presents a well-ordered
appearance. The north end is commanded by the
solid-looking Perpendicular church of St Giles, composed of
a variety of building materials: local grey sandstone
combined with Hamstone and Blackdown chert. Well-
preserved stocks are on display in the graveyard which
adjoins a parish club, crisp as a penguin in black and white.
The White Horse Inn dominates the other side of the road,

and the old pump is preserved in a niche nearby. To the south are rows of low-slung grey stone bungalows, yawningly familiar, varied by traditional survivals such as the thatched Orchard Cottage.

The church, originally Norman, was substantially altered in the period between the late fourteenth and early sixteenth centuries. One medieval survivor, however, is the effigy in the south wall, probably Sir John de Meriet, who endowed the chantry chapel in the south transept in 1387. He is fittingly dressed for his period with armour, hauberk and basinet.

The present parish club occupies the same site as the Blackboy Inn in 1841. The pub may have formerly been the old church house where ales were brewed for fund-raising and revelry, such structures often reverting to local taverns after the Puritan Interregnum. The banning of such festivities had an adverse financial effect because, as one bishop put it, 'Many poor parishes have cast their bells, repaired their towers, beautified their churches, and raised funds for the poor' from the income derived from beer.

Bradford's neighbouring village, West Buckland, occupies a remoter but more conspicuous position on a rambling spur of the Blackdowns. Sawyer's Hill rises to the west, and to the north-east Lipe Hill gently ascends to its trig point. A tiny stream from Luxhay Reservoir dribbles through the village, which probably inspired Collinson when he observed in 1805: '... in part of the parish which lies on Blackdown rise many springs, the waters of which unite in a little rivulet which turns a great mill called *Rugging mill* and falls into the River Tone. Another stream runs by the common and has over it a stone bridge of two arches. The roads are very narrow, deep and strong and the hedges meet in an arch above the head.' But the majority of people's first – and probably only – sight of West Buckland is of the church tower raised high on a green plinth above the M5. It is certainly well worth straying from the pulsing, relentless traffic to look over the building. The church of St Mary the Virgin has a square, rugged tower of grey, red and yellow stone, all speckled and studded with glinting flint nodules – a texture which delights the eye. Above there is a fine show of fat, vulture-like gargoyles hanging from the finials. What is immediately apparent is that it is a 'skew' church, meaning the chancel is set slightly askew in deference to the tradition that, when Christ died on the Cross, His head leant to the right.

Backing the church are housing estates of dark-brown and pale-brown brick arranged in patterns. The remainder of the community is a trim testimony to rural pride. Dyer's Close is a small red-brick estate, and Peacock Close has some Victorian cottages. There is an obelisk to the slain of the First World War, a phone-box, post office, primary school and, set apart from the rest, the cream and scarlet Crown Inn.

On the other side of the Tone is Nynehead, which, like so many parishes in the Deane, belonged to the Bishops of Winchester at Domesday and which was known as 'Nichenhede' or 'Ninehead Flory'. It is a place that retains its quiet tempo and, wandering around its lanes and tracks on summer evenings, one has that sensation of deep, concentrated greenness like a cocoon. Tiny pricks of light glitter from farms like glow-worms, and the stubby little church and elegant Court are transformed into bloated charcoal silhouettes.

Entering the village from the east is memorable. The way penetrates a deep cut in the sandstone called Nynehead Hollow. Steep banks of flaming red stone, canopied by overlapping leaves, create the atmosphere of a cave or passage through a canyon. The cut was implemented by the Sanfords, who came to Nynehead Court around 1600 and sponsored many improvements, including the building of the local school and the widening of the Tone. A chapel in All Saints Church contains busts of John and Henrietta Sanford. In 1830 they presented the church with the blue-and-white reliefs of the Madonna and her Child by della Robbia.

The village is loosely strewn around. Clavengers Farm, Hornshay Farm and Blockhouse Farm are separated by a distance of over a mile in different corners of the parish. Then there is Poole on the railway line where there is a brickworks founded in 1842 by William Thomas. Otherwise no definite nucleus exists, save for the church and the Court, which create a marked contrast. The former is a stout sandstone building with an unusual stained glass window illustrating the story of Mary of Bethany. Nynehead Court (1675) is now a luxurious home for old people. It is soberly elegant with its formal gardens and restrained classicism, and the dazzling palatial freestone is utterly different from the coarse local sandstone. Many windows have been skilfully blocked in to avoid the window tax that was from 1695 to 1851 such a bane to the wealthy.

Hillfarrance lies north of Bradford across the valley. It is named after the Ferons family, distinguishing their 'hill' from the property of the Bishops of Winchester at Bishops Hull. A brook waters the central part of the village, which presents a scene of intense rural calm. There is a green by the church and attractive houses such as the cream and red Burgine – a sturdy Georgian building – and the slated post office with its cheerful letterbox outside. There is one tiny thatched cottage with pale primrose walls, green window-frames and a sprouting red-brick chimney; it might have been purpose-built for pixies such is its scale and quaintness. The church is mainly interesting because of its west tower which was partly financed by John Peryn of Wellington (will of 1509) and is dressed with Hamstone. The freshest feature is the ceiling by the altar, which is blue with gold stars. The south chapel was built by William de Vernai (d.1333) who is buried here, and in the porch are the remains of a holy water stoup.

From Hillfarrance the lanes wind in and out, by Allerford ('ford by the alders') and Pontispool Farm, joining the Taunton road at Norton Fitzwarren, a very early settlement sprawling beneath an extensive Iron Age Camp. Large finds of Roman pottery were unearthed here, and a Romano-British settlement called 'Theodunum' has been affirmed. Its antiquity provoked the local rhyme, 'When Taunton was a furzy down, Norton was a market town.' The name arose by yoking the Saxon 'north tun' ('north farm') to the name of the Norman family who inherited the manor after the Conquest. Taunton has infiltrated Norton, which has been described as its 'unlovely suburb'. This is not fully justified. Outside the town are some extremely handsome sandstone barns and seventeenth-century farmhouses of wonderful texture and strength. The main street is bold and bare, with several houses favouring a pinkish-brown exterior-grade paint which gives them a loud but faintly monotonous look. Victorian sandstone buildings and slated whitewashed cottages vary this bias.

Norton's church occupies an elevated position on a side-road. The Perpendicular battlemented tower supports a team of fat, stealthy gargoyles. A famous interior feature is the 'Dragon Screen' carved by the local churchwarden Raphe Harris (d.1509). During the 1829 restoration this was taken to pieces, smeared over with a filthy brown varnish stain and reassembled wrongly. Part of it, depicting the killing of the monster, found its way to a curiosity shop in Taunton and had to be rescued by the local rector. The screen shows naked men and women disporting themselves in an imaginative way, fields being seeded and the dragon devouring a praying woman. The beast was alleged to have been spontaneously generated from the fumes of thousands of corpses after a battle on Norton Camp. It ravaged the valleys and villages as far as Williton but was eventually slain by a member of the Fitzwarren family. There is a batch of dragon legends in Somerset, and it has been suggested that they originate from the memory of the dragon-headed longships used by the Vikings who invaded this area during the Dark Ages and later.

Further down the hill is Norton Manor, an early seventeenth-century building with mullions and dripstones, a roof of ancient mottled slates, a balustraded porch and gate piers on which two handsome Hamstone lions recline.

Industry has a firm foothold at Norton, which is the home of an immense industrial estate, and the mecca of the cider-making in the district. Today cider is sold throughout Britain and overseas, yet its taste has remained remarkably consistent since the days when the Norman cider-makers (who accompanied the Conqueror's armies) introduced it. Cider apples bear piquant and amusing names: Yarlington Mill, Dabinett, Chisel Jersey, Slack Ma Girdle and Tremlett's Bitter are examples. The beverage remained confined to the West Country until the early 1800s, when

the Reverend Thomas Cornish produced a cider appetizing
enough to find its way onto Queen Victoria's shopping-list.
Years later the Heathfield gardener and cider-maker Arthur
Moore teamed up with George Pallet and founded the cider-
mill at Norton Fitzwarren. A company was registered in April
1921 and had six employees producing about 10,000 gallons
of draught cider per year. Today they employ nearly 500 who
make millions of gallons per year. The company is now
owned by a consortium of brewers and develops traditional
orcharding schemes to produce the right type of crop. The
old rite of 'wassailing' – singing in a good crop – is maintained by the company. Cider-soaked toast is put into the
branches of the chosen tree for the robin (who embodies the
good spirit), and cider is poured around the roots to appease
the Goddess of Fruits, Pomona. The trunk of the tree is
banged to expel evil spirits, and then everyone gets down to
the business of rendering themselves insensible.

On the south side of the river but heavily developed in a
comparable manner, Bishops Hull takes the surge of traffic to
Taunton. Lights have been installed to control the flow of
heavy goods and commuting vehicles. Extensive new settlement is evident in the number of estates that encase the road:
Meadowside, Badgers Close, Gillards, Heron Drive – names
often invoking, mildly ironically, a rural nostalgia effectively
negated by their very presence.

East of the main road, mounted on an even slope, is the
octagonal-towered church – an unusual building with red
pebbly filler material worked into the walls. It has a curious
extension that resembles a Methodist or Baptist chapel. This
was added in 1827 and, as Robert Dunning observed (1980),
'The contemporary Gothic box pews and gallery create an
unbalanced but by no means unpleasing effect.' But Bishops
Hull's truly outstanding building, facing the local school, is
the manor house built 1586 by Simon Farwell which was used
as a court house for the court barons of Taunton Deane. It is
based on an E-plan, and the entrance arch is flanked by Ionic
columns, details that do no justice to this wonderful rosy-red
building with its tall gables and air of dilapidated distinction.

The 'hull' (hill) after which Bishops Hull is named overlooks the Tone. One can ascend it, passing numerous fine

Georgian buildings, adapted as administrative offices for banks and building societies, and, by way of maddening, frustrating lanes, reach the village of Trull, another place which has undergone excessive improvement. Today Trull is incorporated with the residential suburbs of Taunton. Along the main road sprawl big modern bungalows, Victorian villas with high-walled gardens and ultra-spick thatched residences. They are not ugly or cluttered, being everywhere leavened by space and greenery. Trull church and village lie east of this infilling and form a sedate, compact nucleus. A row of yellow houses with red-brick quoins stand near the church in a lane called Wild Oak, and there is a terracotta-tiled parish room and the pink and thatched Church Cottage. An ample primary school occupies a prominent situation, emphasizing the community's considerable growth, and there is also a recent memorial hall besides many substantial stone dwellings – all giving the solid, intact feel of a community that is securely prosperous.

The glory of Trull is the church of All Saints, originally dating from the thirteenth century, when the parish was known as Trendle. It is set in an extended churchyard; an old schoolhouse, cottages and stable were pulled down, and in 1887 the bishop consecrated the additional land. Bold, dramatic, dappled with grey and gold stonework, the church is arresting and scrupulously maintained. Its prize possession is the medieval pulpit with carved figures of saints, including Pope Gregory, St Augustine of Hippo and St John the Evangelist. The figures are sensitively done though by no means mobile or vigorous. Pevsner found them wanting in the 'consummate skill or power of characterization of contemporary German wood-carving' but nevertheless they are unique in Somerset.

In 1872 Francis Kilvert, the Victorian clergyman whose diaries have now attained classic status, visited Trull in the company of his Cornish friends the Hockins, who owned Northtown Nurseries in Taunton. He made no brilliant remarks about Trull and did not even go inside the church but managed to summon a faint snigger at the sight of an 'antediluvian parson' trying to keep up with a group of archaeologists who were examining the building.

About two miles south of Trull, sunning itself beneath the beechwoods of the Blackdowns, the civil parish of Pitminster extends over an area of 5,500 acres. The boundary was first fixed by Saxon charter (834) and has hardly altered since. The parish embraces the hamlets of Pitminster, Blagdon Hill, Staplehay and Lowton. The M5 motorway cuts across but does not destroy the peace and remoteness. Laying the road brought to light a Bronze Age stone which is today set up by the playing-fields at Sellicks Green.

Blagdon Hill is a tidy, open hamlet with some individually attractive houses. Blagdon House has a classical entrance porch and red-brick window-dressing contrasting with the warm, mottled stonework. The Mission Room (1878) is a sturdy Nonconformist meeting-house; the Lamb and Flag Inn displays the paschal lamb on its spick, renovated exterior. 'Blagdon' may hold the clue to the name of the hills. Some derive it from 'black', alluding to their dreary wintertime appearance, but others see 'blagdon' as meaning 'wolf hill', the area being formerly noted for these creatures. No great population explosion has taken place over the years, although infilling continues, and on the slope of hills, in somewhat unnecessarily grandiose positions, big chalet-style homes have appeared with genteel names like Kentia Lodge.

It is not known whether there was ever a minster at Pitminster, which was called Pipeminster in the Domesday Book. The church of SS Andrew and Mary has an octagonal tower crowned by a lead spire and weathercock. The effigies of the Colles family are noteworthy for their detail. Humphrey Colles (1570) is carved in alabaster with his cloak flung open. A monument to John Colles (1607) shows him in armour together with his wife and kneeling family. There is a waxwork-like creepiness in the painted detail of beards, eyes and links in the armour. Humphrey Colles was given Barton Grange when it was taken from the monks.

Less remote the Pitminster, the aspect of Creech St Michael is workaday rather than picturesque, squeezed between the River Tone to the south and the northern curve of the M5. The village follows the long straggling road, looping and undulating beside garages, inns, churches and business premises. There is the feel of being in the vicinity of a large town. Facing the main street, next to the cheerful Women's Institute, there is a big red-brick Methodist church going up that recalls a modern arts centre. A little to the south, at Sycamore Walk, a cycle path cruises between squat, oblong bungalows which are functional rather than aesthetic. But despite the brashness and bustle of fairly continuous traffic, Creech is leavened by brilliant watery ways and green lanes that dawdle and lose themselves among fields and trees. Mill Lane dips down past colour-washed cottages and a ponderous Victorian red-brick block to confront a paper-mill with looming flues and a notice proclaiming 'TAUNTON DEANE'S ANSWER TO THE RECESSION'. The mill has now closed, and so, regrettably, the answer is a surrendering sigh of impotence.* Curvalion Lane leads to a house of that name and was once known to locals by the coarser title 'Pigs Barrel Lane'. Hereabouts the roadway crosses the old Bridgwater and Taunton Canal, beside which the paper-mill is situated, and then the railway line and the Tone itself.

These industrial features account for the mid-nineteenth century expansion of Creech. The village formerly comprised a mainly agricultural population of basket-workers, cider-makers, maltsters and farmworkers, until the construction of the canal in 1827 brought new employment. Items as varied as coal, wine, flax, grain, timber and pitch were borne up the waterway, and for a period there was a price war between the canal traffickers and those who held the river rights. The building of the railway in 1842 struck a blow to the livelihood of both concerns: trains shunted away with the profits, tonnage dropped dramatically and in 1907 canal and river trade ceased. Today the inhabitants of Creech commute to work in Taunton or Bridgwater. The only village industries remaining after the loss of the paper-mill are a slaughterhouse and a commercial apple orchard, plus several shops and smallholdings employing mainly casual labour.

* The premises at present accommodate ten small firms including Woodland Resources, the new company formed after the closure of Creech paper-mill.

St Michael's Church hides from the bustle and new building, tucked away at the south-east corner of the settlement. Its short golden tower has a mellow, battered look, very venerable and weathered, although the oldest feature is the twelfth-century aisle. There is an altar tomb to Robert Cuffe, an Elizabethan yeoman who occupied a nearby farm, and in the churchyard are a renowned thousand-year-old yew and the village stocks. Initials can be seen on the walls, which was part of a custom called 'wall-work tenements' wherein the use of common land was linked to the upkeep of portions of the churchyard wall.

A very fetching if little-visited village, some two miles north of Creech, West Monkton is studded here and there: farms, robust cottages and consequential manors strung along winding tree-shadowed lanes. A stream hurries along by the road, and there is a quiet central street with a post-office stores, Georgian villa and, at the west end, stark yet appealing in black and white, the Monkton Inn flanked by a large lawn occupied by wooden tables and benches.

Originally part of the administrative hundred of Whitleigh, owned by the abbey of Glastonbury, which acquired it by royal grant in 682, after the Dissolution West Monkton came into the possession of William Poulett, Marquess of Winchester, who is alleged to have occupied the present rectory. The latter building is a fragment of a 'very considerable mansion' known as Court House. A distinguished former occupant was Matthew Brickdale, who started out as a woollen-draper's apprentice and rose to become Tory Member of Parliament for Bristol on three occasions between 1768 and 1790.

The situation of St Augustine's Church, high above the marshy meadows of the Tone, is striking. Fitted with plain double buttresses and severe string courses, its tower seems higher than its eighty-eight feet, lack of ornamentation making it more assertive, like a long bare neck of stone. Old stocks are in the churchyard, together with a whipping-post originally portable and probably installed when the commons at Bathpool or Monkton Heathfield were enclosed in 1812. Items of interest are plentiful in the church records. The eighteenth-century burial register provides a grisly picture of the ailments which culminated in permanent leave-taking from this pleasant village. They list things like consumption, water on the brain, King's evil, putrid fever and measles. Poor Sarah Hewer is recorded as having died in the snow on 13 January 1797; Sarah Major, on the other hand, died in 1792 at the age of one hundred.

The largest – and certainly the most elegant – of villages in the upper vale is Milverton. This is indeed the aristocrat among small settlements. The Georgian style is always attractive, but here it is enhanced by the use of rugged red sandstone which produces a contrast of marvellous richness: delicate white window-frames and glazing bars, scalloped porches and pilasters, juxtaposed against this earthy solidity.

This is a very ancient settlement, known to Stone Age man, and traces of flint-working have been found in a field near the Quaking House. At the time of the Conquest it belonged to Queen Edith and was considered relatively prosperous, having a market – there were only seven then in the whole of Somerset – and a lucrative mill. By the reign of James II the market had 'totally decayed', but in 1708 Queen Anne granted a charter restoring the market and allowing 'two fairs in the Burgh of Milverton' and also 'a Court of Piepowder at the time of the fairs'. The latter name derives from the French 'pieds poudres', 'dusty feet', an allusion to the fact that it dealt with trading irregularities on the spot before the itinerant trader moved on. In medieval times the wool trade flourished here, and the weavers of Milverton became famous for their serges, druggets and baizes. The industry declined with the expansion of the steam-powered mills of Wellington and increasing competition from Yorkshire and Lancashire.

The days of prosperity left behind some remarkable houses. North Street is called by locals 'Quality Street' on account of its attractive Georgian terraces. Behind the façades there is earlier work, dating back as far as Tudor times, and the raised cobbled pavement was adapted from the houses' forecourts. The main street, called Fore Street, is where most of the businesses are concentrated, including the bank, post office and Globe Inn. Here too is the Congregational chapel (now a private house), the Victoria

Rooms (1887), with a concert hall and several adjacent rooms, and the Fort, a big house alleged to be sited on the Saxon foundation of Milverton. At the end of Fore Street is the space where the village cross formerly stood. It was removed in 1851 because many people were said to be loafing against it instead of attending church. Prominent by the cross is Lottisham House, a fine Georgian building where Mr Lottisham, an intensely poetic young man, signalled to his sweetheart from the top window. Fore Street curves into Sand Street, where many of the older cottages stand. The Victorian school, a county primary, looks across to the Venetian-windowed Netherfield. Outside the village is Olands, the headquarters of Somerset Social Services, with the Wessex dragon emblazoned on the notice-board. The parish church challenges from its hilltop, its tall red tower looming stark and assertive; the big cedars in the churchyard are said to mark the burial place of plague victims. The bench-ends are carved with portrait busts of notables such as Mary Tudor, Cardinal Pole and Bishop Gardiner; more playful are the bird pecking grapes and the man quaffing wine.

A lane worth exploring leads to the Old Mill, about half a mile beyond the village. The site has been used for this purpose since Saxon times, and the mill did not stop grinding until the twentieth century. Channels and leats may still be seen, and the holes in the wall near the bridge denote that pigeons were kept inside; doves and cornmills went hand in hand, the birds feeding off bits of scattered grain and providing meat in times of need.

One other building of note is Quaker Lodge, where Thomas Young was born of a Quaker family in 1773. In 1802 he became the colleague of Davy as professor of natural philosophy at the Royal Institution, having made the discovery of the interference of light and laid the groundwork for the wave-motion theory. He also preceded Champollion in the discovery of the alphabetic characters on certain Egyptian hieroglyphs, unravelling the mystery of the Rosetta Stone. France honoured him; all the renowned Continental scientists applauded his research, but in Britain he was regarded as a mere dilettante.

On the south side of the valley, north of Milverton, stands Fitzhead. From the larger village one climbs the hill and descends past the ancient buttressed wall enclosing Fitzhead Court. The core of the village comprises the old schoolhouse (1846), the post office adapted from a former smithy, sandstone cottages, a farmhouse and the Fitzhead Inn. The history of settlement here is long and continuous: a flint hunting knife has been found in the field behind Knight's Farm and records reveal that in Saxon times it was known as 'Fyfehide' and formed part of the manor of Wiveliscombe.

A medieval tithe barn is easily recognized from the churchyard. Adapted as a parish hall in 1908, when a large fireplace, inglenook and stage were installed, formerly it had double doors in the south wall through which wagons passed and unloaded there hay, corn and flax for the parson's tithe. Pond Cottage, at the eastern end, marks where the fishponds were leased from the lord of the manor for one shilling a year on the agreement that the tenant would supply the parishioners with fish during the winter months.

Going south from Milverton, the road climbs Burn Hill and descends past Chipley Park (where John Locke wrote part of his *Essay on the Human Understanding*) and into the village of Langford Budville, burgeoning with new luxury homes. Otherwise it is a compact, pleasing place, with a brick school banked above the street, council estates and the familiar pink and cream cob cottages often buttressed for extra security. The church is well sited, commanding a good view over the meadows to the foothills of the Quantocks. Silvery pylons bestride the fields, holding their strands of wire knitting like a queue of robotic grannies.

The church tower is embattled with a stair-turret and is braced by set-back buttresses. Formerly it figured in the Langford Revel (an uproarious ale-drinking festivity designed to raise church funds) wherein a custom called 'clipping the tower' took place. A human chain danced around the church and produced at the strategic moment a terrifying shout which chased the Devil out of the churchyard as far as the River Tone at Harpford. This custom was suppressed during the Puritan Interregnum.

One of the piers in the south arcade has a needle and thread carved on it which may have been a mason's signature but is also a sign associated with Queen's College, Oxford. An alternative theory is that a woman was once a patron of the church, and there is also a possible link with Canonsleigh Abbey, for on the central boss of the wagon roof in the south aisle is a shield with three chevronels, a motif repeated on the arms of Matilda de Clare who re-founded Canonsleigh as a priory for Augustinian cannonesses in 1284.

The local inn, unusually named the Martlett, is seventeenth-century stone and cob with a patio garden and the curious sign of a legless martlett, which in heraldic language indicated the fourth son of a nobleman, meaning he was going to inherit no property. This is thought to refer to one of the Sanford family, former lords of the manor.

The River Tone lies about a mile south of Langford, which marks where it ceases to flow in a flat-bottomed valley and descends from the uplands. This is an exciting if little-known region, replete with homely primitive churches, low plain manor farms, deep-hedged lanes, streams that chase down ferny banks, old mills, cob cottages, slate-walled gardens and sheep of healthy girth. The capital of this region is Wellington, a residential centre and focus of light industry, quite unlike the 'low, dirty place' full of beggars that Defoe saw in the eighteenth century. The Wellington Monument now owned by the National Trust was described by Monica Hutchings as 'a Cleopatra's Needle of an obelisk which often has its head in the clouds'. The 175-foot high monument was erected to 'perpetuate the memory of Wellington' not long after the victory of Waterloo. The foundation stone was laid by Lord Somerville in 1817 and in 1819 the Iron Duke paid his only visit to the town from which he appropriated his title. After remaining in an unfurnished state for years, it was completed by C.E. Giles in 1854.

Some four miles east of Wellington, by way of wriggling, twisting lanes, the tiny hamlet of Thorne St Margaret pursues its agricultural vocation. Its church is set back from the road. It is very plain and of hard red sandstone – redder around the tower than the walls and porch which seem grey. Inside there are oolite pillars, a Saxon font and a brass of John Worth (d. 1610) showing an old man with curly hair and long beard, wearing a ruff, doublet, breeches and gartered stockings and shoes.

Adjoining Thorn, slightly to the south, is Holywell Lake, a hamlet with an inn but no church. It is sited by a holy well and was formerly noted for cudgel-fighting; a platform would be erected in front of the inn, and a rustic Neanderthal would strip and flourish his weapon until a challenger came along. Unconsciousness or excessive bleeding denoted victory.

10

The Quantocks

The main A38 follows the motorway faithfully except that it penetrates the heart of Bridgwater instead of skirting the cellophane-scented town, and then enters the village of South Petherton. The outskirts are not auspicious: red-brick bungalows, drab Victorian terraces, insensitive infilling, the odd petrol-station and bill hoarding. Eventually it brushes by a large, grim, synagogue-type United Reform church (1835) and then the centre of the village. A lofty, golden-grey, 110-foot, pinnacled tower overshadows a big bleak green across which a stream (whose banks could do with a clean) surges – but not to any enchanting effect. Here, in the shadow of the faith, stand two whitewashed pubs, the Swan, actually beside the church, and the Walnut Tree, on the opposite side.

This then is North Petherton, an expanding village, taking much of Bridgwater's overspill and aspiring towards the status of a town. The population is a bracing mixture of aboriginals and incomers. There is even here the glimmerings of an alternative society: complaints about fox-hunting on the Quantocks and the hazards of expanding Hinkley Point power station are topics of conversation that may be overheard among locals. So although North Petherton is not beautiful, it has the kind of bracingness of a rough-cut town. This can be as gratifying to experience as a tweely photogenic village with an entirely static population given over to knitting and socializing with roses.

Although the surroundings are relatively low lying, North Petherton borders on the Quantock Hills. Only two miles to

the west rise this dramatic, compact range, which reach their
greatest height at Will's Neck (1,260 feet), 'ridge of the
Welshmen' (alleged to enshrine the memory of some ancient
battle fought on the summit). The Quantocks have a ridge
walk along the spine and extend some twelve miles along an
axis running from north-west to south-east. Geologically
various, they are composed of grits, slates, limestone and tuff.
The Hangman Grits make a thin, rather sterile acid soil, while
the Morte Slates of the southern Quantocks produce the
rounded hills and deeper, more productive soils. But it is the
valleys or combes which render the Quantocks so distinctive.
Steep-sided, shady, traversed by fast streamlets, they create
an atmosphere of closeted greenness contrasting with the red
rocks and the limitless blue of the sky. Small, compact villages
have grown up at the mouths of these combes because of the
availability of water, grazing-land and shelter from the
elements.

Goathurst is a fine example, sheltering beneath the south-
east slopes, only three miles from Bridgwater, and connected
by a narrow, twisty road that crosses Cobb's Cross Stream
before climbing up towards the main street and halting before
the crossroads by Halswell House. This is a close-focused
village rather than a loose grouping of farmsteads around a
church. The main street is enhanced by a streamlet that once
fed a string of trout-stocked ornamental lakes attached to the
great mansion. Cottages of chunky natural stone or colour-
washed pink, yellow, cream or sand, face each other in
amicable concourse. They are not secretive hives, one feels,
where private affairs and scandals will wilt and die of neglect.
There is the familiar old forge and a post office stores. Lyre
Cottage has a carved porch that effectively mimics Orpheus's
instrument, while the old schoolhouse evokes the music of
swishing canes and juvenescent wails. At Dancing End traditional cottages give way to large-gardened bungalows erected
mainly by commuters to Bridgwater and beyond. Red
almshouses by the church date from 1780 and were founded
by Sir Charles Kemeys Tynte, former lord of the manor. The
old rectory, now two houses, was once the manor house of the
Pawletts and contains a wagon-roofed dining-hall with heraldic murals.

The church at Goathurst, situated near the almshouses, is resilient and sturdy with big buttresses and a stair turret. It is dedicated to St Edward, king and martyr, who was murdered on the orders of his stepmother, Elfrida, in 978 at Corfe in Dorset. This unusual choice of dedication suggests a tenth-century foundation; the plain rectangular nave and chancel may reflect the rudimentary form of the pre-Conquest church. A picture of the death of St Edward by a local artist, Richard Ansdell, is inset in a niche, but this is a subsidiary detail, the interior being mainly taken up with monuments, shields and portraits of the Pawletts, Halswells, Kemeys and Tyntes whose interlocked lives provide much of the narrative of Goathurst history. It was the Halswells who occupied and built the great house on the hill and engirdled it with a park planted with towering Spanish chestnuts, oaks, elms and beeches. Exotic follies were added but these have fallen into disrepair; one of the sorrier sites of Goathurst is the cracked and battered Greek temple marooned in a lonely field not far from one of the ornamental lakes.

A chapel in the church is set aside for the Halswells. There is a splendid early seventeenth-century monument to Sir Nicholas Halswell and his wife Bridget attended by the kneeling figures of their six sons and three daughters. The couple were married forty-four years. Bridget, daughter of Sir Henry Wallop of Farley Wallop, Hants., died on 28 July 1627 and requested to be buried in the Halswell aisle. 'What would I not give that the bones of my faithful and dear Nicke were brought over and buried with me.' Sir Nicholas died in Bristol six years later, and his wife's wishes were carried out. 'I will leave to my cousin Wallop,' the Will continues, 'my clocke, my little Paris worke, my Psalm book, my ring, on which is engraven – shall affliction part friends? – and I desire him to accept these as unworthy remembrances of an unfortunate wretch.'

Sir Nicholas Halswell was Member for Bridgwater and a Justice of the Peace. In 1603 he 'committed to prison one John Gilbert, a fanatical minister for having on a sabbath day attempted to preach naked in the parish church of North Petherton'.

On the walls of the belfry are an impressive collection of hatchments commemorating the Kemeys Tynte family of Halswell House. When a death took place, it was the practice to hang one of these heraldic badges above the front door of the mansion. There it remained for one month after the funeral, and then it was removed to the church. The deceased's side of the coat of arms was painted black.

The churchwarden's accounts for Goathurst reveal a most instructive picture. There are seventeenth-century charity entries detailing the purchase of shoes for Joan Denner 'fir her at Broomfield Fayre' and medical entries listing emetics, laxative potions, worm powder and a 'saturnine lotion for the face'. One gathers that ailments of the scaly, itchy sort were all too common in those pre-hygienic days of yore.

Unlike Goathurst, which occupies the verdant fringes of the Quantocks, Broomfield has a high, exposed situation, about three miles south-west, and is a parish of isolated stock-rearing farms and lonely cottages strewn over 4,000 hilly acres. Some of the farms are of great age: Ivyton and Oggshole, Westleigh and Streams, Lydeard and Rooks Castle. Many of the smaller holdings have become amalgamated with the larger, yet the old field names remain and tell their story: Greenway, where an ancient track ran; Kings Hill and Priors Down, once owned by King John, who gave them to Taunton Priory in 1204; Huntingwell, noted for the pleasure of the chase; Butts Close, where archery was practised.

In 1853 hopes of wealth ran high when some old copper mines (Lodes Lane preserves their memory) were deepened and re-opened. There was even a rumour of veins of gold being found but the gossip proved unduly optimistic and after a year the mines became unworkable and the villagers returned to their familiar stand-by, agriculture.

Andrew Crosse, the electrician and most famed inhabitant of the village, married Mary Ann Hamilton whose family owned 200 acres locally, but it was his second wife, Cornelia, who immortalized his name by preserving his papers and writing a detailed memoir chronicling his early researches in crystallography and electricity.

Apart from the tiny nucleus of All Saints Church, the parsonage and old schoolhouse, Broomfield has no village centre. But exploring the tangle of lanes in the neighbourhood reveals many interesting sites. There is the dilapidated Congregational chapel on Shellthorn Hill, Raswell House (formerly the Caernarvon Arms), Ruborough Camp, the old wheelwright's cottage and the unreassuringly titled Deadman's Well by Durretts' Farm. The early fourteenth-century church has a rugged homeliness and contains an octagonal font, fragments of fifteenth-century stained glass and Andrew Crosse's workbench. Around All Saints Day (1 November) for more than 600 years, until the 1890s, Broomfield held a fair which drew Quantock folk for miles. It was held on the village green and specialized in cattle and coarse cloth trading but later became more diverse. In the 1970s, a local writer A. Mead observed: 'Fair Day meant a day out for folk from miles around and many rode up on their donkeys. There were amusements for all, and stalls selling fairings and goods of every description. Hard-working mothers of big families could buy winter boots for their children with hoarded coins earned by industrious gatherings of blackberries, mushrooms and sweet chestnuts, sold in Bridgwater. Traditionally, toasted biscuits and cider were consumed and the church bells added their music to the day.'

Broomfield borders on both Goathurst and Enmore. The latter is a tiny hill-perched place of farms, cottages and a school of marked historic interest. It went up in 1810, financed by the Reverend John Poole, cousin of Thomas Poole of Nether Stowey, whose educational radicalism moved Wordsworth to write in *The Excursion*:

Oh for the coming of that glorious time
When this imperial realm ... shall admit
An obligation on her part to teach
Them who are born to serve her and obey:
Biding herself by statute to secure
For all the children whom her soil maintains
The rudiments of letters and inform
The mind with moral and religious truth.

A less modest building than Enmore School is the fake baronial castle built for John Percival, Earl of Egmont. The

Gothic embellishments date from around 1790 but the fabric has that vaguely uneasy look which results when solidity (it is all hard red sandstone) is married to theatricality. Here are corner towers, a turreted gatehouse, lancet windows – all the medieval garnishings, but the outcome is more cumbrous than inspiring.

There is an ornamental lake in the grounds of the castle, a civilized strip of water with a tiny island, far less bleak than the Hawkridge Reservoir, about three miles away, holding some 190 million gallons of water. It supplies the urban and industrial areas of Bridgwater and Taunton and occupies an ideally steep-sided site just below the hamlet of Lower Aisholt. Although it is a fairly dull expanse of water, small yachts enliven its surface and marsh marigold, reedmace and yellow flag iris colonize its banks. The main outflow from the lake is a brook which ripples down the combe and forms a small pond in the village of Spaxton, a dispersed community taking in a couple of pubs – the Lamb and Victoria – as well as council houses, a grocery shop, post office and garage.

Spaxton is named after Spakr, an early Norse settler who established a *tun* (farm) around the Peartwater stream in the ninth century. At the time of Domesday the estate was the property of Alured, a Spanish mercenary, and it was owned subsequently by the Fichets and the Hylles. St Margaret's Church stands next to Court Farm, and the two ancient structures exude an earthy, gnarled resilience. The siliceous stone flamingly contrasts with the green of the fields and the pearliness of the sky. The court house is L-shaped, and there is an old mill, now mossy with age, standing near at hand. Just beyond the graveyard are Cooke's almshouses, a somewhat dour charity row equipped with a prayer room. These were originally established for six poor men or women who each got 2s. weekly plus coal, light and clothing. The church shows traces of early Norman herringbone work in the north wall but the structure was rebuilt in the fifteenth century. Sir John Hylles, whose effigy is preserved inside, left money for the tower, which was built after his death in 1434. A feature regularly noted is the fuller's bench-end, its carving demonstrating the tucking tool used for beating the freshly woven woollen cloth. The tucker lived at the house called Tuckers between the Old Quarry and Splatt Mill. The name of the hamlet of Splatt, only half a mile north-east, is derived from old Saxon meaning a strip of land. Similarly 'Pightly', another tiny hamlet by a brook, means 'a little plot' (of land).

At Four Forks are a group of private houses where the Agapemone – the Abode of Love – was established by Brother Prince in 1859. This hypnotically attractive man began his career as an Anglican priest. His sermons were well-attended and afterwards he might kiss the female members of the congregation, purely as an expression of Christian fellowship. Megalomania set in when he declared himself Messiah at Charlinch church, but this did not deter his disciples, who tended to be young and pretty or old and rich females. He built a chapel at Spaxton, now converted into a puppet theatre, and surrounded his community with a high wall which flew a flag bearing 'The Holy Lamb'. He professed immortality, and letters were sometimes addressed simply to GOD – SPAXTON. His effect on the tiny village must have been akin to that of Dionysos entering Thebes, for he tapped passions imploded beneath genteel Victorian exteriors in a manner that would be almost impossible today when inhibitions themselves are regarded as sins. He divined the link between suppressed sexuality and religious fervour and created a sect which attractively combined both. But although the passions they crystallize are eternal, the gods themselves are mortal, with individual identities subject to the mutations and effacements of time passing. Brother Prince passed away in 1899, to the dismay of his more credulous disciples, and leadership was transferred to the Reverend J.H. Smyth-Pigott, a priest of the Church of England. In 1962 builders knocked down the high wall which had concealed the Agapemonites' antics and challenged the athletic prowess of newspaper reporters.

Lanes connect Spaxton and Nether Stowey, which lies to the north amid farming land and at the head of a small valley named Bin Combe. The settlement grew up around a Norman motte-and-bailey castle built on an imposing mound where sheep graze and gorse grows in fat clumps. It was held by William FitzOdo in the eleventh century and besieged by King Stephen in 1138. Later it became the headquarters of James (Touchet), fourteenth Baron Audley, who was one of the leaders of the Cornish insurrection of 1497; in the encounter which took place at Blackheath between the King's forces and the insurgents, Lord Audley was taken prisoner, and shortly afterwards he was executed on Tower Hill. This tempestuous history is not reflected in modern Nether Stowey, which is pervaded by a feel of brisk routine and bustle. The main street, St Mary's, leading from the church to the George Inn, shows irregular rows of colour-washed cottages variegated by Victorian gables and Georgian sash windows. A former market town, this is a place where farm machinery is repaired, foodstuffs are purchased (for animals and humans), and queries about the hills satisfied by the Quantock Information Centre.

Collinson observed in 1791 that the basic shape of the settlement creates the letter Y. St Mary's Street forms the stem, another fork being provided by Lime Street, where Coleridge Cottage (National Trust) is situated, and another by Castle Street ascending steeply to the fortress beside rustic cottage rows. The heart of the village is the Jubilee Clock (1897), on the site of the old market cross, from where the stems branch out.

Castle Street is appealing. A brackish brook buoyantly gurgles down it which Coleridge referred to affectionately as 'the dear Gutter of Stowey'. Thomas Poole's brick-built Georgian house lies in the same street but his old bark house has been converted into a private dwelling. Aside from being a tanner, farmer and philanthropist, Poole was an intensely altruistic countryman of liberal opinions who entertained Wordsworth, Charles Lamb and his beloved Coleridge. A neat pen-portrait of him is provided in one of De Quincey's essays: 'I found him a stout, plain-looking farmer, leading a bachelor life in a rustic, old fashioned house ... with a good library, superbly mounted in all departments bearing at all upon political philosophy; and this farmer turning out a polished liberal Englishman, who had travelled extensively and had so entirely dedicated himself to the service of his fellow countrymen – the hewers of wood and drawers of water in this southern part of Somersetshire – that for many miles around he was the arbiter of their disputes; the guide and counsellor of their difficulties: besides being appointed executor and guardian to his children by every third man who died in or about the town of Nether Stowey.'

The cottage which Poole procured for Coleridge stands opposite the Ancient Mariner Inn. The poet was well pleased with its pretty garden and clear brook of soft water trickling beyond the front door. That period (1796–8) was for Coleridge one of idyllic equilibrium – if that word can ever be used of good poets! – when much of his best work was achieved.

The Stowey bypass has severed the church, farm and court from the pulse of village activity. Stowey Court has weathered elegantly. The smartened façade dating from 1588, the barbered yew hedge and the walled garden with the eye-catching gazebo, create an impression of rejuvenated antiquity. Garrisoned during the Civil War, earlier it had been the property of that Lord Audley who was executed for supporting the Cornish rebellion, and it incorporates stone from the castle.

Two miles from Nether Stowey, at the north-east corner of the Quantocks, Holford continues to attract the tourist and walker. It is a vivacious jumble of improved thatched cottages, guest houses, hotels and rustic businesses grouped at the mouth and along the verges of two deep combes: Hodder's Combe, leading to Lady's Edge and Bicknoller Post (1,000 feet), and Tannery or Butterfly Combe, twisting round the spur of Dowborough Fort (1,093 feet). Yellow, cream and pink façades – some with a disconcertingly pixified appearance – sprout amid woods of beech, oak and hazel. The silver hiss of running water is seldom out of earshot, and portentous ghosts of Eng. Lit. (Wordsworth, Coleridge and Thomas Poole) haunt the shades.

Huguenot exiles settled here early in the sixteenth century and set up a silk factory at the head of the glen. Anyone valiant enough to make a Gurkha-style assault on the foliage may uncover the part known as the factory wall. Soft Quantock water took well to dyeing, and the concern flourished until 1789, when the French Revolution blocked the import of raw silk. The factory adroitly switched over to blanket-making, until 1820 when a disastrous fire closed it.

Tanning was another local concern. A local man, James Hayman, established the first works early in the nineteenth century. The regal-looking waterwheel (1893) at the luxurious Combe House Hotel is the descendant of his original which helped process both local bark and valonia from Asia Minor. The tanyard fell into disuse for a period but was revived in 1886 by J.J. Hayman, nephew of the founder. The days of this localized concern were numbered, however, and Continental competition forced its closure in 1900. The younger Hayman was not defeated by this reversal of fortune, and soon he was harnessing the waterwheel to produce electric light and to operate a stone-cracking machine, a chaff-cutter and even an automatic boot-polisher.

Although the church is comparatively modern with its saddleback roof and 'mean and incomplete' tower, it is set astride a pre-Christian trackway and has a homely, primitive appearance. Its rebuilding was finished around 1842. In the churchyard lies Frederick Norton whose musical extravaganza *Chu-Chin-Chow* had a London run of 2,238 consecutive performances.

Hodder's Combe skirts Alfoxton Park, the name deriving from the big classical manor house, now a hotel with a loggia, where Wordsworth stayed and was suspected of spying for the French – his most suspicious habit being his penchant for taking long walks during the hours of darkness. One of his favourite places of retreat was locally known as 'the Mare's Pool' but afterwards renamed 'Wordsworth's Glen'. 'It was,' he wrote, 'a chosen resort of mine. The brook fell down a sloping rock, considerable for that country, and across the pool below had fallen an ash tree from which rose perpendicularly boughs in search of the light, intercepted by the deep shade above. The boughs bore leaves of green that for want of sunshine had faded into almost lily-white; and from under the side of this natural sylvan bridge descended long and beautiful tresses of ivy, which waved gently in the breeze that might be called the breath of the waterfall.'

The southern rim of the Quantocks north of Taunton provides the sylvan setting for Kingston St Mary, an exciting, hilly place famous for the Kingston Black, a cider apple of exceptionally fine quality. The parish is watered by darting streamlets that once fed mills and tanyards but now run sparkling and uninterrupted. There is a modern village hall, a resplendent Elizabethan manor house of 1560 and a scatter of farms with names like Tetton, Winpenny, Yarford, Dodhill and Pickney. What a solid agricultural ring these names have, evoking the crunch of cattle hooves on tarmac, roseate complexions and windfalls of dropped aitches for the middle classes to retrieve. Bertha Lawrence, a noted authority on the region, wrote vividly of the 'sturdy old barns and stables, built of sandstone that has weathered to many gradations of red, and roofed with russet tile overrun by lichen'. Copper was mined at Kingston over a century ago, as the name Loads Farm attests, and its presence accounts for the greenish tinge in certain blocks of local stone. A more enduring and widespread occupation was weaving by hand loom, and this is carried on today at Church Farm, where craftsmen specialize in tweeds, rugs, furniture fabrics, stoles and wall-hangings. The local inn is called the Swan and was listed in the 1930s as the residence of the Ancient Order of Druids. What this noble sect got up to is none too clear: did they wassail apple trees in flowing robes, dress white bulls with floral garlands, cut sprays of mistletoe off ancient oaks with bronze sickles?

A.K. Wickham, author of an important book on Somerset church towers, described St Mary's Church as 'the perfected model' of a group of buildings. He was referring to the tower, which is celebrated for its rustic grace: rugged sandstone walls and yellow Hamstone angles culminate in an embattled and panelled parapet with flying pinnacles. The interior demonstrates Tudor carvers at their most assured. One bench-end shows a weaver's shuttle, another oxen yoked to the plough, a third hands holding a rosary. The setting of the church on a hillside above the Kingston Brook, looking across to the manor and quilted meadowland, is fittingly placid and pastoral.

In contrast to the agricultural tang of Kingston, such a village as Bishops Lydeard, several miles to the west, is very much in transition. Strictly speaking it is not a Quantock village but occupying the remoter reaches of Taunton Deane, for straggling streams trickle through it and join up with the Tone. Since the war, several new estates have arisen: catering for their needs are a library, health centre and police station. All the regular businesses are here as well as more exotic establishments such as the health hydro at Cedar Falls, a large Georgian mansion of 1740. Building has greatly altered the character of Bishops Lydeard, particularly in Mill Lane, formerly a delightful rural enclave and now blocked out with new development. At Hither Mead similarly the new houses dominate the scene, necessitating a children's play area by the road.

The main streets, Church Street, Mount Street and West Street, link up and the numerous ranked pastel façades have been called 'one long pink and yellow street'. This does not apply to the deep ruddy flush of Richard Grobham's almshouses which went up in 1616. The centre of Bishops Lydeard has an almost suburban feel with a host of distinctively named pubs: West Street has the Bell Inn with a painted mural of itself on its wall; Church Street's inn is called the Bird In Hand, and the bright-plumaged finch sign drives home the point, as does the Zeppelin-sized marrow announcing the Gardener's Arms. Towards the outskirts of the village is yet another pub, the Lethbridge Arms, named after a once-prominent landowner and with a lofty, slablike fives court outside.

Bishops Lydeard church deserves its share of superlatives. The pinnacled tower with golden Hamstone dressings shines like dying embers in the sunset, and the branching mullions in the belfry windows make fine Gothic tracery. The building dates from 1470, but considerably older is the churchyard cross. One of the steps is concave, forming a basin – probably for holy water – and round the base are carved the blurred forms of the Apostles with the risen Christ. No less enchanting is the interior of church. The bench carvings have a primitive, rippling energy and show a childlike delight in visible things. There is a stag on a hill, a miller, a sailing-ship – all locally observable Quantock scenes. In the arch of the porch there is a panel honouring an eighteenth-century vicar, John Geale, who asked to be buried under the flagstones of the porch, giving the reasons: 'My parishioners have tried unsuccessfully to walk over me while I am alive; they shall not be denied this pleasure when I am dead.'

Only two miles north of Bishops Lydeard, occupying the valley of the same stream, Combe Florey invitingly reclines. Sequestered in a woody glen, graced by running water, rambling rose-walled cottages with irregular plots, and presided over by a dignified pedimented manor house, it is precisely the type of spot Coleridge and Wordsworth delighted in discovering during their intrepid intellectual hikes. The formal and the rustic are blended here artlessly, and the varying elevations and aspects of the houses – hidden among trees, astride a dashing streamlet, on a steep slope – enhance the total effect.

The first mention of the settlement occurs when Baldwin de Cume installed himself in the manor house in 1100. Around 1313, Walter de Meriet founded a chantry in the combe. The site of this long-crumbled foundation may have been near the grassy mound known by villagers as 'the monks' garden' which lies opposite the gabled Elizabethan gatehouse, formerly owned by the Francis family and bearing the date 1593. The gatehouse, also bearing the family's coat of arms, seems a little abrupt and isolated minus the original complex, but extending above it are the grounds of the classical manor erected by Thomas Francis in 1665. The novelist Evelyn Waugh spent his last years here after looking over several houses, including a building near Stroud 'inhabited by a poor mad German chemist' and a 'decayed, odd house named Bridon, near Nutcombe'. Finally, in 1956, he settled for Combe Flore – 'cosy, sequestered, with great possibilities', as he noted in his diary. After he moved in, he decorated it in accordance with his specialized taste. His biographer Christopher Sykes (1975) commented on 'the extraordinary and individual atmosphere given by Evelyn's taste for Victorian portraits and narrative pictures, for Victorian furniture and style of decoration, for atrocities of Ethiopian art including a large macabre wooden carving of a squatting camel, an object I could never pass without a tremor'. As a crowning glory to this oppressive anthology, there was a painting by Richard Eurich depicting passengers inside an aircraft just before the moment of crash, the purpose of which was 'to appal those on a first visit'.

Above the church are the walled grounds of a handsome Queen Anne manor where Sidney Smith, a former Canon of St Paul's Cathedral and notable wit, retired after abandoning London life. Although he called the countryside 'a kind of healthy grave' and concocted a list of tediously prosaic events to stand for the most exciting weekly happenings within the village, he enjoyed himself greatly, on one occasion fitting antlers to a donkey's head in response to a lady guest's remark that the view from his window would be improved by the presence of deer. His anatomical ideas were also interesting: 'There are three sexes, men, women and clergymen.' On falling ill, he retired to London and died there in February 1845.

The road from Bishops Lydeard to Cothelstone travels across the valley and surmounts the uncompromising scarp slope of the hills. Here are copses of immense beeches, exposed roots showing like the limbs of gargantuan wrestlers, and in between are wastes of bracken, fern and whortleberry bushes. But Cothelstone, or East Bagborough, lies at the foot of the high uplift, on a gentle incline, and takes in the old manor of the Stawells, a real Tudor grandee of a building. A craggy yet decorative house, solemn but elaborate, it has distinctive baluster and candelabra motifs repeated around the mullions and colonettes of the doorways. Pevsner liked its mellow eccentricity; another writer was put off by its air of 'brooding unease'. Originally it covered a larger area, but during the Civil War it was partially destroyed.

Cothelstone church is dedicated to St Thomas Becket. It has a small but massive embattled tower and a pillar of Saxon date supporting two arches. The fifteenth-century stained windows displaying six English saints – Cuthbert, Dunstan, Aldhelm, Richard of Chichester, Thomas of Hereford and Thomas Becket – are a rare feature.

Students of English literature might be drawn to Cothelstone, not to gaze over the church or manor, but to examine a certain tombstone with a dove carved on it and the words:

In Sweet Memory of
Ianthe
the attached wife of
Edward Jeffries Esdaile
of Cothelstone
She lived to die June 23rd 1813
She died to live June 6th 1876
Until the day break and the shadows
flee away
Daughter of the Poet Shelley

There are indications that the last line had been tampered with, for Ianthe married into a family who were not eager to flaunt their connection with the poet. In those stiffly snobbish times, Shelley's reputation was that of an atheist, adulterer and political agitator. But a contemporary wrote that, 'A greater contrast could not have existed than that between Shelley and his daughter. Mrs Esdaile ... was in no way exceptional except for being a good wife and mother.'

Commanding an extensive view of the Deane, slightly north of Cothelstone, West Bagborough is a close-knit, elevated community, predominantly agricultural in character. Modern times have varied this tendency to the extent that a significant number of residents find work in the nearby Tone Vale, Sandhill Park and Lynchfield Hospitals. There is a local pottery, two racehorse-training establishments and a regular private bus service to Taunton. The popularity of riding around these parts is a bane to motorists who do not always succeed in keeping a discreet distance from those metal-shod hooves, particularly on roads more suited to animals than humans.

The parish incorporates some markedly idiosyncratic features, such as the naked, emasculated statue of a man and his dog occupying the parkland of the demolished Cothelstone House. The latter replaced Tirhill House built by Thomas Slocombe who is commemorated in Bishops Lydeard church. He was an eighteenth-century landowner who created a splendid park, with several follies, and the statue of the poor naked hunter is the vestigial remnant of a once-impressive group.

Bagborough House lies in parkland to the north of the main settlement – a slated Georgian mansion with Ionic capitals at the entrance. Wordsworth stayed there with his wife Mary in 1841 when he briefly returned to the area to attend his daughter's wedding in Bath. He was put up at Bagborough House by the Pophams and revisited the Quantock haunts he had explored in earlier and more sunlit days with Coleridge.

The narrow road which twists through West Bagborough can be followed past Triscombe House and on to Crowcombe. It is a good route, conveying well the feel of the Quantocks: carved green hills, not astoundingly high but adequately dramatic and often strewn with ruddy-fleeced sheep. Trees variegate the scene, oaks, elms and muscular beeches, and the ploughed fields shine like massive flags.

Probably the most impressive sight is the elaborate red-brick Court (1725) begun by Thomas Parker of Gittisham, Devon, and completed by Nathaniel Ireson of Wincanton. (Parker was fired for stealing a treasure-trove of coins hidden in the previous house on the site.) The Court was built for young Thomas Carew, the lord of the manor (after whom the local pub, the Carew Arms, is named). The giant Corinthian pilasters of Hamstone, crowned by a triangular pediment, establish a note of graceful bombast further emphasized by lofty trees and an ample driveway. Visitors are not welcome.

Less imperious than the Court, but an even rarer building, is the old Church House (1515), an austere, slated fabric where the holy bread was baked and the holy ale brewed for consumption at the local revel – an event followed no doubt by a holy hangover. The building survived the onslaught of Puritanism, and the upper floor was used as a school from 1661 to 1871, the lower part becoming almshouses. A broken blue gate opening onto a tangle of undergrowth, adjoining the Church House, indicates the present condition of the village pound where stray animals were kept until their owners claimed them by paying the fine.

The Perpendicular church of the Holy Ghost is a tensile, elaborate building. It has superb Tudor carving on the bench-ends: fish-tailed monsters, naked men fighting a dragon, a Green Man with grape stems protruding from his mouth (a symbol of fecundity) and a wild man with bludgeons poking from his ears. In December 1725, on a Sunday afternoon, lightning struck the spire, causing the top section to crash through the roof, and it was removed to the churchyard as a decoration.

A village quite different from Crowcombe, nestling on the Brendon side of the Dorniford Stream, Stogumber fits compactly into a fold in the hills by a brook which joins the larger river at Vellow. This has been rightly declared a conservation area, basic yet compelling, and it is rail-connected – a rarity these days. Terraces of thatched cottages climb up to the dominant pile of St Andrew's Church. Cobbled pavements line the way, and several houses – notably Seven Crosses – have medieval doorways and wrought-iron rails leading to them. Opposite the church are the White Horse Inn and market-place served by a flight of stone steps. Another feature is the Sydenham almshouses which originally housed six old women, who were given a shilling a week from the owner of the estate. They are now called the Almonry; burials recorded from them go back to 1668.

Different ways of spelling Stogumber in the past have led to argument over its derivation. The Domesday Book called it 'Waverdine Stoke' and King Harold, a former landowner, called it 'Royal Walver de Stoke.' After the Conquest came the de Gomers who tagged their title onto Stoke – hence Stoke de Gomer, which, when slurred by the murky vowels of Somerset, emerges as Stogummer or Stogumber. 'Stoke' has been prosaically translated as 'stock farm' and reverentially interpreted as 'holy place'. The issue of pronunciation posed a mild problem to Bernard Shaw, who having a John de Stogumber appearing in St Joan, wrote to the local vicar presumably enquiring whether to emphasize Sto or Stog as the first syllable.

A quiet place today, with some provision for camping, caravanning and bed-and-breakfast, despite new antique and craft shops, it is a relatively depopulated community, but during the fifteenth and sixteenth centuries Stogumber prospered as a collecting place for wool. The market house was open-sided then and used for fleece trading. Many consequential families – notably the Sweetings of Hartrow and the Dashwoods of Vellow – became involved in the woollen industry. They organized distribution to the cottages where it was spun or loom-woven in cloth, then it was laden on packhorses and carried over the Quantocks to Combwich, whence it was shipped up the Parrett to Bristol. The plenitude of waterwheels in the vicinity, harnessing both the 'home' stream and the Dorniford Brook, were used for fulling (plumpening) the fibres.

Throughout the nineteenth century, despite periods of agricultural depression, Stogumber continued as an important market centre. There were eight shops and several inns in which the iron-ore miners of the Brendons immersed their enthusiasm on Saturday nights. Later Stogumber became renowned for its ale, which was advertised as 'good for the clergy and others with weak lungs' and believed to cure flatulence and fever. Congestion was caused in the lanes by the drays carting the barrels to the station – the ale's price in 1901 was 10d. a gallon. The water for its manufacture was drawn from the local Harry's Well, now neglected and overgrown, which was said to have cured a case of leprosy.

St Andrew's Church stands at the highest point of the village. The tower is big without being particularly high and is diagonally buttressed. It is of rosy red sandstone and has a carving of a writhing, virile dragon, a curious cylindrical pig and fish. The climax of the interior is the Sydenham Chapel, separated from the chancel arch by a wrought iron screen. Here is the tomb of Sir George Sydenham (d. 1589) – endearingly spelt 'Sr. Gorge Sidnum' – and his two wives. He slumbers beneath a vaulted canopy, and at his feet are three small babies and a nurse.

11

The Quantock Seaboard

Dominated by an immense Iron Age hill-fort, straddling a feeder of the Parrett and bounded by marshy meadows to the east and the low Quantock foothills to the west, Cannington continues to expand. A large nucleated village, surrounded by rich farming land, there is a good deal of red-brick development around the outskirts and recent industrial development. It is on the main road to West Somerset and Exmoor – hence it is more often passed by than appreciated.

Probably the best vantage-point is entering the village from Bridgwater along the A39. One sees the gaunt but graceful tower of St Mary's dominating a cottage row of red-brick, whitewash and Regency façades. The cheerful sign of the Blue Anchor Inn centralizes the scene, which is enhanced by the foreground of a tiny river, packhorse bridge and lofty chestnuts – a flashback to the rural core of the settlement.

Tractors can be got here, at Kelland's, and other agricultural merchandise, for Cannington is the home of Somerset farming. The Agricultural and Horticultural College has its base in a former priory lying north of the church. The present building is a rambling red Elizabethan edifice with a pilastered gateway, four-light windows and a Georgian chapel of octagonal design. A priory of Benedictine nuns was established here by Robert de Courcy (*c*. 1138) which originally comprised a princess and twelve nuns, one of whom was Dame Maud de Merriet of Hestercombe, whose heart is entombed in Combe Florey church. Fortunately life at this nunnery was not all prayers and penances. Lapses appear to have been fairly frequent and invoke shades of St Trinian's. They resulted in a commission of enquiry being appointed by the bishop, which revealed such incidents as two nuns, Alice and Matilda, creeping out at night to meet two chaplains in the church, a third nun, Joan Trimlett, giving birth to a child, and, more seriously still, the prioress accepting bribes and allowing into the establishment ladies with more wealth than religious fervour. The last abbess, Cecilia de Verney, came from local gentry and surrendered her position in 1536. The priory then passed to Sir Edward Rogers, whose family connection ended with the passing of Henry Rogers in 1672. The Rogers almshouses, near the centre of Cannington, were established by Henry not long before his death, to accommodate twelve poor women; in 1972 they were repaired and improved, but they retain that utilitarian starkness endemic to such structures.

Opinions differ on the merits of St Mary's, Cannington. Many find its stark, soaring interior daunting rather than reassuring. Others are exhilarated by its spaciousness and majesty. The tower is fourteenth century and retains stones from the old Norman church. There are seventeen consecration crosses around the outside wall, marking where the bishop touched the stone with holy oil.

North of Cannington lies a forgotten corner of England, the isolated villages and hamlets of Combwich, Stert, Stolford, Otterhampton and Stogursey, ranged around the Parrett estuary. Of the latter an old saying went:

Out of the world and into Stogursey,
Out of Storgusey and into the sea.

Combwich is the most accessible from Bridgwater. It sits on the sludgy left bank of the tidal river. The combination of wind and high water frequently makes the river burst its banks, and a notice by the creek informs 'ROAD LIABLE TO FLOOD AT HIGH TIDE'. One might have imagined this abandoned port on a singularly unglamorous estuary to be a forlorn, run-down sort of place, a grouping of battered cottages, worm-eaten jetties and derelict wharves, but the reverse is true: Combwich is an alert, attractive spot, with many neat colour-washed cottages, two pubs – the ancient Ship and the more recent Anchor – and a lively array of yachts and cabin cruisers. The salt-sharp breeze is tart and invigorating, and the inhabitants appear brisk, courteous and hale; a few of them manage a nautical swagger as they exit from the bars, amble down to the river and admiringly survey their crafts. Aside from sailing-facilities, there is a Victorian parish church, a Methodist church (with a thriving Sunday School), a garage-cum-stores, unobtrusive modern red-brick estate houses and a factory making brooms and small brushes which occupies the site of a former flour-mill. By the river is a stark children's play area consisting of a pair of swings on the coarse, rutted grass. The old fishers' cottages here are in fine order; façades gleam with that snowy, fresh-set look, as if DIY perfectionists had just applied the finishing touch.

Walford House brings a certain Regency lightness to its setting, and the Folly, an unclassifiable building with a timbered tower, introduces an agreeable element of modulated madness: I was told it was built by a merchant who wished to view his ships breasting up the river. This harks back to a period when the Bristol Channel was a hive of minor ports: Wick St Lawrence, Uphill, Lympsham – all such anchorages were active, as well as Combwich, taking coal from South Wales and exporting dairy produce across the water and upstream to Bristol. There was a brick and tile-making business at Combwich, and it was possible to fish salmon out of the Parrett, a river which Samuel Taylor Coleridge referred to as filthy, 'as if all the parrots in the House of Commons had been washing their consciences in it'.

The parish church stands on the side of a fairly steep hill. It is usually treated rather glacially in this county of outstanding churches, but for all that it is an attractive essay in Victorian Gothic, with a jutting spire and unmellowed look. The dedication is suitably Piscean – to St Peter, and the carved oak and walnut lectern were designed and crafted by the Reverend C.G. Anderson, rector 1871–98. There was an earlier church at Combwich dedicated to St Leonard (like the church at Otterhampton) which was an important stopping-place for pre-Reformation pilgrims to Glastonbury who would rest and pray here, and perhaps take refreshment, before boarding the boat ferry across the Parrett. The route they followed is still traceable: on Dame Withycombe's Hill an old track is called the Pilgrim's Way.

Beyond Combwich is the type of agoraphobic East Anglian landscape that some find inimical. The flat, salty fields, studded with isolated farms, fade into saltmarsh and sea. A kind of bleak spaciousness strikes the dominant keynote: no sheltering woods or hills, hardly any hedgerows either, just this flat expanse bordered by causeway and embankment. The roads tend to be narrow and ruler-straight. They run past bleak battery farms and fields grazed by Friesians to the desolate hamlet of Stert or to Stolford itself, where the last of the mudhorse operators plies his lonely trade: sledging over the wastes to stake out his nets and catch elvers and congers.

The coastline is broken by the distant cuboids and rectangular cooling-towers of Hinkley Point, about as aesthetically interesting as an arrangement of empty milk cartons. Attitudes to such structures are changing, particularly when news items regularly report radio-active leak-outs at Windscale. The few local eel-fishermen left complain that, after the station was erected, the fish stocks depleted and it was no longer worth the effort.

Some two miles to the north, implanted on a gentle rise above the marshes, the hamlet of Otterhampton beckons like a medieval oasis. It is powerful in its sheer simplicity: only a rectory, manor house and poetic pond glimmering in a field beside the road. All Saints presents a grave and orderly interior. The stonework is skilfully pointed, the white-was-hed parts glow softly, and the Elizabethan altar rail stands secure. In the porch hangs a list of rectors; the earliest, Robertus (1144), is called Chaplain. Elsewhere one sees a Norman font with a Jacobean cover, an arch marked with a Tudor rose, a carved pre-Reformation screen and the figures of Adam (with a fig-leaf apron slung over his shoulder) and Eve occupying two niches. A floriated cross in front of the organ marks the burial place of a medieval priest. Until 1894, a note informs us, a village pound stood where the present lych-gate is and the entrance to the churchyard stood nearer the main road. A painting of the church by J. Buckler dated 1843 in Taunton Museum shows it with roughcast walls; otherwise it is almost exactly the same, guarded by the strange dark yew that casts its mournful shadow near the door.

Some three miles west of Combwich, on a gentle rise of meadowland, Stogursey continues to function in its self-absorbed fashion. Incredible as it may seem in a village situated two miles inland astride an insignificant brook in a remote agricultural region, it once made a bid to become a centre of sea-borne trade. Under the tutelage and endowments of the powerful de Courcy family, it prospered as a medieval borough, sending two representatives to Edward III's Parliament, but eventually relapsed into a stolid farming community, augmented by tanning and candle-making, and finally the modern settlement with working interests shared between agriculture and Hinkley Point power station.

Stogursey is not pretty in the flowerbox sense but exudes robust charm. A long street of joined cottages using a variety of roofing materials – red tile, thatch and slate – straggles and ascends a gentle incline that levels out by the school at the west end of the village, the east end being marked by the dominant, barnlike church. Four roads converge near the centre by the market space, and behind the façades the plots of the medieval burgesses can still be traced in the gardens and backyards. The cottages are colour-washed rather than bare stone, Devonian in character, and their faded pinks, sand yellows and pale greens create an impression of cheerful utility.

Standing slightly back from the old market square are the pebbledashed Poulett almshouses built for six old women in the reign of Henry V. They bear a descriptive plaque and a bell called 'ding dong darling' which originally had to be rung 'at six o'clock, morning and evening, every day' for a quarter of an hour to summon the occupants to make prayers and thanksgiving to God. Charity in those days had a sanctimonious sting in its tail.

On the other side of the street, a more urbane feature is Stoke Courcy House, adding a dash of Regency élan to the vernacular atmosphere. It faces St Andrew's Road, where the blunted stump of the old market cross protrudes like an ancient fertility emblem.

Local children attend the ornate school designed by John Norton (1865). Sir Peregrine Acland donated it to the village as a thank-offering for the recovery of his daughter, Isabel, from consumption, and a portrait of her is kept inside. The red sandstone building is exuberantly creepy. Here are turrets, lancets and Gothic doorways in abundance, and it seems curious that something so joyously neurotic should embody something so stolidly worthy as the three Rs. On the other hand, madness and the classroom have strong traditional connections, so perhaps the style is apter than first impressions suggest.

Stogursey started out as Stoke Courcy after the Norman family of de Courcy who found a branch of a French priory here in the twelfth century. The institution prospered and waned with the changing political situation. The Hundred Years War with France brought heavy taxation, and around 1440 the priory was made over to Eton College. It had never been spectacularly rich, often jogging along with a prior and two or three monks, and an inventory of conventual buildings (1324) listed a hall, prior's chamber, storeroom, kitchen, brewery, bakery and barn. This does create a picture of a modest, self-sustaining community, and the dovecote (the single remaining priory building) was an additional asset.

The former priory church of St Andrew is bulky and austere, with a leaded spire jutting incongruously out of the heavy square tower. The fabric effectively evokes its original builders, partly owing to the efforts of the late Reverend Basil Tucker, who believed the Victorian restoration (c. 1863) 'was too humanistic, too self-confident, not expressing enough of the majesty of God'. So during the 1940s Mr Tucker, assisted by Mr Cridge, a mason who lived on Tower Hill, removed walls and floors in an attempt to re-discover 'the tri-apsidal shape of the building before the Benedictines altered the east end in about 1180'. The result is the present-day interior, awesome, bare and lofty, with a massive crossing and powerful arches decorated with beading and zigzag work.

The table tomb of John Verney (d. 1447/8) is worthy of detailed attention. He lies in armour with a helm bearing the Verney ferns, and his feet rest on a dog. He was a man of consequence in his time and precipitated a local dispute, in July 1442, when a charge was brought against him that, 'Forgetful of his own salvation, in contravention of the sacred canons and the institutions of the holy fathers, at the time of high mass in the parish church of Stoke Courcy aforesaid, after the prayers and preaching by the vicar ... in word and deed he preached in a manner unheard of; and he spoke to the people in English.'

On the south side of the village are the remains of a partly Norman castle. The moat is fed by an artificial channel from the Doddington Brook and is still an impressive sight. Traces of the bridge are still visible, and portions of the drum towers, some walls and a sally-port remain. Originally the stronghold of the de Courcys, it passed to the tyrannical Fulk de Bréauté after he married Alice de Redvers. She was a frail match for the 'ferocious and sanguinary ruffian' to whom she had vowed allegiance. De Bréauté was uncontrollable. He made the castle a stronghold of robbers and used his power – he was sheriff of seven counties – to intimidate and oppress those under him. Finally he was expelled by order of Hubert de Burgh, Chancellor to King Henry III, who had the fortress dismantled. But the next reign saw it rebuilt and occupied successively by the FitzPaine and Percy families. During the Wars of the Roses it was stormed and burned by the Yorkist Lord Bonville, brother-in-law of Richard, Earl of Warwick, after the first Battle of St Albans, 23 May 1455. Since then it has stayed a ruin, an ivy-clad mound of mouldering stonework, until recently, when Stogursey, suddenly conscious of its heritage, cleaned up the moat, renovated certain adjoining cottages and transformed the whole plot into a delightful retreat.

To the east of Stogursey the little lanes wind in and out, gradually ascending the gentler 'dip' slope of the eastern Quantocks. The main A39 skirts the foothills, winding perilously between walls and woodland beyond Kilve and East Quantoxhead. Sudden glimpses of the sea, green, grey or metal blue, can be had between trees and tongues of greenery, and the coast here has a bracing aspect, again recalling East Anglia. The cliffs are dark and bluffy, with a tendency to recede beneath the regular tidal batterings. After the cloistered seclusion of a Quantock combe, it is enervating to stroll along Kilve beach where the wind attempts to flatten you against walls of rock. In rough weather the sea is boiling, boisterous, shooting shivering tongues of foam over the dark drifts of seaweed and sharp slaty ridges.

The beds of shale forming the cliffs here are oil-bearing and richly fossiliferous. In 1914 deep borings revealed that oil-shale beds extended to a thickness of over a thousand feet. This compared with the Colorado deposits, and the possibility of commercial exploitation was researched. The investigator's report observed that no mining – in the sense of tunnelling – was required: 'The hills can be blasted down, great faces opened up hundreds of feet high, the rich oil fuel picked up by steam shovels and loaded on rail trucks'. This is not the type of language to make a conservationist's heart glow with fondest elation, and fortunately, owing to the high sulphur content of the shales and high proportion of waste matter involved in the process, the project was quickly abandoned, although relics of it, in the form of a brick-built retort above the pill, a borehole and a kind of metallic masthead on the beach, remain to intrigue the sightseer.

Kilve, from the Celtic 'clive' ('cliff'), is noted for its ruined chantry founded in 1329 by Sir Simon de Furneaux. A modest establishment for five priests, it was dissolved long before Henry VIII blasted and besieged all monastic buildings and, quite inadvertently, created the cult of the picturesque ruin. Its brief appearance and sudden eclipse created the speculation that its closure may have been the act of Sir Richard Stury, a Lollard who married Alice, heiress of the Furneaux estate; he, being of a heretical disposition, directed his wife's spending elsewhere. Nevertheless, the chantry was abandoned by priests and subsequently patronized by farmers for hay storage and by cattle who resorted to it as a substantial umbrella during heavy storms. Today it hardly constitutes an eloquent ruin. The grey-blue mollusc-like walls wear a rustling cloak of ivy, and its paneless Gothic windows gape morosely. Around it are a string of ponds – remains of monks' fishpools – fed by a stream overhung by the twisted trunks of willows.

The ruin later gained some celebrity as a storage-place for contraband. Hindsight endows smuggling with a certain brawny glamour – remember the dashing Dr Syn? – but during the Napoleonic Wars, when luxuries were scarce, its status must have been as commonplace as tax-dodging today (although a far healthier, more physically demanding activity). Allegedly smuggling at Kilve – the concealment of brandy kegs in the pool on the beach, the retrieval and hiding of them in the chantry – was a flourishing trade until an unfortunate carter drank himself to death on bottles of neat spirit. This aroused the suspicion of a local magistrate, who decided to investigate the source of his liquor supply. But before any enquiries got underway, the chantry caught alight on a night in 1850. The friskiness of the conflagration, and the vivid emerald and blue colouring of the flames, suggested that more was burning than wood and hay.

East Quantoxhead, bounded on the north by the Channel and about 4½ miles north-east from Williton station, is one of those villages that persuade prospering businessmen to retire and immerse themselves in rural oblivion. The soil is stony rush, producing a good crop of wheat, barley, mangolds, oats, potatoes and turnips, and the parish itself embraces 2,338 acres of land. But apart from its agricultural richness, the community presents an image of harmonious interaction with the landscape upon which it grew. The brook that rises on the slopes of Longstone Hill scurries past a row of thatched cottages, many of them fitted with tiny footbridges, and feeds a capacious millpond, dark, tranquil, brooding, yet enlivened by the constant skitter of mallards and their goslings. Rising above the water, overlooking the Channel, is the church of St Mary and beside it the Court House. This austere Elizabethan pile, with its square-headed, lead-lined, stone-mullioned windows, exudes an aloof dignity. The present building is largely the work of Hugh

Luttrell (d. 1522) but the house – and the family incidentally – dates back to the time of Domesday, when Ralph Pagnell held the manor; relics of its great age include a hefty oaken door and beams, a cockpit, a Jacobean staircase and a wooden ox-plough. Formerly a lamb's heart stuck over with pins hung above the vast fireplace in the kitchen in memory of its efficacy when used generations ago to break a witch's curse. Unfortunately a visitor in the 1940s stole it – for what purpose, one asks? A singularly unutilitarian object except for someone intent on founding a black magic museum.

To the right of the broadly moulded porch, inscribed on the lead pipe, is the Luttrell shield, the date 1628 and the initials G.S., perpetuating the memory of George Luttrell (who built Dunster's yarn market) and Silvestra Skory, husband and wife. Silvestra, by all accounts, was a termagant. Her second husband after George was Sir Edmund Skory. In what must have been a truly spectacular eruption of rage, she threw him out of one of the lower windows, a spirited act which caused him much glum and rueful brooding, for when he died, he left 20s. to his servant George Baker 'who hath lived under the tyranny of my wife to the danger of his life' and to Silvestra a prayer book entitled *The Practice of Piety*. Other wrangles followed the passing of Sir Edmund, including a suit issued by her Luttrell stepson, Andrew, for damage to deer and timber in the park. A pitched battle was eventually fought within the grounds but nothing could unseat Silvestra, who acquired a third husband (whom she also outlived) and that awesome dignity characteristic of those who combine an unbreakable will with stubborn longevity.

St Mary's Church, though small, has features of interest including a fourteenth-century tomb chest commemorating two Luttrells, Hugh (d. 1522), who fought on the King's side against Perkin Warbeck in 1497, and Andrew (d. 1538), who detested his wily stepmother yet died before her, leaving a silver cup to Thomas Cromwell to induce him to be a 'good lord' to his widow and children.

The old village of West Quantoxhead, formerly St Audries (after St Ethelreda, the virgin twice-married Saxon queen), was renovated by Sir Peregrine Acland, who purchased the manor in 1836 and provided much-needed work by commissioning lodges, a new school and a Gothic gasworks. He generally enlivened the community with the new expansionist outlook. He also paid for the rebuilding of the church, the rectory and the manor. St Audries Church is the work of John Norton and rises like a romantic aspiration from the emerald trough of its setting. He used red sandstone from the Samford Brett quarries for the new church and monolithic piers of Babbacombe marble for the arcades of the nave. Berta Lawrence considered it 'the least attractive of Quantock churches': I find it colourful yet unexceptional. Underneath there is a crypt housing a Norman font and a stone coffin accompanied by a tabular monument to G. Malet, a former lord of the manor whose antecedent, William Malet, served as both parish priest and member of the chantry. Contrasting with the neat church, the manor is one of those bombastic edifices that make humans crushingly conscious of their physical puniness. The Tudor front, facing south-west, is entered by a crenellated tower served by an octagonal staircase and lit by a three-stage oriel window reaching to the top. Go through the tower and there is the hall, forty feet high, with an oak roof and minstrels' gallery. Formerly this was hung with portraits of the Verneys, Palmers, Wroths and Aclands – ancestors of Lady Acland Hood – but the property was auctioned in 1924 and its paintings were removed.

The beach by the village has been partially annexed by the holiday camp on the cliffs. The rocks are red here, striped by green malachite and blue alabaster, vivid geological warpaint contrasting excitingly with the dull bluish lias of Kilve and beyond. A cascade pours over the cliffs onto the beach; it has the distinction – rare in these parts – of not having a poem attached to it by William Wordsworth. In dull weather it does not amount to much, only a slack dribble of grey water, but during or after heavy rain (vile weather brings out the best in waterfalls) it is transformed into a slender sash of falling foam.

12

The Brendon Hills

At King's Brompton Common the Tone has its source, high on the summit of the Brendon Hills, a range geologically similar to Exmoor but less visited. They are one of those pockets of intensely rural Somerset which have evaded the attention of the tourist industry. The villages have been described in one guidebook as being 'of little or no historical interest' – an amusing put-down that assumes that charm or interest is derived from sensational events, bombastic Tudor mansions or *outré* Georgian folly parks. The Brendon villages lack such characteristics. Their churches are modest compared with the swaggering pinnacles of the wool magnates of Mells and Huish. Usually they have embattled sandstone towers, not particularly high but stout and plain, with fine oolite piers, and all (or most) are situated on the swelling cushion of a hillside. Around them cluster the dwellings that make up the hamlet: a sprinkling of utilitarian cottages, several colour-washed or bare sandstone slated farms (Wiveliscombe and Williton have long provided roofing materials from the Devonian rocks), a short row of council dwellings, a homely little schoolhouse, a post office and some Victorian houses with cement renderings. The countryside encircling the scene is the epitome of tree-studded greenness: fields traced out with trees and hedges, sheep strewn like gold-crusted loaves on curving slopes, the subdued reddy-brown of ploughed fields and the swooping spaciousness of the horizon.

Clatworthy is a hamlet set beside the banks of the infant Tone. There is little to the village, save farmsteads and

Nynehead Court

Bishops Hull: the manor house

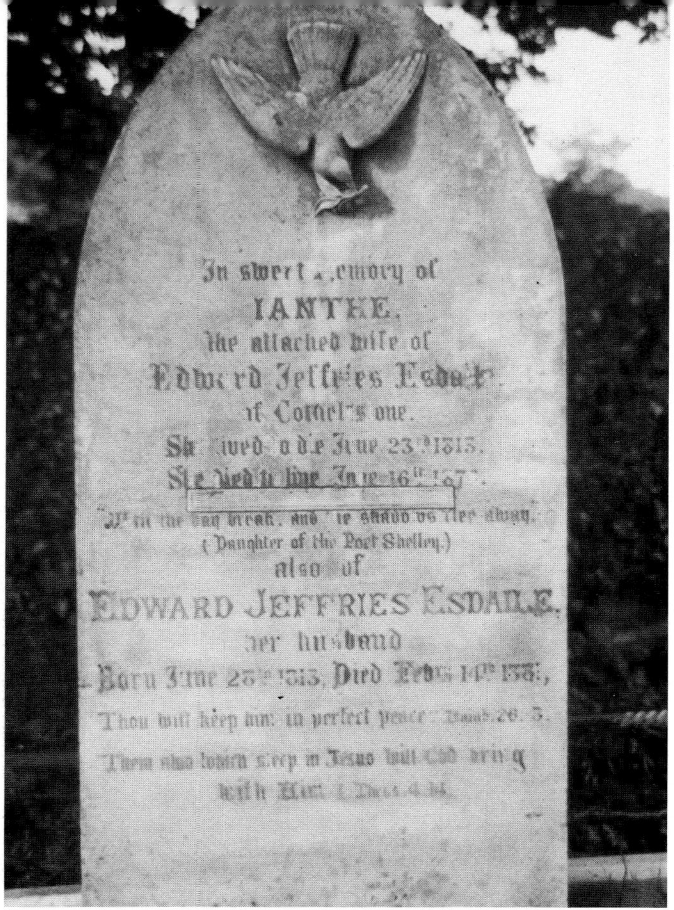

The Cavalier at Bishops Hull

Grave of Ianthe Shelley at Cothelstone

Stogursey Castle

The pond and church at East Quantoxhead

Cannington

Porlock Weir

The sea at Lilstock on the Quantock coast

Yarn market at Dunster

A cottage at Selworthy

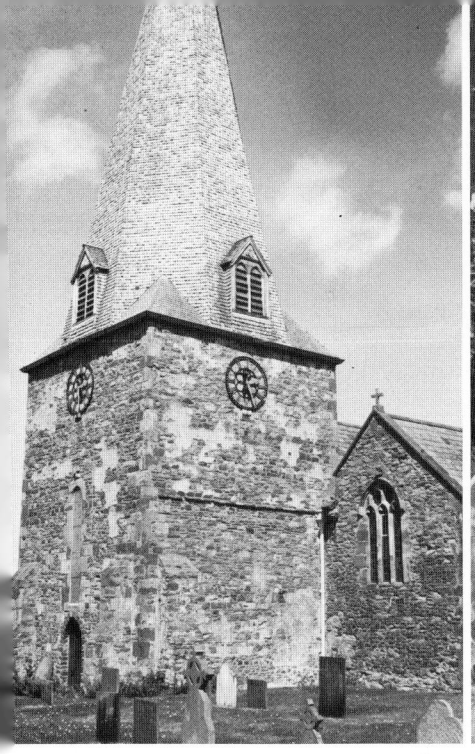

Porlock church

St Margaret's, Spaxton

Culbone Pottery

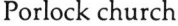

Gateway to Cleeve Abbey

cottages, but the church demands attention – literally, that is, for decay and damp are in the air, eating away at this once-beautiful church with its peeling whitewash and large Norman font. The red star-patterned tiles do not show the nineteenth century at its best, and many of them are cracked.

A lane from Clatworthy goes over the hill past Hele Farm and Westcott Farm, finally plunging into Brompton Ralph, a larger settlement which looks across to the red sandstone arch of Willets Tower. It is prettier than many of its companion villages. The greenery sprawls over the verges with casual vigour, and hydrangeas foam in gardens like extinguishers on a spree. Even the houses have an added streak of self-consciousness. The revamped old forge displays a sign with a fat Thelwell pony. St Mary's Church stands high and haughty on top of a hill and has a fourteenth-century oak screen which was restored at the cost of £140, the money being donated by an American, Arthur C.K. Toms, in memory of his grandfather Robert Toms, late of the parish.

Huish Champflower lies downstream from Clatworthy, about four miles south-west of Brompton. The village, strung along the slope of a hill, has several daisy-white and rose-pink cottages plus a liquid fortress called the Castle Inn. The name derives from a Norman family, and its floral overtones are apt considering the many fine gardens with ferny, moss-cushioned, slate walls. There is a post office stores, an old post office (now a private house) and a church with a charming notice mounted on the door – 'PLEASE SHUT TO KEEP OUT SWALLOWS.' The tower is rendered with pink cement, and the eagle lectern has been patched up and fitted with new wings.

To the south, on the slopes of Heydon Hill, Chipstable has a church perching securely on a hill above a few cottages and farms. Alfred Poole was born here to his wheelwright father in 1874. An inventor, mechanical engineer and photographer, he has been described as 'a small, round, dignified man, bristling with energy, intelligence and full of good humour'. When he died in December 1957, he was the sole surviving partner of W.H. Poole & Sons, mechanical engineers, of Chipstable. After leaving school, Alfred and his brother William began making turnip-cutters, hay rakes, harrows, threshers and reed combers – but this by no means expended their ingenuity. Alfred's interests were far broader than agricultural machinery, and he invented a steam car and later a petrol-driven engine 'with no outside Vaporiser or Volatiser or small passage to choke up'. He also designed one of the earliest West Country telephones, with the earphones and mouthpieces made of elm on a lathe.

Tolland lies between Brompton Ralph and Lydeard St Lawrence. Its name derives from the old English 'Tan land', 'land on the River Tone'; on Saxton's map of Somerset (1575) it appears as 'Toollande'. The chief feature is the church, which is approached by a iron-railed path beside which a stream flows and daffodils grow uninhibitedly in spring. The thirteenth-century building is neat, dignified, with a low tower and immaculate interior. The graveyard is tended like a favourite garden, and eight new trees were planted in 1981: three oaks, hornbeam, beech, horse chestnut, lime and sallow. In the west wall of the tower is a two-light window in memory of Henry Wolcott and his wife Elizabeth who left Tolland in 1630 and founded a distinguished line in America. They appear to have lived on the estate of Gaulden Manor, about a mile from the church, which is open to the public from May to September. It originated in the twelfth century, but most of the building is seventeenth century, the best feature being the Great Hall with its plaster ceiling and oak screen. It was eventually acquired by the Turbevilles of Bere Regis, a family name made famous by Thomas Hardy in his chronicle of ensnared innocence, *Tess of the D'Urbervilles*. John Turberville, a lawyer, wrote to his father-in-law in April 1647, of the Parliamentary faction: he said that his mansion 'hath been full of soldiers this fortnight, such uncivil drinkers and thirsty souls that a barrel of good beer trembles at the sight of them, and the whole house nothing but a rendezvous of tobacco and spitting'.

North of Tolland, by the source of the Hillfarrance Brook, the hamlet of Elworthy is neither populous nor prospering. The church stands very much on its own, occupying a bluffy rise and looking across the valley to Towell's Farm.

Its isolation and condition are such that it has been entrusted to the Redundant Churches' Fund, a charity set up by the Church of England in 1969 to finance historically interesting buildings needing assistance and repair. Elworthy's church has several good features: a painted screen with faded roses on it dated 1632, a marble font with a carved lid and an old pulpit.

The road penetrating Elworthy heads north by Combe Sydenham (National Trust), a most imposing-looking Elizabethan house (1580) with a russet-red tower. In the grounds fallow deer run wild, and there is a herb garden, cornmill and peacock house. It was erected by George Sydenham, father of Lady Elizabeth Sydenham who became the second wife of Francis Drake. He had these words inscribed in Latin above the entrance: 'This door of George's is always open except to ungrateful souls.' After becoming engaged to Lady Elizabeth, Drake is said to have abandoned his betrothed and gone off looting Spanish gold. During the interval, she became engaged to another, but the wedding was interrupted by a cannonball landing at her feet. This was Drake's manly version of a telegram.

Only a mile north of Combe Sydenham is Monksilver village. This is another calculated allurement with cream houses, white houses and houses suggesting the texture of pink coconut-ice. There is a shipshape pub called the Notley Arms, a pair of cottages called Meadowsweet and Limewalk (with new thatched bonnets), an old schoolhouse with a long gabled porch of cobbly red sandstone, a church with a Norman tower, impish gargoyles and a tombstone addressed to the unidentified psychopath who murdered Elizabeth Conibeer, aged 88, and her two daughters, Anne, aged 45, and Sarah, aged 43, in the hamlet of Woodford, 5th June 1775:

Inhuman wretch, whoe'er thou art
That didst commit this horrid crime,
Repent before thou dost depart
To meet thy awful Judge Divine.

To the north of Monksilver, at Woodford, a turn down a lane brings one to a long drive and series of ramps that culminate in Nettlecombe Court and St Mary's Church. The Tudor manor house, seat of the Raleghs and Trevelyans, is a remarkable sight surrounded by tall, rooky oaks in a big park. Above it are laid out stables, courtyards and outbuildings which have been converted into studios by various artists and craftsmen. There are remains of walled and terraced gardens and stagnant watery patches, vestiges of ornamental ponds. A brook trickles down the hill and spreads out to form a lake at the bottom.

Outside the wall of the stable courtyard can be seen one of the gatepost horses in a rampant posture. The leaping horse motif is repeated in several of the plaster ceilings of the Court, where the beast is seen springing out of the waves. A legend states that the first Trevelyan came to live here from Lyonesse and was saved from drowning by a swimming horse. The Cornish Trevelyans inherited the manor by the marriage of John Trevelyan to the great-niece of the Raleghs in 1452. John Trevelyan was known as 'the Cornish Chough' and considered by some to be a dangerously influential figure at the Court of Henry VI. Probably he built the earliest part of the house, which was added to by subsequent owners, such as John Sydenham, who rented it in 1531 and erected the hall. The Great Hall, oriel and porch were put up by another John Trevelyan around 1600, and other chambers were added some forty years later. During the Civil War the Trevelyans were Royalists, and the rector of the parish church, a rooted Parliamentarian, gathered a band of ruffians and tried to burn down the Court. Hence extensive rebuilding was necessary, and the combination of calm Georgian regularity and vigorous Tudor asymmetry is highly effective. The present-day field centre here offers one-week courses for amateur naturalists and artists and provides a useful supplement to academic activity.

The font (dated 1470) in the church is famous for its depiction of the Seven Sacraments, and the chalice, formerly preserved here, is a priceless example of the goldsmith's art. The stone effigies of two Raleghs, Simon and John, lie in the chapel like immense stone logs. John Ralegh is a seven-foot-giant with a sword strapped to his side. His ancestor Simon lies near him beneath the shield which protected him at Agincourt. On top of the Brendons, at the convergence of four roads, stands Ralegh's Cross Inn, so named, it is alleged, because when Simon Ralegh's body was being taken to Nettlecombe for burial, the cortége rested at this spot.

The villages on the northern side of the Brendons – Kingsbridge, Roadwater and Luxborough – are best dealt with summary fashion in a book of this size. Kingsbridge has a group of thatched cottages sheltering below woods and a bright brook close at hand; Roadwater is thinly straggled along a narrow valley and is known for its inn sign – the Valiant Soldier – rendered in painted metal relief. Luxborough's inn is called the Royal Oak but was known as the Blazing Stump after its association with the iron ore miners of the Brendons who made heavy demands on local woodland. It is divided into two parts: the nineteenth-century church in its elevated setting, with a few farms dotted around, and Pool Town where the inn is situated. The valley is an idyllic ramble among watery meadows, conifers and bulbous sheep-grazed hills. Steep-sided fields slant down to the stream's edge and around Roadwater are traces of the iron ore railway which ran from the top of the Brendons to the main line at Washford. The industry began in the second half of the nineteenth century and continued up until the First World War, the ore supplying the foundries of South Wales.

13

Exmoor

Simonsbath tends to conjure words from the bleak spectrum of the vocabulary to all who have visited the place in the dead of winter. Remote, lonely, cold, windswept, forbidding – all these adjectives can be true, yet it lacks the savagery of remotest Dartmoor. The buff-green hills sing in summer, clothed with blue moor grass, rusty deer-sedge and acres of ling, bell and cross-leaved heath. There are khaki pools where moss, sundew and asphodel grow, and peaty channels are discoloured by iron ore. This is the setting for the village described in 1938 as 'just a tiny hamlet in a wood, with an ugly little church, a handsome yellow-washed rectory, a farm or two and the lovely Barle'.

Situated in the upper reaches of the river, Simonsbath formed the headquarters of the Knight empire. The Knights, father and son, were the first to attempt to farm the moor in a systematic manner. They planted hedges and trees, laid down new roads, worked out a system of stock-rearing concentrating on Black Galloway and Red Devon Cattle and experimented with planting roots and corn. They helped transform the sterile, unproductive ground by establishing some fifteen farms with thick walls, big rectangular courtyards and purple roofing slates, all built in that late-Georgian style combining sober elegance with solidity. Their attempts to develop Exmoor's mineral resources were less successful. Although they located pockets of iron ore and copper, the lodes proved uneconomic to work even after they had established a private mineral railway. Simonsbath stands as the hub of their enterprise, the engine-house of their multiple activities, being the focus of a new settlement – an agricultural oasis amid 'forest, baren, and morisch ground, where ys store and breading of young cattle, but little or no corne or habitation' (Leland). In 1897 the Knights sold their properties to Devon neighbours, and an era on Exmoor came to an end.

After Simonsbath, the River Barle curves along its deepening valley, rounding knobbly spurs, flowing beneath fords, passing by the towering hill-fort of Cow Castle, then under the magnificently bold and buttressed Landacre Bridge and finally reaching Withypool, an exemplary village with a hospitable inn, thatched cottages, shops, a garage and an Early English style church. The knightly family of Withipoll, or Withipole, said to have originated in Italy, settled here and acquired their name. Once there were four harvests a year here – turf, whortleberry, hay and corn – but now the emphasis is more on sheep-rearing and dairying. Typical Exmoor names adorn the surrounding dwellings: Higher Blackland, Waterhouse, Foxtwitchen, Weatherslade and Holmbush, all evoking lean moorland rather than lush pasturage. Withypool Bridge, like Landacre, is many-arched and overlooks a broad weir; a pebbly beach fringes the stream in which children sometimes paddle.

The Royal Oak is a well-known hunting pub – not so insistently photogenic as its Winsford counterpart – where four packs of hounds meet. The interior is aptly decorated with antlers, hunt-buttons and horsebrasses. R.D. Blackmore stayed here while he was writing *Lorna Doone*. Sir Alfred Munnings was another distinguished tippler – he installed a studio above the stable in the 1930s. Hot on his heels came Dwight Eisenhower, taking a break to plan the course of the war, and also perhaps to immerse himself in whisky and Zane Grey. Withypool is said to have more horses than people and should be an ideal place for those desirous of reviving an equine cult.

In 1905 Walter Raymond, tiring of city life, rented a cottage in Withypool for a shilling a week, and there spent some of the happiest years of his life. His genial fire-red face crowned with prematurely white hair became as familiar as the sunset. He tramped over the moor with a knapsack and sat in the Royal Oak listening for stories. Locals regarded him first as 'a furriner' and his frugal eating-habits – he consumed nettles and dandelion leaves – provoked the comment, 'Why he do eat rabbit victuals!'

Winsford also lies on the Exe but is prettier in the conventional sense. Considered by many to be 'Exmoor's most beautiful village', it has no fewer than seven bridges, ranging from the cobbly and amateurish to the strong, durable packhorse bridge. A road leads up a steep narrow lane, honeysuckle-scented in summer, to the church, which is a strong-lined Perpendicular building comparable with a Cotswold wool church. The outstanding feature is the panel bearing the arms of James I dated 1609 and a text from Ecclesiastes: 'Curse not the King, no not in thy thought; and curse not the rich in thy bedchamber; for a bird of the air shall carry the voice, and that which hath wings shall tell the matter.' Other buildings are the old malthouse, now a hotel and restaurant, the nearby Wesleyan chapel and the photogenic Royal Oak Inn, one of those rambling former farmhouses going back to the twelfth century. The thatching is imaginatively tailored to the pub's structural whims: tongues, Vs and moustachios of straw slant down, shawling each dormer, lintel and bulging window. Obligatory roses twine outside the door, horses sedately trot by, and the *status quo* stalks about with rod and gun.

On the wall of a rather undistinguished house is a tablet stating 'ERNEST BEVIN, STATESMAN, WAS BORN HERE.' He was born at Winsford in March 1881, attended the local Sunday School when he was three, became an orphan at the age of six, left school at eleven, worked at cutting mangolds and scaring birds off crops, married in his twenties and then embarked on a career in politics. On 30 November 1946 the *Picture Post* published a photograph of him at the age of three, together with a photograph of the house where he was born. 'Dominating the political scene,' the article ran, 'is the massive figure of the Foreign Secretary. He dominates foreign affairs through his office and energy. Even the MPs' revolt is a tribute to his power. In a little West Country village there are still some who remember him as a rather weakly small boy.'

The next major settlement, travelling upstream from Winsford, is Exford, where the kennels of the Devon and Somerset staghounds are situated. In the centre of this spacious, salubrious village is the cricket and football pitch, pleasantly tree-shaded and attended by the Exmoor stores, a branch of Lloyds Bank, the gabled and tile-hung Crown Hotel and a necessary if visually prosaic garage. There are other aspects such as the sturdy packhorse bridge and the converted Exmoor cottages with lofty cylindrical chimneys and inglenooks; also the slightly forbidding church of St Mary Magdalene, situated on rising ground east of the village, with its seventy-foot embattled tower. The fifteenth-century font was taken from the old church of St Audries, demolished in 1858, and put aside for forty years until taken to Exford. Queens' College, Cambridge, contributed the choir stalls, and the fifteenth-century oak screen is extraordinarily elaborate for Exmoor. Like Withypool and several other moorland retreats, Exford is a horsey place, with the animal being shod in the smithy, turned out for hunting or merely available for tourist trekking.

Porlock is a name synonymous with Exmoor. The picture it conjures is not one of starved, sterile moorland, for it belongs to the lush, fertile periphery of the National Park, where Somerset assumes the soft, verdurous airs of Devon. One imagines deep-sculptured, chalk-white cottages and roofs of soft-shadowed thatch absorbing the lustrous light. The truth is slightly different from this dream haze. Nevertheless, it is the latter image – of a quaint rural retreat where life is an endless round of clotted cream teas and where the plaster pixie holds court – that persists in posters and holiday hand-outs, so it is worth a brief, critical examination.

The village lies between the hills and the sea in the north-west corner of Somerset, only a few miles from the Devon border. It is recessed in a lush, wooded amphitheatre and, as Collinson (1791) noted, occupies a 'finely romantick' situation 'being nearly surrounded, on all sides, except towards the sea, by steep and lofty hills intersected by deep vales and hollow glens'. Overlooking a serene stretch of arable, long famous for barley growing, the name means 'enclosure by the sea'. The water here normally has a greeny-grey tint; only in Cornwall does one find that shock-blue iridescence. The sea left Porlock open to attack during the tenth century, when it was the site of a royal palace of the Saxon kings. In 918 the Lidwiccas, from Brittany, launched an attack here after an abortive attempt to invade the mouth of the Severn, but they were beaten back, the survivors escaping to Steep Holm, where many died of hunger. A more successful raid was accomplished by Harold Godwinson in the midsummer of 1052. After a failed attempt to unseat Edward the Confessor, he sought refuge in Ireland, where he raised troops sufficient to occupy nine ships and landed at Porlock and set about plundering, slaughtering and burning. Some scorch-marked stones in the church are said to be relics of his incendiary tendencies.

These historic events do not weigh heavily upon the present-day settlement, for Old Porlock, that picturesque if unsanitary nucleation of chunky thatched cottages, survives only in fragmental relics and the sepia-brown plates of nineteenth-century photographs. What we have today is a briskly competitive holiday resort.

There has been a dramatic rise in property prices since the speculators moved in, and Porlock became a desirable place for retirement. Local couples can no longer afford the prices demanded in their own village and either move out or acquire a council house. William Rayner, a citizen of Porlock, wrote in 1975 of a 'geriatric invasion' and complained, 'There is an aesthetic danger in too much renovation, too much smart white paint, too much double glazing, too many roses in brass-bound tubs, as well as shabbiness and dilapidation.' He also commented angrily on the destruction of a thatched cottage, which added nothing, only laid bare 'a desolate area of garages and parked cars'. And, of course, cars themselves are a problem as they stream up the narrow high street past the Ship in never-ending chromium queues. They clog the air with their ceaseless exhalations and surge up the steep 1 in 4 hill which prompted Southey to call Porlock 'the end of the world' because 'all beyond was inaccessible to the carriage or even cart'. But it should be noted that there is a popular alternative route, a well-graded toll road owned by the Blathwayt family which ascends the incline in a series of cautious loops.

Porlock High Street is narrow and winding, occluded by shop signs, AA and RAC recommendations, oriel windows, telegraph poles and projecting porches. Despite the modern clutter, there are houses with medieval cores and thatched roofs served by tall, buttressed chimneys typical of West Somerset. Others are pure recreations and belong to no known century save twentieth-century twee. One of the best buildings, on the outskirts of the village, is Doverhay Manor, now the local information centre, with an ornate traceried window and a billiards room. The village hall nearer the centre also deserves a second glance. It is a plainish structure, faced with pebbledash, obtrusively buttressed and notable for being designed by Voysey, a leader of the modern movement in British architecture, who managed to combine geometric diversity with an improved utility.

Many visitors flock to the celebrated Ship Inn, honoured by Southey, who stayed here in 1799 and wrote a poem praising the village and vale which appeared in the *Morning Post*, 26 August:

Porlock thy verdant vale so fair to sight,
Thy lofty hills which fern and furze embrown,
The waters that roll musically down
Thy woody glens, the traveller with delight
Recalls to memory, and the channel grey
Circling its surges in the level bay.

The Ship is mainly eighteenth century with a small carved oak window at the north end, rustic porch and cosy, unprettified interior. A popular venue for folksinging, one hired cockhorses here in the nineteenth century before climbing the hill. Outside there an old four-step mounting-bar and central lighthouse-like chimney.

The fifteenth-century church of St Dubricus, first Bishop of Llandaff (d. 612), is reminiscent of Stogursey, with a low, square, bulky tower from which springs a truncated steeple faced with oak shingles. Inside there lies an effigy of Sir Simon FitzRoger (d. 1306), who helped build the church. His feet were amputated so that he might fit properly into the recess in the wall, and his leonine companion has been taken from him – such are the assaults of time. John, fourth Baron Harington (d. 1417), lies under the easterly arch of the arcade with Elizabeth Courtenay, his wife. The knight, who joined Henry V's second expedition to France and never returned, is in full armour, wearing cuirass, bawdrick, belt and sword and is clad in a mantle and surcoat. An additional feature is 'the silly names of many ignorant louts scratched over it, even on the forehead of the fair lady' – Arthur Mee, 1940.

Porlock Weir is the name given to the tiny harbour that once served as a lifeline to the villages of the hinterland. Essentially it was a lagoon fed by a stream, where the piling up of pebbles by wave-action created a natural inlet. This was developed in the early nineteenth century by the creation of a quay, warehouses and a wall with lock gates thirty feet wide. The master of a Porlock sloop during the Napoleonic Wars kept an account book recording cargoes of barley to Swansea, timber to Bristol and limestone from Aberavon. Nowadays the harbour is full of pleasure yachts, some of which stay the winter snugged under tarpaulins, and no longer a trading post but an architectural composition featuring high wooded slopes framing salt-crusted cottages, an inn, hotel and car-park. After the close-packed atmosphere of Porlock, one registers the sudden expansion of light and space broken by a moody headland thrust into the sea. A tiny forest of masts, gulls, shingle ridges, big lock gates – the drama has its special *frisson*.

From Porlock Weir it is well worth taking a walk to Culbone, which lies hidden in a massive green womb amid hills shawled by deciduous woodland. The walk is a revelation and varied by the presence of sudden walls, tunnels and castellations, all erected by Sir Thomas Acland III, who transformed the Holnicote estate into a model essay in the picturesque. The Culbone woods enclose the walker.

A veritable ambush of sprawling ferns, galaxies of clustering leaves, fusillades of foxgloves – and green-gold light breaking through interfused with the grating whisper of the sea. The atmosphere is strong here. It seems one of the few places in England where the nature spirits still hold sway. One can well picture these woods as the last outpost of Pan, the grinning, hairy face seen between bracketed leaves, the horned and lust-exulting one, and sure enough, on reaching the tiny church, there is a two-light Saxon window divided by a mullion at the top of which is a carving of a horned face.

Culbone church lies 400 feet above sea-level, and its walls may date from the twelfth century. It has a quaint slated spirelet (which humorists claim to have been snipped off the top of Porlock church), a reredos designed in 1927 by C.F. Annesley Voysey, and room enough to seat thirty (in great discomfort).

A stream trickles past the church and pottery, intensifying the muffled quietude of a place many use as a spiritual retreat, particularly those who have harassing jobs in the city. I have met a police superintendent who visites Culbone regularly in order to re-charge himself with a dose of the restorative tranquillity that few places can now provide. But one cannot be over-sentimental about Culbone. It once played host to a colony of charcoal-burners and lepers, and violence has erupted here from the most unexpected quarters. The Assize Rolls of 1280 record that Thomas, the chaplain of Cattenor (Culbone), was prosecuted 'for that he had struck Albert of Esshe [Ash] on the head with a hatchet, and so killed him'.

The name is an enigma. 'Kitnor' was the old form, which has been translated as 'cave by the shore', but the usual derivation is from 'Kil Beun', 'the church of St Beuno', a Welsh saint. Joan Cooper (1978), a local mystic, has stated that the place was originally called K'SH'B'H, pronounced 'Kasheba', after a Sumerian sage.

The tiny village of Oare, some three miles distant as the crow flies, also occupies an isolated, enchanting setting, except, unlike the relatively inaccessible Culbone, it has a twisty road going through it, along which stream some 50,000 visitors per year, mainly bound for the small

Perpendicular church where R.D. Blackmore's grandfather once served as rector. The scenery is shining, verdant, jauntily tempestuous, with wooded cleaves, bumpy packhorse bridges, breakneck trout-streams and farms with tall flue-like chimneys.

Oare is hidden in a deep valley, within earshot of the pounding sea. In winter a deep, shuttered silence pervades this spot but in summer lark song electrifies the breeze, and the scurrying gurgle of Oare Water is a persistent accompaniment. Oare church has a small, crenellated tower, horsebox pews, memorials to R.D. Blackmore and several generations of Snows and an Elizabethan chalice. King Edward VII, a great huntin' fishin' monarch, visited the church in 1879, an event commemorated by the late Nicholas Snow (himself described as 'Lord of the Manor of Oare, an upright man greatly skilled in woodcraft, Master of Hounds, and churchwarden of this Parish') who put up a tablet inscribed with the Prince of Wales' feathers in bold relief. Snow (1827–1914) himself is honoured by a stone showing a kneeling knight in a wood and two hounds looking at a stag with a cross between its antlers – an illustration of the St Hubert legend. The long, low Oare manor house, the seat of the Snows, stands by the church and had a large ash at its entrance with hideously bent branches, the outcome of 'girt Jan Ridd' having a difference of opinion with it. Local names preserved in the church – Ridd, Fry and Vellacot – enforce the verisimilitude of Blackmore's romance, and Kemp's Farm has been declared the original for Plover Barrows Farm idyllically evoked by Blackmore: 'Almost everybody knows ... in our part of the world, at least, how pleasant and soft the fall of land is round about Plover Barrows Farm. All above it is strong dark mountains spread with heath and desolate, but near our house the valleys cove, and open warmth and shelter. Here are trees, and bright green grass and orchards full of contentment, and a man may scarce espy the brook, although he hears it everywhere. And indeed a good stout piece of it comes through our farmyard, and swells sometimes to a rush of waves when the clouds are on the hilltops.'

Selworthy lies two miles east of Porlock in a snug little niche, pillowed against the pumpkin-fat, afforested hills. Its setting is fine enough to set camera-shutters blinking and paint and horsehair furious stirring. The picture postcard scene *in excelsis* depicts a group of big, tall-chimneyed cottages, with leaded panes and rustically coiffured thatch, grouped around an unwrinkled green shaded by walnut trees and presided over by a bold and handsome white-painted church. It is just too sturdily authentic to be described as 'twee' although at times one might expect to see Snow White and the seven dwarfs emerging from the gabled porches clutching utensils and affirming the work ethic in tuneful chorus. It all looks artless and effortless, but, as with many fine effects, there lurks a cunning stage-manager in the background. The buildings did not just emerge gradually over the years like the shrubby lichen on the old oaks but were planned in accordance with an approved design, possibly based on the hamlet at Blaize Castle, Henley, Bristol, which was the work of Richard Nash. The Selworthy group were erected by Thomas Dyke Acland III, lord of the manor, and went up in 1828 to house retired workmen belonging to his estate; his wife, more pretentiously, provided these retainers with scarlet cloaks to standardize their debt of gratitude.

Sir Thomas Acland III (1787–1871) planted the oaks, chestnuts and silver firs which render the lanes and drives of Selworthy a delight and set up the walled carriageways and castellated arches in Culbone woods. A friend and contemporary of Gladstone, the winner of a double first at Oxford, he was an energetic improver of property and local benefactor but marginally less popular than his father, Sir Thomas Acland II, who died on 17 May 1794, a gusty country squire who held port-swilling banquets at his Holnicote mansion where the guests performed such druidical rites as drinking toasts from a silver goblet which had been previously implanted in the mouth of a decapitated stag. Nevertheless, it is the handiwork of Sir Thomas III which is valued today above the excesses and eccentricities of his hunting father.

The Acland family are commemorated in Selworthy church, a capacious Perpendicular building perched on a green eyrie above the hamlet. Its most admired feature is its south aisle, probably endowed by the Steyning family, which has rich, dextrous window tracery and arch mouldings of striking grace and strength.

Descending from the church, on the left there is wonderful rosy red fourteenth-century tithe barn, softened by sprouting valerian in summer and with a window opening, now blocked, through which the sheaves of corn were passed. Lambs, pigs and sheaves are worked on the terminals of the hood mouldings, a pictograph of the former rector's payment, and on the west gable is a two-light window (originally above the church porch) inserted there by Mr Stephenson, friend and tutor of Sir Thomas III, in 1826.

Dunster is in many ways the most popular and least typical of Exmoor villages, lying on the blossoming, fertile edges of the National Park in the valley of the Avill. Deciduous woodland masks the towering slopes, and on Grabbist Hill, above the village, Mrs Alexander composed the hymn 'All Things Bright and Beautiful'. People congregate in large numbers at Dunster because it possesses the quintessential appeal of a fairytale. Its High Street is long and broad, retaining its medieval market space, and the ranked cottages cluster and climb up to the dramatic slopes of the tor on which the castle stands. It is a magnificent climactic pile with turrets, curtain walls and vigorous buttresses – a combination of solidity and fantasy.

The Luttrell Arms Hotel, essentially a sixteenth-century coaching inn, was formerly the private residence of the abbots of Cleeve. It has a porch pierced by loopholes, enabling archers to fire askance as well as straight, and the upstairs rooms display many curious features, including a plaster overmantel depicting Actaeon being torn to pieces by dogs which Edward Hutton (1910) found 'very ugly' and which other commentators found unidentifiably crude. It featured in the Civil War as a boarding-house for Colonel Blake's Roundheads during the 160-day siege of the Royalist-held fortress. Cannonballs whizzed up and down the main street. One struck the famous octagonal Yarn Market erected by George Luttrell in 1609. The hole made in the beam is still traceable, but the damaged roof was repaired

after the cessation of fighting in 1646. The weather vane
bears the initials G.L. (George Luttrell) and the date 1647.
Ironically, there is a portrait of Oliver Cromwell in the castle.

The sixteenth-century priest's house forms the entrance to
Dunster church, built as a priory church for the Benedictines
of Dunster, which was a cell of Bath Abbey, founded in the
reign of William I by William de Mohun, to whom the
Conqueror had given Dunster and fifty-five other manors in
the country. The dominant outer feature is the massive
square tower, buttressed and embattled, about which a good
deal is known. In 1419 William Pynson of Dunster, 'seeing
that the shadow of death has fallen upon me', asked that his
body should be buried in the church of George the Martyr,
before the image of St Christopher. Also he bequeathed 40s.
towards the building of a new tower, an enterprise not
completed until 1443 when the parishioners contracted John
Marys, mason of Stogursey, to carry out the work. They
provided the muscle-power for rough stone haulage, and the
necessary pulleys, ladders and winches, while he did the
skilled building at the rate of 13s.4d. per foot. The tower has
three stages, and its pillars are set 'diamond-wise' on the
foundations of the old Norman tower.

Several notable memorials occupy the church, especially
the bombastic Elizabethan monument to Thomas Luttrell,
high sheriff of Somerset, 'who departed this lyfe in sure
hope of a most joyful resurrection' on 16 January 1570.
Flanked by columns, crested by coats of arms, three ruffed
recumbent Luttrells lay stricken in alabaster repose; a third,
still alive, is industriously praying.

On the north side of the church are remains of certain
conventual buildings – traces of a cloister, a wooden
almonry, a tithe barn (now a Crown Estates workshop), a
lofty, walled garden (now a Garden of Remembrance) with a
hushed and haunted atmosphere, and an immense, round
dovecote capable of lodging some 2,000 birds and dating
from the twelfth century. A tragedy once happened inside
the dovecote: one spring, when it was full to capacity with
birds and fledglings, someone shut the door and forgot to
open the window through which the pigeons obtained food,
and all the birds starved to death.

Aside from the castle, monastic and domestic buildings, Dunster has an old flour-mill, mentioned in the Domesday Book (1086), which was repaired in 1979 by West Country craftsmen and is now turning again under the encouragement of a steady flow of admission fees.

Dunster Castle (National Trust) has been described as 'the quintessence of baronial might', a view all too understandable when one sees the fortress, like some grand stone patriarch, rising above the steep wooded slopes of the tor. The site has been occupied since Saxon times, when it served as a frontier against the Norsemen. At the time of Edward the Confessor, when it belonged to Aluric, it was known as a 'torre', a fortified tower. Afterwards it acquired a prefix 'Dun' or 'Dune', meaning a ridge of hills stretching towards the coast. There is a twelfth-century account describing it as 'inaccessible on the one side where it was washed by the tide' – a reminder that sailing-ships could actually dock at Dunster before the waters receded and the deer park was created. After the Conquest, the fortress was granted to William de Mohun, who built the Norman castle of which no trace remains. In 1376 Lady Joan de Mohun sold the castle to Lady Elizabeth Luttrell, and it was Sir Hugh Luttrell who erected the gatehouse in 1420. But the most decisive alterations were inaugurated by George Luttrell, who in 1868 engaged the fashionable architect William Salvin to enlarge and enhance the castle. Salvin had worked at Windsor, the Tower of London and Warwick Castles, so he was by now adept at producing three-dimensional essays simulating what most people would prefer such structures to look like.

A village celebrated for its cider-orchard rites, Carhampton is about one mile from the Bristol Channel and about $1\frac{1}{2}$ miles south-east of Dunster. Situated on the A39 northern Exmoor route, it is a fairly stark, workaday place, with sturdy blocks of cottages. But the surrounding orchards and farms act as rural compensations. The towering bastions of Bat's Castle and Withycombe Hill overshadow its southern aspect, and on the outskirts of the village are the kennels of the West Somerset Foxhounds. They are found on the lane leading to Withycombe, and many people gather to see the hunt, sometimes blocking the way for other

road-users less interested in the spectacle of the frankly
incredible pursuing the rankly inedible.

The screen in the parish church is a remarkable survival,
with its stem-frail fan vaulting. Instead of being polluted by
layers of beetle-brown Victorian slime varnish, it glistens
silver, red, green, gold and blue. Jubilance, delicacy and
grace combine in this marvellous carving, where wood
assumes the finery and tractability of precious metal.

East of the church there is a big red sandstone house,
formerly the vicarage, where in 1928 workmen dug up
stones and skeletons arranged so as to suggest the site of a
former graveyard. This aroused much interest: Carhampton
is named after the Celtic St Carantoc, whose feast day fell on
16 May. He was the heir to the kingdom of Ceredigion
(Cardigan) in Wales but renounced the luxury of court life to
become an evangelizing ascetic. Folklore claims he
dispatched – or should one say tamed? – a fierce sea serpent
which ravaged the countryside around Dunster. He merely
threw his scarf around the creature which trundled along
docilely by his side. For this deed King Arthur granted him
the land called Carrum – Carhampton – where he built an
oratory which developed into a chapel. It served as the
parish church until as late as Edward II's reign (1307–27),
and Leland visited it when it was in decline.

Still keeping to the A39, between Carhampton and
Williton, Washford spreads across Vallis Florida, the flowery
valley dedicated to 'Our Blessed Lady of the Cliff'. The
masts of a big transmitting station disfigure the outskirts,
but the eye is quickly diverted by the pink and grey walls of
the Cistercian abbey founded in 1188 by William de
Roumara, youngest son of the Earl of Lincoln. Chapter
house, sacristy, dormitory and rectory – the complex is a
poem in well-honed stone. It is an expression of the
landscape itself, a building that seemingly has grown
whelk-like from the rock. At Old Cleeve, of which
Washford was once considered part, there was another
shrine to the Virgin called Our Lady's Chapel. This village is
more secluded than Washford, but time has not injected it
with new vitality. Instead the village school has been lost,
and young couples have moved on to Minehead or Taunton.

The church is Perpendicular, famous for its blacksmith's epitaph:

> My sledge and hammer lie reclined,
> My bellows too have lost their wind;
> My fire's extinct, my forge decayed,
> And in the dust my body's laid;
> My coal is burnt, my iron's gone,
> My nails are drove, my work is done.

George Jones, village blacksmith, d. 1808

Two miles north of Washford, Watchet is the only port of consequence in Somerset and of some economic importance to the villages of the area. The name comes from the Welsh 'under the hill' but also lent itself to a fashionable colour (Charles I was described as wearing a waistcoat of 'Watchet blue') possibly derived from the distinctive shade of the cliffs which were formerly worked for alabaster. The town has the blunt, salt feel of a harbourage, with houses presenting a harsh scrubbed look from continual scouring by wind and spray. It is functionally laid out, as a port should be, with the Washford River walled-in to avoid flooding, the railway linking up with the harbour complex, two car parks near the centre, a coastguard look-out by Splash Point and swings and memorial grounds set over to the east. An old Saxon settlement, the site of a Royal Mint, it was sacked by the Danes (one of whom, according to legend, decapitated the town's patron saint Decuman) and developed by the Normans. It imported Welsh sheep, cattle, coal and salt in the sixteenth century and harbour trade still thrives today with a cargo-liner service to Portugal and the export of items like building materials, motor car parts, tyres and caravans.

14

Hamstone Country

If Glastonbury Tor is the ancient nodal point of spiritual
energy, guarded by St Michael, lord of the high places, Ham
Hill for hundreds of years was the centre for toilsome
temporal activity. The sprawling uplift of shelly limestone,
crouching above the villages of Montacute, Tintinhull,
Stoke-sub-Hamdon, Norton-sub-Hamdon and the Chinnocks, has been sawed, hacked and blasted for over a
thousand years. The huge coppery-brown slabs have been
planed and shaped to provide building-material for
churches, mansions, tombs, statues, troughs, gateposts and
stiles. Characterized by its golden shade, the Inferior Oolite
also has a grey bed producing a hard, coarse-grained brown
limestone more durable than the yellow. Only about 400 feet
high, Ham Hill affords views across the Yeo and Parrett
valleys; one glimpses too the blue and purple bastions of the
Mendips and Quantocks. The Romans found the camp on
the summit useful for keeping a watch on the Fosse Way.
They acquired it by defeating the Durotriges, a Celtic tribe
centred around Dorset who had earlier fortified its ramparts.
They left behind their strange Modigliani-like stone heads
and a wonderful bronze knob-horned bull. The Romans left
a chariot wheel, metal plates from the reinforced tunics of
legionnaires, brooches, weaving-implements, toilet articles
and a steelyard. Traces of Roman building can be identified
on the hill as well as medieval remains. The Somerset
historian Gerard wrote in 1633 that the quarrymen had
created 'a pretty kind of commonwealth' including their own
courts, and made their quarries 'seeme rather little parishes

than quarryes, so many buildings have they under the vast
workes to shelter themselves in wet weather, and their
wrought stones in winter'.

At the turn of the century the quarry trade dwindled.
Only one stonemason was working in the parish of
Montacute in 1902, compared with four in 1897. Eight years
later the remaining quarries were being worked by the Ham
Hill & Doulting Stone Co, who were eventually bought up
by United Stone Firms Limited. Desultory quarrying
continued until 1968, when all the economic beds had been
virtually worked out. So it was decided to make the area a
country park, an inspired concept, for it makes an exciting
place to explore and ramble over, full of grassed-over bumps
and declivities, cliffs and gullies, hillocks and humps, and on
its scarp slope there is rich woodland.

Montacute can fairly be regarded as the capital of the Ham
Hill region. Strategically situated on the old Exeter-London
coach road, a former centre for quarrying, gloving and the
cloth trade, it is dominated by the almost arrogantly
imposing mansion begun by Thomas Phelps in about 1590
and completed about ten years later by his son Sir Edward
Phelps, Speaker of the House of Commons. But this
building, though impressive, represents a mere particle of
Montacute's history. The origin of the settlement can be
traced to the seventh century, when an estate known as
Logworesbeorh was already established. By the ninth
century this had become the present-day Bishopston, which
encompasses part of the main street and runs northwards
from the church. After the Conquest it was acquired by
Robert, Count of Mortain, who built a castle on the conical
hill. This struck a humiliating blow at the subjugated
English, for the hill, like Glastonbury Tor, was a holy place.
In the days of Canute, a smith had a dream wherein
Christ appeared to him, bidding him go to the priest and
climb to the top of St Michael's Hill and dig. He ignored the
dream twice but the third time he contacted the priest. They
both reached the summit and began to dig 'and came upon a
great stone which was suddenly cleft in twain and in the cleft
they saw a great Crucifix of glistening black flint and
beneath it another, smaller, of wood, with a bell very old,

and a very old book'. They loaded these on a farm wagon and harnessed up twelve red oxen and twelve white cows to see where they would go. They began to move with great determination; nothing could stop them until they reached Essex and halted before a cottage at Waltham. There a church and abbey were built around the Holy Cross: Harold is said to have knelt there before Hastings, and 'Holy Cross!' served as the English battle cry.

The core of Montacute is the Borough, a spacious square with many old two-storeyed houses including the old bakery and the chantry which has the initials of Robert Shirborne, the last prior of Montacute (1532–9), carved on a stone panel attached to the bay window. The Phelps Arms was a coaching inn during the sixteenth century and is haunted by a ghost of an old lady who leaves a smell of camphor. The creeper-covered King's Arms in Bishopston belonged to the abbey at the Dissolution: hence the name refers to the confiscation of the property by the monarch. Also deserving of a lingering glance is the thatched Monk's House (formerly the Gables) built in the sixteenth century with soot-black interior timbers. No less distinguished is Montacute Cottage, lying by the entrance of the great house and displaying mullioned two and three-light windows and a four-centred entrance arch. As for the priory, nothing remains but the gatehouse which stands south-west of the church. A gracious example of ornate Tudor workmanship, it has turrets and oriels looming above a fan-vaulted, arched gateway. Around the back is a traditional farm with trees, cattle pond and rambling walls – a favourite postcard composition.

Aside from obvious architectural features, much interest is to be got exploring the lanes and byways of Montacute. Wash Lane joins Bishopston and Middle Street and is a fascinating amble among walls, backyards and boundary stones. The charmingly named Kissmedown Lane joins up with Tintinhull, and its covert is fondly remembered by Llewellyn Powys in one of his essays.

Montacute parish church is dedicated to St Catherine, and the main road runs up against it before merging with Bishopston. It is a proud, handsome building, dramatically

rearing above the huddled Hamstone cottages and containing some Norman work and in the north transept tombs
of the Phelps family, owners of Montacute for over 300
years. The early sepulchres, such as those of David Phelps
and his wife Ann (1484), are moving in their homely lack of
detail – a kind of soft rusticity shines through the
workmanship, while the latest tomb, that of Thomas Phelps
(1500–88) and his wife, Elizabeth Smythe of Long Ashton
(d. 1598), is a far more sophisticated Elizabethan piece of
workmanship with a cold elaborateness of detail.

Montacute's less busy, if equally alluring, neighbour is
Tintinhull, yet another bright star in the galaxy of Hamstone
havens. The quarried blocks have weathered so beautifully
here that many of the buildings might have been composed
of chunks of tarnished gold. Llewelyn Powys loved this
place and recalled in *A Baker's Dozen* how he and his
brother (John Cowper) liked to walk here from Montacute
during their Easter holidays. 'It was a fancy of ours,' he
wrote, 'that in no other one of the neighbouring villages did
the April evenings fall with so charmed a grace upon leaf
and grass and tile and thatch. We never wearied of the scene
presented by Tintinhull in the twilight hour, with the old
sun-bonnet women crossing to the Lamb Inn to fetch cider
for their suppers, with tittering gloving girls idling after
boys with cowslips stuck in their caps, and with the voices of
children floating on the soft Somerset air, on the soft spring
air that seemed to smell of opening buds in unseen gardens,
and of ground ivy banks, and of the sun-warmed feathers of
little hedgerow wild birds.'

How does modern Tintinhull match that flight of delicate
lyricism? Originally an agricultural village augmented by
glove-making (one factory still survives), today it serves as a
convenient dormitory for Yeovil. So inevitably there is a
paucity of genuine milkmaids and youthful farmhands but
no lack of prosperous, sober-suited commuters who enjoy a
pint and *pâté* at the Bull and discuss what is cost-effective,
labour-intensive and prestigiously expensive. Yet there is
still a very special feel to Tintinhull, created by the
mustard-yellow buildings with their sturdy well-squared
gateposts, groves of full-blown chestnuts, neatly barbered

hedges and atmosphere of century-deep repose that instils a feeling of slumbering smugness.

A large triangular green forms the core of the village, circumvented by Head Street, Vicarage Street, St Margaret's Road and the Yeovil-Martock road. On the east side of this expanse is Francis Farm (1603), a two-storeyed Hamstone residence with vigorous window mouldings. The Dower House, at the northern end, is both severe and decorative; a tiny porthole window is set above the classical doorway, which is flanked by regular mullioned windows. In 1687 it was referred to as 'Mr Napper's new house', and today it has a farm and cider-press attached to its grounds. On a wall nearby there is a plaque stating that A. Tooze captained and won the carnival tug-of-war game in 1979: Thomas Gray might be glad to hear that village Herculeses no longer go unhonoured.

Tintinhull church, dedicated to St Margaret of Antioch, stands near the austere, slate-roofed pile of the Court, a stark-lined Jacobean building with numerous round-headed windows and air of lofty detachment. It dates from the early thirteenth century, evidence of primitive workmanship can be traced in the exterior East Wall, and a daub and conglomerate of mud and stones diversify the bonding-materials. In the graveyard are a profusion of massive, mouldering tombstones, bearing the lichenous imprint of their great age and leaning over slightly as if in need of a helping hand.

The floor of the chancel has a brass bearing a half-length effigy of Master John Heth, Canon of Salisbury, Rector of Tintinhull (d. 4 February 1464), who, anxious to advertise his piety to the very last, asks Christ to witness 'that this stone does not lies here that the body may be adorned but that the spirit should be remembered'. As one leaves the church, a carved stone of a curious shape may be seen above the entrance. This is directed at an angle due East and may have been used as a midsummer or midwinter solstice check. But the overbearing yew tree, in whose massive shade it rests, effectively blocks out the sun's rays, preventing the theory from being tested.

The villages occupying the south-facing slopes of the Ham Hill range have a character entirely different from that of the north. Montacute is slightly grand, with its enormous Renaissance mansion and its prestigious history, but the Chinnock villages and the nearby Chiselborough began and continued as modest farming settlements.

There are three Chinnocks, Middle, East and West, and they all are set in exciting, hilly country. East Chinnock is on the A30 about four miles from Yeovil. This has led to some unsightly developments but there are some fine Hamstone cottages in the village by way of compensation. The church clings to the hillside and is dedicated to St Mary. It has a fifteenth-century tower, a strongly moulded Norman font and an east window endowed by the Young family, churchwardens of the parish 1870–98.

The remaining windows were made and installed by Herr Gunther Anton of Leonberg, Stuttgart, Germany. A rear gunner in the Luftwaffe, he was shot down over Southampton in 1944, taken prisoner and sent to the POW camp at Houndstone, Yeovil. Only eighteen at the time and anxious about his parents living in East Germany, he began to visit the church to pray. Shortly afterwards he heard his parents were safe and, as he looked at the church from the farm where he worked, he had the idea of designing a stained glass window for the church as a way of expressing his gratitude to the people of East Chinnock, who had shown him much sympathy and understanding. He returned to Germany in 1948 and built up a stained glass business with his father, who reminded him before he died, 'Do not forget about the window for East Chinnock.' In 1962 Gunther returned with the fine window showing scenes of Christ's life and ascension. He also added the north sanctuary window, of Mary and the infant Jesus and Christ the King, in 1967 and the south chancel windows in 1969. The latter depict the four archangels: Gabriel, the messenger; Michael, the helper of the Chosen People; Raphael, the angel of healing; Uriel, the angel of judgement and mercy.

Middle Chinnock is tiny, barely a hamlet, yet highly attractive with its little roadside church showing Norman work, and with the fine seventeenth-century Manor Farm, mullioned and immaculate, which anywhere else in England, save in this prodigally endowed region, might be considered very special. The same might be said of its parent village, West Chinnock, which is considerably bigger yet equally appealing, following an irregular pattern around a hilly triangle of lanes. The southern part clings to the shoulder of Snail's Hill while the northern part descends the valley of the Chinnock Brook towards Chiselborough. Exploring its byways, one notes in particular a three-bay cottage dated 1604 by Duckpool Lane, council homes at Scott's Way, a Victorian church school (1838) a Norman-styled church of 1889 and a marvellously named pub, the Muddled Man.

Across the valley to the north, the neighbouring village, Chiselborough, nestles securely in its fold in the hills. The approach from West Chinnock is full of writhing, serpentine excitements where the narrow lane enters into the cutting between Brympton and Balham Hills. It is dark, ferny, beset with jutting Hamstone walls and in places thickly over-arched with vegetation – hence Chiselborough bursts on the visitor excitingly, like coming out of a dark tunnel into an explosion of sunshine. The farming community neither thrills nor disappoints. Everything is tidy and composed: litterless streets, weedless gardens and meadowy, willowy footpaths that beckon across the fields. The inn called the Catshead is a protected seventeenth-century building with a doorway with a chamfered head: traditional beer is served here traditionally.

The church is dedicated to SS Peter and Paul; its Perpendicular spire, like the one at Compton Pauncefoot, juts out with just the right degree of emphasis. The interior is light, airy, cool, containing a memorial slab to one of the Gawlers after whom Gawler's Hill to the south of the village is named, and also to Stephen Burridge whose surname occurs in a copse to the south.

From Chiselborough it is only a mile to Norton-sub-Hamdon – a village over which anthologists of rural charm are wont to gloat. In the high ridge overlooking the settlement, Hamstone was quarried, and its varied shades of dark honey and weathered grey enhance – some would say create – its unique appeal. It features in a traditional rhyme alluding to the quarryworkers' habit of taking refreshment:

When Hamstone hears the Norton chimes at midnight
clack,
It rolls down hill to drink at Jack o' Beards, and back.

The approach to Norton from the east is leisurely and
unremarkable, down a long, gentle slope past orchards,
recent estates and some light commercial development.
Eventually the road flattens out and the village centre is
reached. A stream trickles by the side of a road that reveals a
vista of mellow, mullioned windows, sun-warmed thatch
and raised gardens with wall and iron railing surrounds. Tall
firs loom over homely cottages, creating pools of shade, and
one is tempted to cross a bridge and sample the hospitality of
the Lord Nelson, a renovated seventeenth-century inn
which, during the last war, was the centre of much illegal
trafficking, all the whisky being held back for the American
servicemen who could afford to pay more.

Like other villages in this region, Norton was once a centre
for quarrying, gloving and agriculture, but today only the
latter industry – especially fruit-farming – profitably
employs locals. Commuting to factories such as Westland
Helicopters and the numerous offices of Yeovil provides the
most important outlet for the working population. And of
course there are an increasing number of elderly citizens who
enjoy a prosperous retirement: hence the local over-60s club
is well patronized.

If Norton-sub-Hamdon is essentially rural, its sister
village, Stoke-sub-Hamdon, enjoyed an active industrial
history. It was formerly an important centre for gloving,
quarrying and even the manufacture of spats and boxes, but
only gloving continues on a modest scale; the others have
declined or disappeared, along with a number of farms. The
main street rumbles with the persistent thunder of Yeovil
Plant Hire Lorries, and there is an invigorating workaday
feel to the village. Change is accepted here despite its historic
lineage, and no one balks at the consequences. Contemporary estates – Prince's Close (1965), Queen's Crescent (1967),
Hamdon Close (1969) – rub shoulders with ancient buildings
like the priory; working men's institutes function alongside
old clothiers' houses; modern surgeries and health centres

sprout up amid venerable Hamstone edifices.

The main road is West Street from which North Street – originally the old Exeter-London coach road – branches off obliquely. West Street has a large green and memorial hall, opposite which stands the Fleur de Lis Inn. Around the back is a fives court with angle buttresses and roundels at the corner, probably dating from 1754, when the Bishop of Bath and Wells ordered that the game of fives should cease being played against church towers. There is a fine house in North Street called 'The Gables' dating from the second half of the sixteenth century. The interior is absorbing: a drawing-room with a ribbed and floriated plaster ceiling, a dining-room with fine eighteenth-century panelling and a fireplace in the large bedroom surmounted by a shield with a double eagle. This last somewhat Teutonic feature represents the arms of Sylvester Prior Bean (d. 1797) who was Vicar of Stoke 1754–76 and resident owner of the Gables. He is also known to have built a summerhouse inscribed with this legend:

This parlour was built to drink and to smoke
At the foolish expense of the parson of Stoke.

Stoke has two parts, West Stoke, which is the busy commercial part of the village previously described, and East Stoke, separated from it by fields and farms and lying on the Montacute road. The church is famous for its Norman chancel arch where billet, zigzag and lozenge combine to fine effect and where the clustered columns create an impression of massed individual strength. The tympanum shows the tree of life, three birds and the figure of Saggitarius firing an arrow at Leo. The workmanship is bold and childlike yet very satisfying in its emblematic simplicity. A tomb in the church may contain the body of Reginald de Monkton (d. 1307). He was provost to the immensely powerful Beauchamp family, former lords of the manor, who employed a community of priests to say five Masses a day in their manorial chapel dedicated to St Nicholas. Nothing remains of the 'very notable ruins of the great manor' which Leland described except part of Castle Farm at West Stoke. But the house of the provost, Stoke Priory (National Trust)

survives with its Tudor entrance, bellcote and gabled
oratory.

Stoke was the birthplace in 1310 of Matthew de Gournay,
knight. He was the son of one of Edward II's murderers and
renowned as a gaunt, swaggering soldier of fortune. 'The
veneration attached to this distinguished warrior,' Fuller
wrote, 'was so great that his armour was beheld by martial
men with much veneration and his faithful buckler was a
relic of esteem'. Gournay fought at Sluys, Crécy and
Poitiers, then took up a campaign on his own account, for
which he got two years in the Tower.

The track of the old Exeter-London coachroad mounts the
rugged hump of Ham Hill from West Stoke and descends
into Higher Odcombe. Overlooking the Yeovil basin, with
its sprawled estates and smoking flues, this is a soothing,
secretive spot: a junction by a row of venerable Hamstone
houses; a road running past banked bungalows and a post
office towards Crewkerne; a vastly altered parish church
with an abstract stained glass window; and a modern
imitation Hamstone estate called Coryate's Close after the
famous traveller (b. 1577) who, after legging 1,975 miles
through France, Italy, Switzerland and the Rhine Valley,
returned to Odcombe and hung up his boots in the parish
church. His travel book *Coryate's Crudities* is outstanding,
written in an ornate yet vigorous style, characterized by
trenchant observation, turgid humour, mild religious mania
and quirky erudition, all garnished with anecdotes and
marvellous whimsical asides. It is touching to read Coryate,
for, although he had an almost insane will to travel, to excel
other men and confer distinction on himself, he seemed to
have been passionately attached to his native region, and to
the house of Sir Edward Phelps who was his friend and
patron:

'Too much could not be said in praise of Odcombe,' he
wrote, 'whose smoke was dearer to him than the fire of a
foreign place; whose air was piercing and of excellent
subtilty; whose wool was the finest; whose springs were
sweet and wholesome, endued with orient and crystalline
clearness.'

Lower Odcombe is prettier, with many thatched dwellings and a faintly prestigious air. There is a popular pub, the Mason's Arms, allegedly sixteenth century, and the residents are a pleasing mixture of local turnips and imported flora.

The Chinnock and Hamdon villages are engirdled by the River Parrett, which, in its upper reaches beyond the South Petherton sluice gates, takes on a humbler, more picturesque character. It is navigable no longer, and a series of wriggling tributaries join it in the vicinity of Wigborough. One is called the Lopen Brook and has its source in Seavington St Mary; another descends past orchards from Haselbury Plucknett; a third begins at Hinton Park Farm and flows east through the Merriot valley joining the main stream at Snail's Hill in West Chinnock. The hills on the right bank of the river are less knobbly and precipitous than the Montacute range, although geologically similar. Their slopes are gradual and spreading and support strips of mixed woodland and open fields and fruit farms.

The village of Merriot is typical of this region. The parish is bounded by the Parrett to the east, the Lopen Brook to the north, Hinton village to the west and Crewkerne two miles to the south. The soil is compounded of loams and flints and Yeovil sands with outcrops of limestone and clay. Field names in the north-west, Stoneridge and Longmoor, testify to the poor arable potential of the flinty parts contrasting with the fertility elsewhere. A complex village with an abundance of lanes winding in and out and sometimes backing upon themselves, it has a quiet, industrious air with several important businesses, notably Scott's Nurseries and Merriot Mouldings, helping counteract the decline in agriculture. Formerly it was a great centre of flax-growing and sailmaking, and the bellying sheets of HMS *Victory* were produced by local craftsmen. The village concentrates around the main road, called Broadway, and Church Street and Lower Street. The latter has three dated houses (1663, 1729 and 1766) with predominantly Tudor features. Many of the dwellings started out as small farms and retain vestiges of yards and barns at the backs; also there are terraces of double-fronted houses of early nineteenth-century origin. Amply provided for amenity-wise, Merriot has a long-established social club, a squash club, two public houses (Swan and King's Head) and a variety of businesses including a handyman's shop. Curiously enough the place was known as 'Little Ireland' on account of an entirely baseless tradition of colonization by the Irish in the distant past and a predominance of dark hair coupled with a distinctive dialect. One point Merriot may have shared with an Irish colony was in the dogged persistence of certain surnames which resulted in the seventeenth century in a plethora of improvised titles such as 'curlhead', 'noghead' and 'bonehead' – evidence of no great verbal sophistication.

All Saints Church, Merriot, is arrestingly sited above the roadway. Its fourteenth-century truncated tower fitted with a tiny cluster of thistly pinnacles strikes the eye somewhat oddly, like an ambitious concept abruptly abandoned, and the carving of fighting cocks on the vestry wall is a curious detail.

Lopen lies almost exactly between Shepton Beauchamp and Merriot. The Fosse Way here runs narrow, dark and leaf-fringed, but the landscape is attractive, with numerous fruit farms easily identified by the hundreds of white pegs slotted in fields to assist the growth of young trees. The Roman road crosses Lopen village, a place of tumbled cottages and a tucked-away church with a faint atmosphere of foreboding. Lopen is remembered for an incident that took place here hundreds of years ago when a young rector over-indulged at the local feast and was punished by the high sheriff, Sir Amias Poulett, who had him put in the stocks for drunken behaviour. Unfortunately, from tiny misdeeds great vendettas are born. The sportive cleric's career took a series of gargantuan leaps and he finally became Cardinal Wolsey, Chancellor of England. But he did not forget those humiliating hours smouldering in the stocks, so he avenged himself on Sir Amias by forbidding him to leave London without his express permission, an irksome constriction on the Treasurer of the Inner Temple. Finally Sir Amias flattered the Chancellor by mounting his shield on the new Temple gateway. Wolsey relented and let the humbled aristocrat return to Somerset.

South of Merriot and Haselbury Plucknett is Crewkerne, a country town noted for making high-quality sailcloth, canvas

Huish
Episcopi
church

The Rose
and Crown
at Huish

The Priest's House and memorial cross at Muchelney

South Petherton church: the octagonal tower

The lock-up at Kingsbury Episcopi

St Nicholas's church at Combe St Nicholas

Churchyard wall, North Cadbury: The falling figures represent sin, suffering and death, the rising figures joy and redemption through the intervention of Christ

Tomb of the freethinker at West Camel

Jack the Treacle Eater, Barwick

The slatted spire: one of the Barwick follies

Thatched cottages at Shepton Beauchamp

The cider farm at Dowlish Wake

The drang way leading to Queen
Camel church

Church Path House (with dovecote) and the church at West
Camel

Grace Martin's Lane, Queen Camel

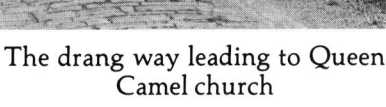

The rectory at Compton Pauncefoot

North Cadbury Court

and webbing. The sails for Nelson's *Victory* were spun here but nowadays synthetic sailcloth, shirts and gloves are the main specialization, augmented by agriculture and dairying.

Over the railway bridge south of the town, Misterton invites a brief inspection. Almost a suburb of Crewkerne nowadays, it grew up at the bridging-point of a combe, spreading up the slopes on either side. It is hardly a village that has been placed under a glass jar, for the A30 blusters fumily through, passing both the incongruously recent and the renovated antique. The novelist Helen Mathers was born at the mullioned Court House in 1853. Her most famous book *Coming Through the Rye*, an adhesive blend of saccharine and narrative skill, went through sixty editions. Although the rye fields in which the lovers gambolled are no more, there are still 'hilly green fields, silvered with daisies' and the house retains its flagstone passages and Decorated window which came from the resurrected St Leonard's Church (1840). The water-colour artist Knighton Hammond lived at the Court House when he turned his skills from the Continent to the rural life of Somerset and Dorset. On the outskirts of the village is Young's, an old-established factory specializing in hunting and trapping devices. The Hong Kong police buy traps from Young's for catching wildcats, and maybe that famous gamekeeper Mellors used them for ensnaring poor defenceless titled creatures.

At Haselbury Plucknett, conveniently situated between Yeovil and nearby Crewkerne, there has been a marked population increase since the last war; estate development, however, has been restrained. Essentially a most inviting village, amply endowed with old clothiers' cottages and several structures of outstanding merit, especially the fine medieval bridge with pointed ribbed arches, Haselbury is often dubbed 'Wulfric's village' after an anchorite who lived here in the twelfth century. Wulfric was born around 1080 at Compton Martin and was much addicted to hawking, hunting and other manly sports. A chance conversation with a beggar is said to have converted him, and he became an ascetic hermit of the same mould as Simeon Stylites, who punished the body in order to pamper the spirit. He ministered at Compton until 1125, when he settled at

Haselbury in a cell on the north side of the church. His regime was stern, necessitating the wearing of chain mail, frequent immersion in cold water and rigorous fasting. He is said to have hailed Stephen as king before the event materialized (compare witches' scene in *Macbeth*), and the knight Drogo de Munci was cured of paralysis by his ministrations. After his death in 1154 many miracles were reported from Haselbury, and his cell became a place of pilgrimage. Leland mentioned his tomb, and John Gerard (1633) stated that his cell was still standing and his memory alive. The church has been modernized and the arcades were removed in 1920; not a trace of Wulfric's tomb survives.

Hinton St George lies on relatively high ground, as its name ('hean-tun', 'high settlement') suggests. Only two miles west of Merriot, overlooking the Fosse Way and covering an area of nearly 1,600 acres, the village has an unbroken agricultural tradition. The former lords and masters of this village were the Pouletts, whose begetters are said to have come over from France at the time of the Plantagenets and to have taken the name from the manor of Pawlett near Bridgwater. The family stayed at Hinton for 500 years, exerting a seigneurial yet essentially benign dominance, until 1968, when the eighth and last earl sold Hinton House. Their influence on and control of village life were profound. In the late eighteenth century, when the fourth earl was carrying out extensive alterations to his property, the village street was diverted so that a new hot-house could be laid in the garden and traffic noise be kept to the minimum. The village then was almost a semi-feudal entity, the inhabitants finding work running the great estate farms or as domestic or garden staff in the manor house, a picture markedly contrasting with today, when the inhabitants commute or are among the wealthily retired.

Hinton is close-set and concentrated, a classic open-field type with farms lining the main street with plots on the north side running up to the escarpment and on the south side bounded by a back lane. The predominant impression is one of rural calm and pride in appearance. Here is a medley of golden thatch, deep-tanned Hamstone and shrubby, high-banked gardens of artless appeal. Interesting buildings

include Tetts Farm, Manor Farm, the seventeenth-century
post office, Old Farm with its Devonian-style chimney, and
the decorative medieval cross with the figure of John the
Baptist on the shaft. There is a lock-up occupying part of the
old green but now privately owned; also the malthouse, a
sixteenth-century structure improved by John Draper,
maltster, in 1798; and the Poulett Arms with the sign of the
naked wild man and woman crowned by oak-leaf garlands –
a markedly barbaric family crest – and a fives wall around the
back.

Hinton House, former seat of the Pouletts, is now split up
into various compartments. Leland evoked it in the 1540s:
'Heere hath Sir Hugh Poulet a right goodly manor place of
fre stone, with two goodly high tourres embatelid in the
ynner court.' Jeffrey Wyatville added the Gothic porch
(1814), but despite such cosmetic additions, the embattled
regularity of the layout, together with the lower rectangular
windows and neat square upper ones, recalls the Georgian
period. Only the south front, with its pierced parapet and
triangular window pediments, evokes earlier days.

St George's is a Perpendicular building of Hamstone. The
tower has been dated 1492 and is four-storeyed with
set-back buttresses tipped by pinnacles. A gilded
weathercock crowns it, over three feet high, made by
Thomas Bayley of Bridgwater in 1756. The interior is dense
with monuments to the Pouletts. There is something slightly
macabre about all the carved alabaster sealed behind glass
partitions, radiating a salt-like glow in the dim light. Here is
a plenitude of carved cadavers enclosed by classical columns,
attended by angels, cherubs and kneeling children – all the
fancy dress of aristocratic extinction.

Against the west wall is a monument to the second Sir
Amias Poulett (d. 1588), who was appointed keeper of the
Mary, Queen of Scots, at Tutbury. His behaviour once
invoked the wrath of Queen Elizabeth, who called him 'a
dainty and precise fellow, who would promise much, but
perform nothing'. This statement was no slur on his virility
but an allusion to his disinclination to murder the Catholic
Queen.

There is a somewhat florid monument to John, Baron

Poulett (d. 1649), an almost ludicrously ornate painted plaster affair. It has as its centrepiece a winged figure standing on skulls and embellished by fruits, flowers, preposterous mannikins, the family arms (three swords in pile) and a wild man and wild woman at the base. This simply implies the soul transcending death, symbolized by the skulls, and rising on wings to immortality. John Poulett was a fervent Royalist, in many ways an intemperate and self-seeking man, who was heavily fined for his allegiance after the triumph of Cromwell's army. The fact that he was the brother-in-law of the immensely effective Parliamentarian commander General Fairfax might have proven a mitigating circumstance.

Subsequent members of the Poulett family led distinguished lives as justices of the peace, energetic sportsmen and local benefactors but never quite achieved the political impact of their predecessors. The eighth and last Earl Poulett (b. 1909) took up mechanical engineering and served an apprenticeship at the Great Western Railway workshops in Swindon. During the war years, in 1942, he sold off 3,000 acres of the estate, relinquishing forever control over tenants and farmers, and also his status as squire. In July 1968 he sold the estate at Hinton and moved to Jersey where three of his ancestors had been governors and where he died in 1973, without an heir.

East of Hinton, at Dinnington, the Fosse Way enters a cutting by a wooded combe, and there is a neat Victorian church (mainly 1863) dedicated to St Nicholas. But the principal village here, apart from Hinton, is Dowlish Wake, also called East Dowlish, which is named after the brook flowing through the settlement and the Wake family who held the manor after the Conquest.

Set astride a valley, where Wall Brook, Stretton Water and other tiny streams congregate, it is a place of shorn lawns, fords and footbridges. Thatched cottages lazily stand back from the curving main street, their gardens bright as painted glass, and women in jodhpurs provide confident directions to motorists who have been led astray by the worming, turning lanes. It is idyllic and unspoilt, the single touristic feature being Perry's cider mill, an old thatched farm building selling stone cider jars, country-style cooking-pottery and basketware. There are also corn dollies for anyone desiring a dash of rustic fecundity. The cider sold at Perry's is excellent: large quantities of it render the world an infinitely more sympathetic (if slightly less distinct) place.

The concentration of farms, cottages and recent bungalows is found by the cider-mill, on the south side of the main brook, but to the north are the church, manor and Victorian Parke House, 'the road running a tortuous course in a sandy hollow way' to avoid the manor grounds. The church is imposingly situated above a steep-backed lane with a railed path leading to it. It has a table tomb of an armoured knight and his wife, thought to be John Speke (d. 1442). He married a descendant of Joan Wake who was burned at the stake for murdering her husband. The most imposing monument is a rather cumbersome Victorian gesture honouring John Hanning Speke, the explorer who discovered the source of the Nile and accidentally shot himself in 1864. His sternly handsome features, rendered in white marble, preside over a gleaming serpentine tomb. But the portrait bust is spoilt by a monstrous floral garland entwining it like a deadly python.

To the south of Dowlish the gradient increases as it mounts the windswept, hilly downland where many small streams feeding the Isle have their source. It is a country of expansive views, large farms maintaining big herds of Friesians and pasturing sheep. The A30 Chard-Crewkerne road looping over the spine of the summits, passes the popular Cricket St Thomas Wildlife Park, opened in 1976. It is a surreal experience to wander around and see crested porcupines, wapiti and llamas sampling the English countryside. Some criticize the development as a flagrant breach of the exclusiveness of this tranquil spot; others see it as a healthy democratizing venture. 'Cricket' derives from the Celtic 'cruc', 'a little hill', and the area was owned by Syrewold the Saxon at the Conquest. Later owners have lent it the tang of tar and salt: Sir Amyas Preston captured the Admiral of the Galeasses of the Spanish Armada and then, in 1595, raided the West Indies, entering the Spanish-held Jamaica and emerging 'with little loss, some profit and more honour'. In 1757 Cricket House was bought by Alexander Hood RN, becoming his family seat until 1897, when it was sold to Mr Fry of Bristol.

Cricket House is the work of Sir John Soane. It was completed in 1804 and is a restrained Georgian building of Hamstone with a classical colonnade at the front and a balustraded garden wall. The church of St Thomas replaced an earlier building that was favoured by couples who wished to marry surreptitiously. It was erected by the second Baron Bridport (Captain Samuel Hood RN, who served under Lord Nelson at the Battle of the Nile, 1798) and contains memorials to his family. In the graveyard is a white angel clasping a sword, which was originally set upright but subsequently laid out corpse-wise because it 'frightened servants and strangers on dark winter evenings'. The interior contains a wooden font carved by Rosa Hood from Sicilian chestnut and the White Ensign flown by the battleship HMS *Nelson*.

Occupying the same golden, hilly country but situated south of the Yeovil basin, the Coker villages, once famous for twine, sailcloth and glove-making, are a powerful magnet to those interested in both architecture and art. There are fine Tudor houses and dignifying literary associations to boot. North Coker is traversed by the A30, which has a drastically de-ruralizing effect but there are many warm, appealing Hamstone dwellings with windowbox geraniums and an exquisite manor house (1455) which belonged to the Earls of Devon.

East Coker, which lies to the south-west of Barwick, should not be missed because it corresponds so exactly to many peoples' idea of a dream village. Here there is a profusion of things to see and admire, from the rows of almshouses (1640) with green doors, iron railings, dormers and mullions, to the idyllic succession of amber-stoned cottages with names like Silverweed, Laburnum, Bay and seventeenth-century Bubspool House. Coker Court, too, with its line of clipped yews and its big bay-window consolidated by diagonal buttresses, is an incredibly stately and impressive fifteenth-century building with later effects. Even the pub, the Helyar Arms, despite its classical entrance, is a fabric originally built in 1491. The long, curving road into the village ambles gracefully past all these and skirts the proud eminence on which the church reclines; a floodlight is mounted outside for winter evenings.

There is an atmosphere about East Coker – congenial to some, claustrophobic to others – of rural sedation, particularly in summer, when the droning of bees mingles with the self-satisfied clickings of well-oiled motor mowers and all seems right with the world. T.S. Eliot, the Anglo-American poet, came here to retire and lies in the lofty dark-gold St Michael's Church next to the wimpled and footless effigy of Lady Elizabeth Courtenay (d. 1375). Perhaps it was entirely in keeping that a poet, who, more than any other with the possible exception of Yeats, had deplored the rootlessness of twentieth-century man, should spend his last years here, in the village of his forefathers, where old cottages doze contentedly and wistaria falls in thick cascades over lintel and doorway: a perfect rural rebuke to those distracting, destructive images – of reeling bells in broken towers, of scorched plains and twisted lilac stalks, of eyes twisting like crooked pins – that make his work so uniquely arresting.

Visitors to Coker are often charmed by the sight of Hymerford House with its traceried windows, thatched hall, kitchen range and Gothic porch. William Dampier was born here in 1652 – 'buccaneer, explorer and hydrographer', as the brass in the church puts it. He fought in the Dutch wars, served as a lumberjack, took up coasting, plundered the shores of Peru, got marooned on Ascension Island, wrote a nautical classic, explored parts of Australia (which he found bleak and forbidding, inhabited by savages and terrifying kangaroos) and died in 1715 in unknown circumstances.

East of the Coker villages, on the Dorchester road, Barwick (pronounced Barrick) now qualifies as a dormitory for Yeovil. The centre has a number of tiled cottages, all heavily renovated with lucky horseshoes above the entrance and twee gabled porches. The effect of the square is not displeasing, just banal, with shops and garages beckoning prominently rather than hiding discreetly. Commuter life is

astir in the number of cars passing in and out and through;
estates spread out and around, creating a suburban feel,
which is left behind on attaining the church. The latter is set
about a mile away from the main concentration of houses, in
the zone of yellow sandstone known as the Yeovil sands.
This is an exhilarating miniature geological region where the
roads have carved deep gorges through the soft rock,
reaching a height of over twenty feet in places and making
the journey to St Mary's, Barwick, an exciting dash among
plunging green-shaded lanes, with precipitous coppery-gold
rock walls on either side.

St Mary's is an attractive church, banked above a narrow
lane in the older core of Barwick. Its lines are very bare and
simple and do not harmonize. There is a plain square tower
with narrow two-light windows, a segment of crenellated
parapet on the north side and some competent quatrefoil
window tracery. But the best effect is simply the biscuit,
oatmeal and gold of the ancient stonework.

An exciting feature of this area is the park of Barwick
House, which contains several famous follies. The house
was built around 1830 in a style which has been called
French Renaissance but is noteworthy for clockfaces, curved
pediments and a palatial plethora of windows. It is now a
reformatory for young offenders, a pleasant place to equate
and balance things out amid rolling farmland and an
ornamental lake of some charm. The Messiter family, noted
glove-makers, built the house and landscaped the park
(during a period of financial depression) with four
extraordinary structures: an arch and tower crowned with a
statue of Mercury known as 'Jack the Treacle-Eater'; a
cylindrical obelisk with a fish weathervane; a solitary cone
slatted with holes and serving the purpose of a dovecote; and
a needle-pointed obelisk with a bend on top. There is also,
by repute, a hideous grotto somewhere in the vicinity of the
lake. It has an air of cold, slithering horror and is jammed
with floating logs that recall dead alligators – see Barbara
Jones's *Follies and Grottoes* for an enthralling account.

The Romans did not neglect Somerset. The Fosse Way,
the most typical of their roads, runs through the county,
crossing the Mendips at Shepton and joining Bath and

Ilchester. East of Ham Hill it forms a fine diagonal stripe
cutting across traditional routes linking Merriot and Petherton, Tintinhull and Ash, Stoke-sub-Hamdon and Martock.
The last-named place, Martock, is highly pertinent to this
fertile region. A growing settlement embracing the hamlets of
Hurst and Bower Hinton to the south, and Highway and Coat
to the north, the plan of the village is polyfocal, with blocks
and squares of development encasing the north-south route
of the B3165 which forms the main street. Traversing this
road, one sees on the outskirts a notice asking the visitor to
drive slowly through the village.

'Village' is dubiously applicable: Martock is nearer a town
than the biggest village in England as it claims. There are
rather too many service industries, banks, bakers and solici-
tors' offices, plus a fine modern library and supermarket. The
atmosphere in the centre has a pace and intentness that smack
of a town; only in freezing winter when the streets are
deserted, or during a World Cup final, does it relapse into a
village once more. There is much new building on the outskirts. Hamstone can no longer be quarried; a cheese-yellow
artificial stone is the local substitute, which is an atmospheric
concession of sorts, though it bears about the same rela-
tionship to the original material as pink seaside rock to
rose-coloured granite. For Hamstone is the cornerstone of old
Martock. All the buildings around the centre are mellow
yellow, tawny gold or a shade of tanned leather. Wandering
down its streets in streaming sunshine is like wandering
through a solidified cornfield. Yellow and gold are the light of
Apollo, and Martock should have produced poets but succeeded only in nurturing rich farmers. Agricultural prosperity fostered its architectural elegance. 'Take a Martock
man by the collar and shake him,' wrote Daniel Defoe, 'and
beans will rattle in his belly.' Earlier Thomas Gerard had
observed that Martock was situated 'in the fattest place on
earth of this county, especially for arable, which makes the
inhabitants so fat in their purses'. But Martock trade has not
been wholly based on agriculture. Industries have come and
gone: glove-making, canvas-making and cloth-making consolidated its wealth, and today it is energetic in the production
of pre-fabricated wooden buildings and tents.

Situated in rich, oozy country, on a hillside above the meandering Parrett and bordering on Martock, South Petherton is more than a village but perhaps less than a town. A bustling, lively centre, with many shops retaining Edwardian frontages, the basis of the community has always been agriculture, variegated by intensive flax-growing in the nineteenth century and glove-making, which was a profitable cottage industry and still continues in a small factory at Watergore.

South Petherton is bypassed by the main road and retains some of its traditional seclusion. Even the old road from Ilchester evaded the settlement by branching off the present A303 at Watergore, following Moon Lane to Frogmary Green, then passing the Traveller's Rest Inn (no longer extant) and on to Ilford Bridges.

The quiet South Petherton, 'the *tun* by the Parrett', was an important place in Saxon times, being the site of a royal palace and a mission centre. The nucleus of the village is found in the vicinity of Crown Lane, Jubilee Terrace, Palmer Street and St James Street. The Blake Memorial Hall (1911), an arched Georgian-style building of Hamstone, marks the meeting of ways and recalls civic edifices at Martock and Milborne Port. The main thoroughfare is narrow and shadowy, but not oppressively so, and dominated by the looming octagonal tower of the church. Many of the businesses around the centre strike a joyfully individual note. Wynn's Stores are painted canary yellow. Little Thatch is suitably petite, selling women's clothes. Global Village, a unique local phenomenon, trades in anything ethnic from the colourful baskets of Upper Volta to tiny enamel badges painted with Chinese cloud-dragons and mystic Yin and Yang symbols.

An interesting building, thought to have been used as the rectory house, stands at the corner of St James Street. Formerly called Holbrook Place or King Ina's Palace, in remembrance of the Saxon foundation at South Petherton, this is the old manor of the Daubeney family, a fifteenth-century building with an elaborate traceried two-storey bay window. Giles Daubeney (d. 1445) is commemorated in the church by a brass portrait in full armour with his first wife and his pet dog. The image of Sir Philip Daubeney (d. 1294) was dug out of the roadside nearly fifty years ago while a pit for a petrol tank was being dug. The church is also associated with the Methodist preacher Thomas Coke, who was curate here and whose radical preaching culminated in his being drummed out of the town by an angry mob.

On a slight elevation, some two miles west of South Petherton, at the source of the tiny Lambrook stream, Shepton Beauchamp is one of those several under-praised Somerset villages that will become increasingly important as the years go by. Predominantly agricultural from early times – although bricks and tiles were made on the north-eastern border in the nineteenth century – it has retained its basic character, being attractive yet with few self-conscious cosmetic touches. There are some thatched dwellings where the straw registers gradations in colour from a kind of stained charcoal to beige and pale gold; the homely fringes overlap the eaves, creating the most enchanting effect. The main street rambles in and out, going through a succession of different names: Lambrook Road, North Street, Church Street, Sheepway and Silver Street. Near the centre stands the village pump, set neatly in a stone recess, and the Duke of York Inn, dating from 1754. The New Inn, at the corner of Buttle Lane and Church Street, closed in 1960 and has around its back an old fives court with a curved parapet and ball finials. Most of the older houses are nineteenth century and built of stone with tiled roofs. Beauchamp Manor, the former rectory, was the spiritual HQ from which V.S.S. Coles (rector, 1872–84) instilled the Tractarian code. His magnetic personality put fresh vigour and confidence into the community during the late nineteenth-century agricultural depression when Shepton lost many of its workers to the colonies and the mines of South Wales.

Formerly the village had a reputation for rural uproariousness. An 'Old Shepton Play' used to be performed on the second Monday and Tuesday after Easter (at 'Hocktide'), and cider flowed freely down gutters and gullets. Cecil Sharp, the composer, recorded the folksongs 'Midsummer Fair' and 'Tarry Trousers' from two local nightingales.

The traffic that streams through Shepton Beauchamp often does not deign to stop until it reaches the prettier, more self-satisfied village of Barrington. The rambling main street has a captivatingly unregimented appearance. Here are thatched cottages built of random rubble, golden-gabled farmsteads, converted barns, art studios, the Royal Oak Inn and St Mary's Church banked above the road. In summer there is an air of expectation about Barrington. Local businesses are poised for the appearance of crowds and road-choking charabancs heading for the Court and gardens. The great house is certainly the tourist honeypot but there are other admirable medieval structures, notably Knapp House, Vinces and the Priory, providing a stark contrast to the humble, squat cottages in Water Street and Copse Shoot.

Barrington House (National Trust) rewards a visit, presenting a splendid fanfare of Elizabethan gables, twisty chimneys and enough mullions, transoms and lights to reduce an apprentice window-cleaner to a state of permanent whimpering dementia. It has a flavour of the Renaissance in several of its details and can be regarded as a precursor of the intensely elaborate Montacute House. Henry Daubeney, first Earl of Bridgwater, 'the most extravagant nobleman of an extravagant age', was responsible for its present appearance; he died in 1548 after spending large sums in self-advancement that did not really pay off. Major restoration was undertaken by Colonel A.A. Lyle in 1920, when salvaged bits of other noble mansions were worked into the decor with tact and discretion. ·

The Barrington Friendly Society was founded in 1807 and dissolved in 1945. It had a brass band and a feast day, originally on the last Tuesday in May, and anthologies of old Somerset photographs occasionally feature participants in this celebration lying flat on their back in fields and ditches in varying modes of alcoholic prostration.

Langport is ingeniously sited at a bridging point of the Parrett, on a thin neck of elevated land, where the upland areas of Aller and the Ham villages protrude to form an irregular bulge skirted by the meandering river. For Langport's history is the Parrett, and the main street, Bow

Street, rests on a causeway built by the Romans. The town had a mint in the tenth century, yet it was still a comparatively minor parish, a fragment of the larger and more important Huish Episcopi. Langport's church was merely a chapel of Huish, and although they were only, as it was said in 1548, 'a bird-bolt shot apart', there was rivalry in their opposing claims. Nowadays of course the tables are turned: Langport's rapid growth has expanded beyond its ancient boundaries and overwhelmed the sister parish. Huish is now a parish dominated by its proximity to Langport. Very little of the rude farming community remains except odd bits such as Pound Cottage, Wearne House and the rubble-and-thatch Cornerways. Otherwise estates strike the visitor's eye from every angle. The local authority erected houses in the 'Garden City' between 1918 and 1929. After the Second World War building intensified and extensive private developments are found north of the church. Huish is noted for its famous nurseries; Kelways is renowned for gladioli and peonies and has a gaudy, swaggering entrance, suggesting the gateway to a floral Disneyland.

No visit to Huish is satisfactory without sampling the hospitality of Ely's or the Rose and Crown, a seventeenth-century stone thatched pub with neat Gothic windows, suggesting it may have been a gatehouse. The sign is striking, for the rose stands out in garish relief, forged by a student of Bristol University for his project. Once it was part of the estate of Lord Devonshire but it was bought up by the Scott and Slade families, owners since 1868; Ely is the name of a former landlord. Huge stone slabs make the interior floors, and the decor is entirely original, like an old farmhouse.

The church of St Mary's can be seen from Ely's, its grey and gold tower, fine stone filigree work, rising up like the finger of God. The south door has Norman work, zigzag and nailhead motifs and was reddened by a fire which destroyed the building 600 years ago. There is a fine Burne Jones design in the east window of the south chapel; it shows kings, shepherds and angels with red wings paying their respects in the Bethlehem stable.

South of Huish, among the flatlands and meadows of the Ivel and Parrett, Muchelney stands out like a beacon. The ravaged stone ribs of the medieval abbey rear majestically above the loamy fields. The surroundings are fruitful and green, and yet, unlike northern Sedgemoor, there is a yellow tinge which flecks the soil, lightens the green, blossoms in the ancient ruptured walling and stonework. 'Muchelney' means 'the Great Island', recalling the period when the whole neighbourhood was marshland excepting one or two gentle outliers. Even today many dried-out fields are only twenty-five feet above sea-level, and it was usual for Muchelney to be cut off for many days during the winter months until the present pumping-stations were established. In the past this caused grave problems with the supply of fresh water. The priory and convent of Bath in 1243 offered a share in the seven Masses said daily in the church for benefactors, alive or dead, to anyone prepared to take fresh spring water to Muchelney.

The Benedictine abbey is older than the church and may have been founded by King Ine of Wessex (d. 726). This claim is set down in charters forged by monks. Archaeologists in the 1950s unearthed a crypt probably built in the eighth century, thus squaring falsehood and fact. So it is a very old abbey, although predominantly fifteenth and sixteenth century in what remains today. The abbot's house, fragments of fresco work, the cloisters with fan-vaulting, and the stone lions crouching on twelve-foot pillars amount to a series of most remarkable relics. The last abbot, Thomas Ive, hailed from Ilminster and was described the King's commissioner, Thomas Legh, as being 'negligent and of doubtful character' – this was on 3 January 1538, at the time of the Dissolution; Legh further remarked that the other monks were 'ignorant and unlernyd and in the manor no servauntes maynteyned or hospitalitie kept'. These comments raised the Catholic ire of crusty Edward Hutton (1910) who observed: 'It never seems to have occurred to Thomas Legh that if the brethren were "ignorant and unlernyd" so was Christ their Master, and that if they "maynteynd no servauntes," neither did He.'

The parish church is also noteworthy, not only for its tower – one of the Somerset towers, bearing the arms and badge of the Daubeney family of South Petherton – but for its ceiling, which is 'most uninhibitedly painted, with the colourful buxom angels wearing Tudor-style costume'. It is very exuberant and naïve, with a backcloth of sun, stars and coiled clouds. Certain angels appear to be spilling out of their bodices, and for once aesthetic reverence gives way to a smile. The sanctuary tiles are worth looking at; they were dug up in the orchard covering the remains of the abbey in 1872 by farm workers. First they came across a coffin lid (now lying west of the font) below which was a tiled pavement. The tiles belonged to the Lady Chapel of the abbey and date from the thirteenth century: designs feature a knight on horseback, an elephant and castle, a double-headed eagle, the arms of the abbey and the arms of the Montacutes.

Aside from the church and abbey, there is the village centre. 'It stands compact and perfect,' wrote W.B. Mais (1938), 'a tiny hamlet at a corner of the road with a little toll gate, a farm with hayricks, the superb little Priest's House, the old church among the yews, and the great abbey now so carefully restored by the Ministry of Works.' This holds true today. The priest's house (1308) is an almost unique fabric with a fine old wrought-iron door-handle simulating interlacing serpents, Perpendicular windows and a bold Hamstone fireplace. This was the former vicarage and is now the property of the National Trust.

Long Sutton is a nucleated village east of Muchelney which grew up around a central green at a convergence of routes: the Somerton-Martock road crossing the Yeo at Load Bridge, which was turnpiked in 1760–1 by the Martock Trust, and the Ilchester-Langport road which may be traced along traditional footpaths and lanes. The impression the place creates is agreeable. It has a bold, bluff, stand-offish air, with most of its citizens involved in the trivial tasks of gardening or shopping or gazing vacantly at sunny blue patches in the sky. In the centre is the big green overlooked by the stolidly Victorian Duke of Devonshire Inn. The manor house has mullioned windows concealed by hedging, and a stern façade blending grey and dark bronze stones. Over all this the very regal church tower presides, ninety-six feet three inches high, with fine Somerset tracery and the date 1622 on the belfry window – referring to the year it was repaired. The coloured wooden pulpit (1455–8) is the most ornate interior furnishing, bearing the initials of John Petherton, Abbot of Athelney. It is a static piece of work with traceried niches enclosing the figures of the apostles, prissily intricate but skilfully managed. The roof of angels and gold stars echoes the motifs of Evercreech and elsewhere but is less startling. A long Quaker tradition is associated with Long Sutton; the Friends' Meeting-House (1717) is restrained with a curved, pedimented doorway and mounting-block for horsemen set just beyond the wedge-shaped gateposts.

Some three miles south of Muchelney, bounded by the Parrett to the east, yet another Hamstone village is found in the form of Kingsbury Episcopi. It is long, straggling, incorporating several hamlets, such as Thorney, Stembridge and Burrow, and situated on a gentle eminence which supports numerous orchards. Commuting to the offices and light industries of Martock, Somerton and Langport has supplanted the ancient agricultural rhythm, but the village is lovingly tended. A Hamstone lock-up sits on a tiny green island near the centre, braceleted with flowers.

The church is set away from the main street down an attractive lane amid clustering cottages. The 120-foot tower soars above the fields and meadows, a glorious fountain of golden stone; one of the niches depicts the martyrdom of St Martin. Coming back from the church, it is worth calling at the Wyndham Arms, set by the T-junction, named after the lords of the manor who lived at Williton, a historically ubiquitous family, related to four of Henry VIII's queens – Jane Seymour, Catherine Howard, Anne Boleyn and Catherine Parr. Francis Wyndham helped Charles II escape after the Battle of Worcester, 17 September 1651: he sheltered the Prince and tried to get him to France. Sir William Wyndham was equally headstrong: he supported the Old Pretender and plotted to unseat the King. When the conspiracy was discovered, he escaped to Williton, where he was found. Asking to say goodbye to his wife, he jumped from an upstairs window to a waiting horse and fled to friends at Blackdown. There he disguised himself as a clergyman and escaped to France. Eventually, after he returned and gave himself up, he was kept in the Tower for six months, then pardoned.

Visible around these parts is Burrow Hill, rising 255 feet and sprouting a single tree on its crest. The view from the top embraces the nearby Lambrooks, East and West, tiny hamlets of modest interest. The Old Manor (1584) at East Lambrook is an attraction, not merely on account of its oak panelling, but because of its semi-wild garden created by Margery Fish and her husband.

A pub at Kingsbury was called the Willow Cutters Arms, this part of Sedgemoor being the centre of basket-making, a craft that once employed thousands of workers, but now there are under a hundred left. Locally grown willows or osiers are cut each spring and processed during the summer – stripped or boiled and stained by their own tannin. Although the various types of rod have names redolent of a certain cruel finesse – Black Spaniard, Long Skein, Blue Violet and Champion Rod – they usually end up as innocent domestic utensils such as shopping baskets or log containers.

15
Cadbury and Caryland

There is a stretch of country east of Ilchester and north-west of Yeovil, watered by the Yeo River, geologically distinctive from the Cadbury area, which is knobbly, well-wooded and underlain by oolite. This other region is scenically undramatic, rich in meadowland and dairy farms and embraces such parishes as Queen Camel, West Camel, Mudford and Marston Magna. The predominant building-material is grey and blue lias, and thatched houses made of uncoursed blocks are fairly common.

The chief village in this region is Queen Camel. The A359 strides through with its telephone wires, distracting slightly from the congenial atmosphere produced by so many neat gardens and well-tended homes. Approached from the south, the road hooks round by a capacious, tiled barn – an admirably professional piece of conversion. The stonework stands out clean and coursed: dormer gables and square neat Georgian windows combine harmoniously. On reaching the Bell Inn, one is affected by the quantity of thatched grey-stone houses, all immaculately upkept, with glinting casements and twining roses outside. Grace Martin's Lane is an example, and the old cobbled drangway leading to the church is a bonus. Near the centre is an Arthurian pub called Camelot, but the Mildmay Arms is more important. The Mildmays were the lords and benefactors of Queen Camel, and their traditional seat was Hazelgrove House – a mock-Veronese palace created in 1732 by John and William Bastard of Blandford. The Mildmays, many of whose tombs lie in the church, were political animals: Sir Hubert Mildmay remarked of Charles I, 'The King is no more to be trusted than a caged lion at liberty.'

A floodline mark on the exterior wall of St Barnabas's demonstrates that the Camel, after which the village is named, can burst its banks and cause problems. Little more than an animated ditch in dry weather, it inundated large areas of the parish in 1917 and 1979. But the trouble seems to have been exaggerated by subsidence, silting and rubbish dumped in the river. Other problems exclusive to the village are traffic in Gason Lane and a dilapidated telephone kiosk.

St Barnabas's Church is an arresting site. It rears up like a towering stone exclamation mark, and its set-back buttresses and pinnacles harmonize finely. Situated at the north end of the village, opposite the Victorian school (built in 1875 by the Mildmays on the site of the poorhouse), it has a soaring spacious interior. In the north aisle there is a grotesque boss of a man's vine-encircled face; this is the 'Green Man', the Celtic Pan, the god of woodland 'panic' – of coarse, vibrant, irrepressible instinct. A far more restrained figure is the stiff, stylized statue of St Barnabas on the west face of the tower, which was done in fibreglass by Charles Hopkins (1971). He is turning his face from sharp flying stones and is flanked by a hayrake, a medieval symbol arising from the fact that his feast day coincided with midsummer in the old calendar.

The other Camel village, West Camel, is grassy, charming and unpretentious. It has an ample, spacious feel, with its own friendly core around a big meadow with a bridge and stream. There is a bus shelter by the roadside and opposite the pretty thatched post office. Across the fields one can see the dainty metal spirelet of the village church, and close at hand is the rectory, a restrained stone building with traces of fifteenth-century work. Attached to it is a circular dovecote (flying doves was a manorial right; unfledged nestlings – squabs – were used in pies for the abbot's guests) and stone barn where the tithe was stored. A church school (now the church hall) was established here in 1818, and Bridge Cottage was built as a house for the schoolmistress in 1869. The local pub, the Globe, is not very old but serves a frisky pint. Essentially the atmosphere is one created by dairy farming: mud on the roads, straw and dung smells, and the soothing drone of working vehicles.

In 1938 the broadcaster S.P.B. Mais alluded to the 'most picturesque church standing above a duck pond by a farm with tall rectangular vertical stones for hedging'. Unfortunately the duckpond was drained some thirty years ago after a small boy nearly drowned in it, but the church is in good repair with its partly Norman tower and a spire added in 1631. There is a sculptured stone inside carved with dragons' faces and interlace work, vestiges of a Saxon cross.

Citizens of West Camel are celebrating the removal of the threat to their ancient packhorses bridge, which was in danger of being drastically altered but now has been agreeably improved by the Water Board. An odder monument is the obelisk on Steart Hill which was put up by a free-thinker, Henry Parsons, who wished to be buried there rather than in an ordinary churchyard – hearsay has it that he was afraid of the rats gnawing into his coffin. He was interned in 1794, and the steeple was adorned by an inscription:

And learn that virtue wheresoever found
In wood, in churches, consecrates the ground.

The Hornsey Brook separates the Camel parishes from Marston Magna to the south. The high, bare hill of Corton Ridge rises to the east, and to the west the Yeo meanders through its shallow valley towards Ilchester. The village presents a very civilized scene. There is a row of modern, artificial stone houses beside a small green and trickling brook, an old schoolhouse by a cottage with Gothic windows, a post office, a pub called the Marston, a church with Norman herringbone work, and attractive thatched dwellings such as Kingsland House. There is also an old mill and the remains of a moat backing the church which formerly guarded a vanished manor house. The present manor (1613) lies south-west of the church and is a Jacobean building with mullions and dripstones. When it was restored in the 1930s, a bullock's heart was found pierced with pins and needles – a charm against sickness in animals.

Geologists may be cognizant with Marston because of the pearly white ammonite stone called Marston Marble. When a seventy-foot well was sunk in the vicinity of the church in 1815, a nodular mass of it was found. The first block had been uncovered earlier in 1778 at the opening of a marl pit.

Walter Raymond, the popular Somerset novelist, was born at Yeovil in 1852 but spent his early childhood in Marston. His books charmed many readers. 'How can we criticize a bunch of honeysuckles?' asked the reviewer of *Tryphena in Love*. Inevitably his work has been compared with Hardy's but he lacked the impulsive narrative thrust and did not occupy the same brooding malevolent cosmos.

Cadbury country, between Castle Cary and Sherborne, is exciting to explore and traced with innumerable deep-hedged lanes. The traveller needs to keep a sharp eye for a puff of smoke against some trees or for the grey glint of a church spire or he is liable to miss what he seeks. Even the detailed Ordnance Survey maps do not prove infallible in this country where signposts start off with the best will in the world and then lose heart and forget about the route previously indicated. The best form of transport for the semi-fit is the motorbike, and for those with strong hearts and big lungs the bicycle.

Golden Hamstone is the most engaging feature of this region. Old thatched farmhouses, with sleepy fringes of combed wheat reed eyelashing their latticed windows, abound and the stonework glows like ripe, dark-gold wheat. In summer this richness of colour, set against a green hillside, the silver flash of rippling stream or the shell-pale sky alone, astounds and captivates the eye. Here is a surfeit of those rose-embowered vistas of rural charm. The Hamstone villages are an estate agent's paradise: for once his language, those wary, circumlocuting evasions, those slum-transcending verbal wands, are endorsed by matter of fact reality: cliché and truism are reconciled.

South Cadbury is not a classic Hamstone village: red-brick development has crept in here and there, and it lacks the rich scope of Montacute or Tintinhull. Despite the number of books and learned articles about it, it remains a quiet little place. The inn here is not called the Excali-bar – an atrocity perpetrated at Tintagel – but the Red

Lion, and it has the king of the jungle perched on the porch. There are some ordinary terraced houses and some Hamstone mullioned mansions, notably Castle Farm (1687), but it is all very unself-conscious. The churchyard is occupied by a tulip, a yew and a ginkgo tree. The dedication is to St Thomas of Canterbury (martyred 1170), and the earliest rector was Peter de Brug in 1265, when the cult of Becket was at its height. There is a painting of the martyr in a cope and mitre in the south aisle on the splay of a window. The stout western tower, with battlements, pinnacles and a stair turret, dates from the fourteenth century, and the arcade is part of the Early English building (c. 1280). Opposite the church is the eighteenth-century rectory, and to the left, capped by a belfry, is a converted schoolhouse. Then there are thatched Hamstone cottages, with ever-attendant cock pheasants on the roofs, but little else in this quiet, contained community, still strongly agricultural, yet with a quota of retired people and commuters.

These features are but a minor prelude to the great Iron Age fort, Cadbury Castle, which Leland (1548) described as 'wonderfully enstrengthened of nature ... gold, silver and coper of the Romaine coynes hath been found ... people can tell nothing ther but that they have heard say that Arture much resorted to Camalat ...'. To climb the fort, one goes up Castle Lane which lies to the right of the road heading south. It is a stony, slippery path, littered with cowpats, and ends by a kissing-gate. Then the track broadens as one attains the dome-like summit. The much-vaunted fortress is shaped like a trapezium and has a powerful atmosphere, green, silent and faintly tense. By comparison the Tor at Glastonbury seems grimy and much trampled but this ancient strategic site, occupied from neolithic to Saxon times, is a genuine stronghold of tranquillity. The hills to the east and south display graceful, feminine contours. On the slopes of Pen Hill there is a group of trees thinly sprinkling the summit known as King Arthur's Men. The great leader is everywhere around these parts. Springs issue forth bearing his name; sunken lanes record his footsteps, old packhorse bridges his places of battle. Arthur's historical insubstantiality has immortalized him.

A stream, which, after performing a series of unpredictable meanders, finally joins the Cam near Queen Camel, marks the division of the parish of South Cadbury from its northern neighbour, Sutton Montis. An attractive hamlet, strung out along a narrow road, Sutton is unmarked by the gaudier aspects of progress: only a post office stores, selling grocery and tobacco, but no central pub, although this is a good place for genuine farmhouse cider. One hears all sorts of creative tales about what goes in to contribute to the tangy, full-bodied flavour, including 'rats in the vats', but everyone must eat a peck of earth before they die, so why discriminate against a fermented rodent?

Abbey House, to the west of the church, is an early Tudor building with a Perpendicular window, a buttressed gable-end and an orchard with a stone-enclosed well fed by a spring. This is a place of legend. On Christmas Eve, Arthur and his men pass this way, veering from the old track called Arthur's Hunting Path to drink at the well. A true-hearted person who bathes his eyes in the sacred water may see the hill become transparent like glass, and Arthur and his band asleep inside. A visiting antiquary in 1902, intrigued by all this knightly lore, was mildly surprised when an old man asked him, 'Have you come to take Arthur away?'

Ruggedly prepossessing, the hilltop church of Sutton sits squatly on its haunches. The graveyard in summer is a petite carnival of daisies, buttercups and speedwells, and the charming classical entrance porch is an unexpected feature. One of the bells is inscribed with a prayer to Margaret, the patron saint of the Mont-Acuto family, after whom Sutton Montis and of course Montacute are named.

North Cadbury is another beautiful village. Even certain of its houses (such as Lovely Cottage) bear titles that are faintly self-congratulatory. The main street is an idler's dream of delicate yellow stone and restful thatch. This is an ideal retreat for a pensive pipe-smoking country-lover or an earnest brass-rubbing cyclist.

The best approach is across the fields and droves from Compton Pauncefoot. Taking that walker's route, one crosses a stream, skirts orchards and rhynes and eventually confronts the swaggering pile of the Elizabethan court built by Sir Francis Hastings (d. 1600). Looming and lofty-gabled, it complements the adjoining church built by Lady Elizabeth Botreaux in 1417. Cadbury was one of the numerous manors held by her husband, Sir William, first Baron Botreaux, until his death in 1391. Inside the church is a tomb bearing an effigy of William with his feet resting upon a lion, symbol of bravery, and his head reclining on a basinet. Lady Elizabeth (d. 1433) lies next to him dressed in a kirtle and horned head-dress. At her feet, two little dogs, symbols of fidelity, maintain their frozen composure. A notable brass hangs inside commemorating Lady Magdalen (d. 1596), wife of Francis Hastings, consisting of ninety-six lines of tiny Roman lettering arranged in verses. The poem amounts to a devout and loving panegyric:

> This lady was well borne and eke well bred
> Here virgine tyme she spente with worthy praise
> When choise of freindes brought her to mariagbed
> With iust renowne she passed those her daies
> And though her youth were tyde to age farr spent
> Yet without spott she liv'd and was content
>
> Her second match shee made by her owne choice
> Pleasing her selfe whoe others pleas'd before
> Her cares shee stopte from all disswaders voice
> Whoe did her tender wealth & goods great store
> With honour greate wch both shee did refuse
> And one of meaner state her selfe did chuse.

The long poem was written by Sir Francis Hastings, a Puritan pamphleteer who was granted Cadbury Court in 1586 by his brother, third Earl of Huntingdon, who became Lady Magdalen's second husband. Under the influence of the Hastings family, North Cadbury became a stronghold of Puritanism, but the stringent self-denying aspect of that religion did not always find favour with the country folk. In 1634 the parson complained that on Midsummer Day morris dancers from Galhampton and district had interrupted the morning service. Accompanied by fiddlers and a drum, they had merrily frisked around the church, and the parson had

entreated them twice 'to leafe makeinge such a noyse' but
they were impervious to his requests.

A special feature of St Michael's are the sixteenth-century
carved bench ends. Executed with marvellous, delicate
assurance, they feature a flute-player, a windmill, a winged
griffin, a dolphin, two lindworms, a cat and mousetrap, and
a contorted face – an unusually varied and vigorous
selection.

North of the church and court, set around a rectangle of
roads, is the body of the village. In the main street is the post
office stores which strives to keep afloat, like many similar
concerns, by dealing in as great a variety of wares as limited
space will allow. Woolston Road travels north past a group
of somewhat raw-looking modern bungalows and Woodforde Cottage. The road can be followed round to the Catash
Inn, supposedly honouring John Catte, who mustered an
army to repel the Danes around 900. The alternative theory
derives it from 'cad', an armed encampment – a likelier if
duller explanation.

Compton Pauncefoot is one of those secluded spots lying
north-east of Cadbury Castle. It has a wonderful freshness.
Watching it unfold is like opening a brand new tin of
water-colour paints. Idyllically situated in a declivity called
Golden Valley (a breath of the cemetery about such
lusciously peaceful name – remember Evelyn Waugh's
'Whispering Glades'), the name is derived from the family
that held the manor after the Conquest; a branch of them
has been previously alluded to in connection with
Cossington. The hamlet is a veritable picture-poem framed
by knobbly green hills sumptuously wooded. Neat-gardened
and very slightly stand-offish (like many that take overmuch
pride in their appearance), the houses emit, to steal Monica
Hutchin's well-chosen phrase, 'a greeny-gold glow reminiscent of young oak leaves'. This is not at all accurate but
captures something of the spirit of the place. Hamstone has
mellowed here and softened: walls and façades are spotted
and sealed with rosettes of white and silver lichen.
Everything appears on the right scale as if the effect had
been exactly gauged, and the sharp-spired church provides
just the right dramatic touch in its sylvan setting. There is an

oak tree by a bench on a green, and in the meadow lumbering Friesians graze beneath shadowing chestnuts and sycamore.

A well-proportioned Georgian rectory, a stream feeding a duckpond, an augustly formal manor farm – these are one's immediate impressions. But there is yet more if one follows the twisting road above the hamlet and finds the picturesque castle, complete with angle turrets, bay windows and twisting lake fed by ornamental cascades. This was built by Mr Hussey Hunt in 1825 and is now owned by the Showering family. Not far from the main entrance are a crescent of five big workers' cottages with wooden porches and latticed windows. They have a kind of functional decorum and were originally estate workers' houses.

Compton is one of a group of eight rural parishes, legally established in 1976, which are served by a team of clergy and wardens meeting in the Group Council. They co-operate in a number of ways including group services, joint training, missionary and social activities and bring out a magazine entitled *Excalibur*. The other parishes are North Cadbury, South Cadbury, Yarlington, Holton, Blackford, North Cheriton and Maperton.

Maperton lies east of Compton in gently exciting hill country. It is named after the maples (vindication of the long 'a') which take well to the clayey soil underlain by fullers' earth and overlooks the A309 towards Higher Clapton Farm and Elliscombe Wood. In the twelfth century there was a castle on the high ground behind the church, probably an 'unlicensed' fortress built by supporters of Empress Matilda against King Stephen, subsequently demolished by Henry II when Stephen died. In the thirteenth century Maperton was the seat of Nicholas de Moels, right-hand man of Henry III, but since then its importance has dwindled. There are remains of a far larger medieval village to the east of the present settlement, which probably shrank during the agricultural depression. The church is situated a little above a handsome classical manor house with pilasters dating from the early eighteenth century. Dedicated to SS Peter and Paul, it was rebuilt by Henry Hall in 1869, excepting the tower and the Norman piscina in the chancel.

Holton has a Celtic Hamstone cross erected in 1921 on the base of the old parish cross, as a memorial to those who fell in the First World War. St Nicholas's Church was restored 1884–7 when the old oak roof, long concealed by plaster work, was opened and repaired and the remains of a stone pulpit were discovered.

The Cheritons, North and South, are villages with all the paraphernalia of rural desirability: salubrious settings, Hamstone cottages with flowers ablaze in the gardens, and within quick driving distance of Sherborne, Wincanton, Yeovil and Castle Cary. North Cheriton church occupies a hillside ledge beside a manor of bronzy-gold Hamstone. South Cheriton, sometimes called Horsington after the hamlet to the south, has an old preaching cross with skulls and bones carved on it – emphasizing the calcareous reducibility of man. There is a rectory here built in 1686 by the Wickham family who inaugurated a long line of rectors serving the parish for over 200 years. The church has been rebuilt but keeps its octagonal font and Perpendicular window foraged from the manor house of the Gawens. There is also a church house at Horsington dated 1611, erected not long before the Interregnum suppressed most of the fund-raising activities.

Blackford lies between Maperton and South Cadbury, a delicate, delightful hamlet with a brooklet flowing through. It has a miniature gem of a church, Hamstone barns and a beautiful spring known as the Nun's Well. St Michael is the patron of the church, which has a Norman doorway with zigzag carving and spiral fluting on the colonettes. The damaged figures of St Michael and Christ were found when the rood loft stairs were uncovered. St Michael is shown wearing scale armour with traces of gilding, and his left hand is placed on a shield with dabs of green and red paint. Probably the figures were once part of the reredos.

Sheltering under Jack White's Gibbet (a hill named after a notorious eighteenth-century murderer) Yarlington retains its air of sleepiness. The Berkeleys of Gloucestershire had a mansion by the church, and the moat is still visible. Yarlington House is brick-built Georgian, and St Mary's Church is pinnacled and contains a font with fourteenth-century carvings. In many ways Yarlington's situation is its chief point of interest, for it lies on the Hardway, a three-mile stretch of road extending from Alfred's Tower, Stourhead Gardens, to Redlynch crossroads between Bruton and Wincanton. The earliest traders used this path carrying a stock of flint implements, then later bronze and iron, and after them came medieval merchants with bales of cloth woven in the villages around Castle Cary. When wheeled vehicles became the fashion, the road would have rutted badly, becoming glutinous in winter when rain and dirt combined to form a boggy cocktail. Celia Fiennes (c. 1690) travelled this way on horseback: 'As we returned from thence we came to Bruton, a very neat stone built town, from it we ascended a very high steep hill all in a narrow lane cut of the rocks, and the way is all like stone steps; the sides are rocks on which grow trees thick, their roots run amongst the rocks, and in many places fine clear springs bubble out, and run a long way out of the rocks, it smells just like the sea, we were a full hour passing that hill, though with four horses and a chariot ...'

The Hardway was actually a small part of the Harrow Way, one of the three oldest roads in England, beginning on the Kent coast near Dover and joining the Dorset Ridgeway to end at the mouth of the Axe in Devon. During the winter months, rain, snow and ice made such roads impassable, cutting supplies sometimes for months and necessitating the stocking up of food. When spring came, it was time for housewives to replenish their larders – hence the plethora of fairs in what might now appear small, obscure places. Yarlington Fair was famous throughout Wessex for hundreds of years and was discontinued only in 1900. A late account (1882) tells of fat and lean cattle on sale and 'an unusual show of sheep'. A prize was won by 'Mr Shittler's pony, beating five others; and the purse of sovereigns on the second day by Mr Lewis's *Sober Tom*'. Pickpockets were active and 'succeeded in obtaining considerable booty', but at least one was found out and committed for trial.

Moving towards the Dorset border, the countryside undergoes a subtle change, a difference not merely of geology – although that is undoubtedly a factor – but of purity too. No motorways bulldoze through these parts; no sizeable towns or cities pollute the atmosphere, and the cleanness of the air is reflected in the shrubby lichen found on trees. The hills seem to have acquired that almost wounding edge of distilled greenness, and the roads are a pleasure to drive along. They take long, curving swoops and snake into the most delightful villages.

Such a road runs south of Blackford and into Charleton Horethorne, where the kennels of the Blackmore Vale Hounds are kept. The centre is by a confluence of roads going to Milborne Port, Sherborne and Wincanton. It is fairly high and exposed, and the surrounding place-names are evocative and beautiful: Windmill Hill, Dark Harbour Farm, Seven Wells Down, Golden Valley Farm, Silver Knap – names that the late poet laureate John Masefield would have relished. There is a small enclosed green with a chestnut tree, and nearby is the Victorian King's Arms. Across the way big barns overlook the road; they stand beside a fine gaunt manor house of the seventeenth century of dark local stone with Hamstone dressings. The church, with its powerfully buttressed tower, has a carving of a woman with a horned head-dress and two smaller stone heads above her. On the outskirts of the village, moving towards Milborne, the road goes by a row of houses called Waterloo Crescent: a long pinkish block, framed by stone walls, hardly elegant but striking in their setting.

Exploring the hilltops around can be a fascinating exercise for the amateur archaeologist, for this is the heart of the Wessex Culture, the name designating that enigmatic transitional phase in prehistory when Stonehenge as we know it was constructed, when men began to work with bronze, and the bell barrows appeared.

Set among these tumuli-dotted hills is Milborne Port, a place of great antiquity. Six mills are mentioned in the Domesday Book (1086), and it was listed as the third town in Somerset. The name is derived from 'mill on the borne or brook', and 'port' signifies a town. From early days it has been associated with the manufacturing of sailcloth, dowlas (a coarse cloth used for clothing, especially in workhouses for the poor) and linsey-wolsey.

A nucleation rather than a roadside straggle, Milborne is built on the south-facing slope of a hill which plunges to a small if rather attractive feeder of the Yeo. The houses wander up and down, and parts of the main street have elevated pavements with iron railings. The rows of houses are composed mainly of light, creamy oolite, not so rich as Hamstone but the effect is equally entrancing. The village has a civic feel befitting a former royal Saxon borough and site of an Anglo-Saxon mint (at a London acution in 1971 an Ethelred II coin from here was sold for £820). The town hall, originally arcaded but now blocked in, emphasizes the dignified tone with its Tuscan pilasters. Of equal note are the guildhall with its Norman herringbone work around the door, a tannery of 1800 and an impressive brick-built glove-factory dating from 1850. Since early in the last century, leather-dressing and glove-making have been the principal local industries, supplemented more recently by boat-building.

Milborne is essentially a quiet village, yet by no means a dead one, for lorries charge through the centre fuming carbon (a bypass is urgently needed) but fail to destroy completely the charm of such features as the Big Ball Court (1847) erected by Sir William Medlycott for the 'health and amusement of the town' – or the appeal of the old coaching inns, the King's Head and the Queen's Head. At right angles to the High Street runs South Street, featuring grey-stone houses with red-brick quoins and North Street containing the Commonwealth Club rebuilt in 1898. The shops around these parts have a cloistral cosiness and modesty of scale one associates with Victorian lace caps and ticking tongues. Probably the best walk in Milborne is down Lower Gunville Lane towards Rosemary Street. This bridges a tiny cressy stream at Millbeck Cottage where there is an open space backing the sheepskin factory graced by leaning willows and haunted by mallards and their chicks – an enclave of pure rural sweetness. From this point one can climb the hill and admire the pinnacled exuberance of the County Video Library (a former Victorian schoolhouse) or proceed along Paddock Walk and view the old factory buildings and the spectacle of crates of salted New Zealand lambskins. The whole aspect is hilly, green, rural, yet pleasantly tempered by a solid workaday atmosphere – definitely one of the finest villages in Somerset.

It is of incidental note that Milborne possesses the oldest fire-engine in the country, now housed in Taunton Museum, bearing the inscription 'Given to the Borough of Milborne Port by T. Medlycott, of Ven, Esq., 1733'.

The parish church overlooks a meadows and is unique because of its massive pillars with their intriguing capitals dating from the eleventh century. A powerful, capacious building, like a Norman abbey, its south transept has an oak-panelled wagon roof with heraldic emblems and angel corbels with shields. The inner south door, of Norman date, has a frame of carved capitals and a tympanum of two lions, and there are more creatures fixed to the buttress pinnacles, including a horn-headed demon with a protruding tongue.

Milborne is teetering on the very edge of the Dorset border, which behaves erratically hereabouts, cutting back on itself as it moves east, then striking south and claiming a sizeable chunk that constitutes the parish of Henstridge. Two main blocks of development stand out: the northern sector bordered by the A30 and the southern nucleation around the church and green. Another main road, the A357, crosses the A30 looping south to Blandford Forum. A local correspondent complained that residents 'dice with death' as they walk about the main street and suggested a bypass. There is an A357 Action Group seeking a change of route or a weight restriction on heavy traffic.

On the A30 stands the Virginia Ash, an eighteenth-century two-storeyed inn reputed to be the first tavern in which tobacco was smoked. It was said to be here that Sir Walter Ralegh, taking a maiden pull on his pipe, was interrupted by a waiter who attempted to extinguish him with a bowl of water. In 1752 this inn was advertised for cudgel-playing in the *Western Gazette*. A fine display of railway memorabilia can be seen in the public bar, garnered partly from the Templecombe station. East of the main settlement, near the hamlet of Henstridge Marsh, the gaunt, weed-haunted runways of the old World War II base crisscross the fields. Mainly used as an Advanced Flying Training Unit, using Spitfires and Master aircraft, it continued up to the 1950s as a satellite of Yeovilton and was then employed by a firm of whale-hunters using (appropriately) Walrus aircraft. Today private planes use it sporadically. Like Milborne, Henstridge has traditional connections with gloving that have declined, but agriculture – mainly dairying – continues and there is some light industry. The church of St Nicholas stands amid an open space and has been energetically restored; only the chancel is of special interest, for the tomb of William Carent (d. 1463), High Sheriff of Somerset. His name is preserved in the distant Toomer Farm, a fascinating building with battlemented gables and a pair of stone watchdogs at the door.

Early eighteenth-century church records of Henstridge demonstrate the apathy of a nation which had been Anglicanized, Catholicized and Protestantized in successive spasms. The abrupt switchbacks subverted the credibility of religion itself. Hence we find the sexton being told 'to walk the church with his whip and bell in the time of divine service to observe that people did not sleep, to keep out dogs, and to look after the boys in the churchyard'. But later, in 1714, he himself was criticized as 'an idle, drunken, disorderly fellow' who had failed to weed the churchyard and assist the clerk at ringing the bell at the proper hours. His apathy had caused a bell to fall out of its cage, which 'broke the bell wheel to pieces to the great damage of the parish'. He was removed from office for his negligence.

North of Henstridge is the hamlet of Yenston, formerly 'Endeston'. From the twelfth to the fifteenth century a priory of Benedictines was based here, a cell to the monastery of St Server, Normandy, and there is a field known as Priory Plot.

Over the hill from Yenston, strewn along a wandering slope, Templecombe marks the edge of Blackmore Vale. The main street directly links up with Abbas Combe, with which it is now incorporated. Formerly it was called Combe Templariorum, a name derived from an ancient preceptory of the Knights Templars founded here before 1185 by Serlo FitzOdo. The remains of their house lies to the south of the village at Manor Farm: a long range, formerly the Templar's refectory, and to the east a fragment of a chapel.

As for the village, it is an uneasy mixture of old cottages, new estates, big nineteenth-century houses with entrances set in high-walled gardens and such endowments as the hospital (1906) which Lady Theodora Guest, a noted philanthropist, financed in memory of her husband. The church of St George is set astride a perilous hill striped by continuous white lines – to secure parking-space is almost impossible. Opposite are a hair salon and defunct fruit-and-vegetable shop. The main road descends under the railway bridge and past a fish-and-chip shop (where the massive church key is obtained) and up a hill winding between shops and poker-faced houses. In the other direction it climbs above the church and between huddles of colour-washed cottages, outside of which the stocks are displayed, and past an enormous pinkish Georgian building due for conversion to an old people's flat complex. The feel is faintly grimy, unself-conscious, with new brick estates laid out in a blunt, basic way. Below the church is an open space by the cycle shop and railway station (receiving around seven trains per day) where a road runs leading to the Plessey Marine Research Unit.

The church is gaunt, grey-stoned, clinging to the hillside like a barnacle to a rock. Inside there are old seats with holes in them to take candles, but the feature which excites current controversy is the panel painting of Jesus. It came to light as a result of a gale in 1951 which caused a ceiling to collapse in an outhouse of a cottage belonging to Mrs A. Topp in Templecombe High Street. This exposed the panel painting, covered with coaldust and bearing keyhole and hinge marks – indicating it had been used as the door of a small coalshed. The painting was dated at 1314 but other experts put it earlier and connect it with the Templars, who had a West Country headquarters here.

The Knights Templars, whose order (established 1118) had its origin in the Crusades, took vows of poverty, obedience and chastity and dedicated themselves to the Christian faith. They also regarded it as their task to preserve and protect holy relics. Kings had no power over them; only to the Pope himself did they vow allegiance. Their combination of mysticism, military prowess and chivalric elitism proved irresistible to young aristocratic knights, who eagerly joined and funded the order. But strange rumours also circulated which King Phillip IV of

France employed as evidence against them. What did the Templars do in private? It was said that each member, far from being a devout believer, was compelled to spit upon the cross, to submit to indecent ceremonies, to worship grotesque four-footed figures, to kill children who had accidentally witnessed their nightly orgies. In England children told one another to beware of Templars' kisses, and in France they were said to roast their illegitimate children and smear their idols with burning fat. The upshot of this was a ferocious inquisition (1310) in which confessions were extracted from the Templars under torture and the order was suppressed.

The Preceptor at Templecombe managed the order's estates, trained knights and horses for service in the Holy Land and may also have stored religious treasures brought back from foreign parts. The painting of Christ in the church bears a marked resemblance to the Holy Shroud of Turin. It has no halo (which was considered an idolatrous omission), and the expression is not one of wan passivity. Instead the gaze has a blue-eyed searching solemnity; the face is not emaciated but full-fleshed and strong; and there is something else too – an eeriness that haunts and unsettles. Is this then a copy of the image on the Holy Shroud which was brought to England and hidden at the time of the great persecution?

The Templars' lodgings at Templecombe eventually went to the Knights of St John, an order of hospitallers, whose work for the sick was popularly acknowledged, leaving no scope for rumours of black magic or heresy.

After Castle Cary the principal town in this south-western corner of Somerset is Wincanton, formerly a re-mount point for couriers betwen London and Plymouth and an important staging post on the main route from London to the West, some seventeen coaches a day stopping and resting. The prosperity of the town was built on weaving, and in the eighteenth century more than eighty looms were working in the town, producing the material used for mattress ticking. Loom windows are evident in several buildings, although much of the old town was destroyed by fire in 1707. Thatched roofs assisted the conflagration, and now the oldest remaining cottages are in Mill Street to the west of the market-place. The parish church contains a medieval carving of St Eligius, patron of metalworkers and farriers.

The Wincanton region is the very threshold of Somerset. One does not associate the polished, close-cropped smoothness of chalk downland with the county but towards the Dorset border the landscape has just this quality. It shelters villages like Cucklington with a church prominently situated beside the road, containing a chapel to St Barbara but dedicated to St Lawrence. Old Somerset rustics were known to exclaim 'Lawrence' before removing their shirts and jerkins, alluding to this unfortunate saint's martyrdom by being barbecued on a gridiron. Cucklington stretches up and down hill and has a well called Bab Well where St Aldhelm is said to have baptized converts. Stoke Trister is another compact village nearby with a hilltop church (1841) replacing one that was burnt down. North of the A303, still amid the hills, Charlton Musgrove has a church dedicated to St Stephen with pinnacles, battlements, a turret and some deliciously repellent gargoyles.

But to end this book, let us abandon impressive architecture and travel east to Bourton, just over the Dorset border. The River Stour flows through some boggy woodland here, and in the middle of a thicket is the object of our enquiry. A walking-stick is necessary, for those who delight in taking scimitar swipes at clawing brambles and nettle patches; Wellington boots also, for those averse to paddling in mud, but press on to the centre of the thicket until a plain grey stone, about 3½ feet high, is reached. Egbert's Stone this is called, after the grandfather of Alfred the Great, and it stands on the border of Somerset, Dorset and Wiltshire. Grey, undistinguished, mossy, pitted with holes, this marks the rendezvous point of the men of three counties whose combined efforts defeated the Vikings. They met here, wild-clothed, grimy, desperate but determined, in this forest, which would have been a wolf-ridden retreat of robbers and rejects. The men came, arriving in scattered drifts and pockets, then waited tensely, wondering if their leader would arrive. A sunburst of joy and applause on seeing him, Alfred, aged twenty-nine, a slender figure, not cast in the heroic mould but prone to sickness, piles and fever. But courage transcends its mortal casing, and it was here, in 878, that England began to achieve something near a definition of its future identity.

Bibliography

Atthill, Robin, *Old Mendip* (1971)
Atthill, Robin, *Mendip: A New Study* (1976)
Burton, S.H., *Exmoor* (1978 edition)
Collinson, Reverend, *The History and Antiquities of the County of Somerset* (1791)
Connor, A.B., *Monumental Brasses in Somerset* (1970)
Down, C.G. and Warrington, A.J., *The History of the Somerset Coalfield* (1971)
Dunning, Robert, *Christianity in Somerset* (1976)
Dunning, Robert, *Somerset and Avon* (1980)
Farr, Grahame, *Somerset Harbours* (1954)
Fraser, Maxwell, *Companion into Somerset* (1947)
Greenwood, Charles, *Famous Houses of the West Country* (1977)
Holt, Alan, *West Somerset – Romantic Routes and Mysterious Byways* (1984)
Hutton, Edward, *Highways and Byways in Somerset* (1912)
Kelly's Directory of Somersetshire (1931)
Knight, Francis, *The Heart of Mendip* (1915)
Lawrence, Berta, *Quantock Country* (1952)
Lawrence, Berta, *Coleridge and Wordsworth in Somerset* (1970)
Lawrence, Berta, *Somerset Legends* (1973)
Mais, S.P.B., *Walking in Somerset* (1938)
Mee, Arthur (editor), *Somerset* (1940)
Pevsner, Nikolaus, *The Buildings of England: Somerset* (two volumes, 1958)
Powys, Llewelyn, *A Baker's Dozen* (1941)
Reid, R.D., *Some Buildings of Mendip* (1979)
Sampson, Aylwin, *Somerset Scenes* (1980)

Victoria County History of Somerset (3 vols., present editor Robert Dunning)

Webber, Ronald, *The Devon and Somerset Blackdowns* (1976)

Wickham, A.K., *Churches of Somerset* (1965 edition)

Woodforde, C., *Stained Glass in Somerset* (1970 edition)

Index

231